Understanding Understanding

Natural and Artificial Intelligence

ROBERT K. LINDSAY

ISBN-13: 978-1466450585
ISBN-10: 1466450584

DEDICATION

I dedicate this work to Maija, Griffin and Logan.

CONTENTS

ACKNOWLEDGMENTS

I am indebted to several people who have generously given me their time and shared their expertise in an attempt to improve my explanations and writing. The work has been substantially improved through their help, although the limits of my ability still remain.

Computer Scientists Bruce Buchanan, B. Chandrasekaran and John Laird, and Philosopher Maija Kibens have read the entire manuscript and offered many improvements in detail and organization. Psychologist Henry Wellman has helped me improve my treatment of animal intelligence. My thanks to all of these friends and colleagues.

I thank my daughters for their contributions to the cover design. The author photograph is by Griffin Reames. The cover image is by Logan Kibens.

I also wish to thank the United States National Science Foundation for sponsoring some of this research.

1 UNDERSTANDING

The noblest pleasure is the joy of understanding.
– Leonardo da Vinci (1452–1519)

1. Introduction

In 1997 a computer named Deep Blue beat the world champion chess player Garry Kasparov in an extremely close contest: two wins, one loss, three draws. This fact is remarkable for two reasons.

First a computer was able to best a human at what many had considered a classical example of an intellectual task requiring a high level of intelligence.

More remarkable still, at least in hindsight, is the fact that the computer did not win easily. A game such as chess requires that a player look ahead to examine the possible replies to a potential move, and the replies to the replies, and so forth as far as one's ability allows. If this were all that were required for excellent chess play the computer should have won easily, for Deep Blue could examine 200,000,000 chess positions every second. A human chess expert, being limited by slow and imperfect biologically based memory, typically is able to examine only a few hundred positions before selecting a move. Why, then, could a human play Deep Blue to (almost) a draw?

Modern, computer-based Artificial Intelligence (AI) has produced other achievements in its over half century history, although probably none that captured the public's attention to the extent of the Deep Blue/Kasparov contest. Many find these accomplishments to be Good News – amazing and important, auguring yet more life-enhancing achievements of modern technology. Others find them to be Bad News – discouraging and threatening to the special place humans have in the Cosmos.

But why should AI's successes be threatening? Machines have bested humans in many ways in the past. Machines can travel faster, lift more, and see things that people cannot. Still humans run races and engage in athletic competitions with one another, unconcerned that machines, and indeed other animals, could readily outdo them at these activities. After all, these mechanical devices and even animals do things in entirely different ways than we humans do, so let us not compare apples and oranges. In any case, the reasoning goes, humans are the masters of all the animals and all the machines, and we make them do our bidding, so their superior abilities are used to *our* advantage, not theirs.

When it comes to intellectual accomplishment, however, we become uncomfortable. We have assumed that it is human *intelligence,* not brute strength, that allows us to dominate other animals and turn them to our use, and it is human *intelligence* that allows us to create machines for our purposes. If the previously clear superiority of human intelligence is now challenged it is a new and much more serious challenge altogether, for perhaps we would cease to be the masters even of our own creations. The place of humans at the center of God's physical universe and at the center of God's design has been gradually eroded by scientific fact. Are we about to find out that we do not hold a special place in the universe of intelligence either? Are we not at all important to God?

Still, it is only a minority of observers who take either the Good News or the Bad News view of AI. Most, including most scientists, philosophers, and other intellectuals, dismiss the accomplishments of AI because the accomplishments lack some essential element of human intelligence, and, the argument generally continues, always will. What might that element be?

I propose that human intelligence is capable of an *understanding* of the world and the self that has qualities not shared by other animals nor any existing machines. For me it is still an open question whether computer-like machines could be developed or arise to achieve the ability to understand in this fashion. Before we can design such machines, however, we must have an understanding of what understanding, itself, means.

It is surely possible to live, thrive, and reproduce without understanding. Even plants do these things all the time. It is also possible to behave in complex ways without understanding. Mammals interact successfully in quite varied and complex environments. Chimpanzees can solve a variety of problems, interact socially with their fellow chimpanzees, use tools, distinguish large quantities from small, and can be taught to use symbols for rudimentary communication. However, humans also have an additional ability: they can understand what they are doing and experiencing in a way that other animals cannot. It seems to me that understanding is the fundamental feature of *human* intelligence.

My ongoing personal scientific quest is to understand understanding. In this essay I will attempt to make clear what it is I seek, and to show why neither psychology nor artificial intelligence has provided the understanding I desire.

2. Scientific Understanding

Understanding is a fundamental phenomenon in another important sense: it is the fundamental goal of science. Science is a uniquely human activity, by which I mean that no other organisms or artifacts do science. It is only possible because people have the ability to understand and to share their understanding with others. The drive to understand is the force behind the creation of science.

This characterization of science is not universally accepted. Some scientists and most lay persons would say that the fundamental goals of science are to predict and control the physical universe so that we can eradicate disease, harness energy, predict the weather, eliminate human suffering, travel to other planets, and so forth. While these are often desirable accompaniments to science, my view is that the fundamental goal of science is to explain the universe to ourselves, that is, to understand it. This is, I suggest, a spiritual quest rather than a practical one.

CHAPTER 1: UNDERSTANDING

Prediction and control in many cases follow from understanding, but in other cases they do not. For example, even simple physical processes, such as a dripping faucet, may not be predictable in detail by the deterministic mechanics of classical physics since they involve non-linear relations among the critical physical variables. Such behavior is called *chaotic*. The existence and ubiquity of non-random but unpredictable behavior is a relatively recently discovered fact, and conflicts with what was the conventional scientific view until quite recently.

Unpredictability in this sense is not due to a fundamental randomness of physical processes. In particular it is not due to the indeterminacy of quantum events. Rather, chaos is exhibited by fully deterministic systems. This is because the future behavior of non-linear deterministic systems is sensitive to the smallest possible alterations in the initial conditions from which the equations of the theory produce predictions. Thus future behavior can deviate arbitrarily far from that predicted by the equations no matter how close to the correct initial conditions we began. This is an in-principle unpredictability. There is also an in-practice unpredictability that applies to almost all situations, simply because it is impossible to obtain the initial physical values in the first place. Thus in general we cannot predict whether a train will crash because we cannot measure everything we need to know to feed to the equations while the train is hurtling down the track. Similarly, we have weather forecasts, but not weather predictions. Precise prediction is by and large limited to artifacts that are carefully constructed and controlled.

On the other hand we can often predict and control without understanding. Pre-scientific people built bridges and roads and temples, folk medicine works to a degree, and those successes that modern medicine has achieved come in most cases with only very limited understanding of biological mechanisms. Therefore prediction is neither necessary nor sufficient for scientific understanding. However, without understanding, scientific knowledge is severely limited and deficient, and most importantly it does not address a fundamental spiritual quest of humanity.

It is significant that our best theories do indeed give highly precise and accurate predictions in many situations. In fact the major role of prediction in science is to test proposed theories, because predictions that are shown to be false necessarily require a modification if not an outright rejection of the theory. On the other hand, of course, a theory cannot be established as True in any absolute sense no matter how many predictions it correctly makes, because the refuting observation may lie just around the corner. The distinction between theory and truth is one that large portions of the non-scientifically trained public does not appreciate.

If theories can only be refuted and never proved correct, how then are the non-refuted theories to be judged? The answer is that the best theories among those that have not been refuted empirically are the ones that offer the best understanding, that is, the best explanations. Explanations that are more general, those that cover a wider range of phenomena, are better. They are better because they permit us to understand more. Explanations that are simpler are better because they permit us to understand more easily, which again broadens the scope of what we understand. Most important of all, explanations in one domain that support and extend explanations in others – such as relating biological processes to physical theories – provide the greatest understanding of all. Generally, the more we understand and the more easily we understand, the more control we ultimately have. For an eloquent and more extensive exposition of this point of view see Deutsch (1997).

One important way in which science aids understanding is by reducing the unfamiliar to the familiar. For example, a measure of understanding is achieved by explaining that light bears similarities to water waves or that the structure of atoms is similar to a planetary system. Paradoxically, science often explains the commonplace with counterintuitive descriptions, such as that seemingly solid surfaces are really mostly empty space.

Although understanding through scientific theories is the greatest benefit of science, understanding itself has never been explained scientifically. Thus we cannot give a good account of how science provides understanding, or how it could do better. Furthermore, we need an account not just of scientific understanding but of the ordinary, human understanding by which we find our place in the world.

3. Where is Understanding Bred?

Life, as embodied in a huge variety of organisms throughout evolutionary history and in co-existence with man today, has done and continues to do quite nicely without understanding in human fashion. Living organisms obviously must respond adaptively to their environments or they will not survive.

Do chimpanzees understand in the way humans do? Chimpanzees are very similar to humans. In fact, Diamond (1992) makes the point that to an alien from outer space, humans would be considered another variety of chimpanzee, along with bonobos (pygmy chimpanzees). In terms of biochemistry and anatomy the similarity of man and chimpanzee is striking and the differences readily identified. Cognitively, however, it is more difficult to make comparisons. Perception and motor skills are highly similar in man and chimpanzee and these suffice to account for some complex goal-oriented behavior. There are also major similarities between human and chimpanzee social organization, including a tendency for violence toward conspecifics, although this latter is not shared with the bonobos (Wrangham & Peterson (1996)). Recent work has indicated that the great apes are perhaps even smarter than we thought. They have a limited concept of number. They attend to their reflections in mirrors, and know that the image is of themselves. They construct and use simple tools. These are very sophisticated cognitive abilities that place the primates, especially chimpanzees, well above other animals, including other mammals such as cats and dogs.

Nonetheless, there are cognitive abilities that seem clearly to set humans well apart and doubtless account for the fact that we have no serious competitor for dominance of the Earth in spite of the superiority of other animals in such areas as strength, speed, and agility. Clear major differences are language, literature, art[1], science, mathematics, and religion. These in turn appear to be related to the huge differences in social organization between humans and other animals.

---

[1] There are reports that other animals, including elephants, are capable of 'painting,' but it is not clear exactly what it is they are doing, particularly because the paintings are mostly non-representational, recent anecdotal studies notwithstanding It is unlikely that their works 'mean' anything to *them*, as opposed to their human patrons; see Mayell (2002).

CHAPTER 1: UNDERSTANDING

All of these human accomplishments reflect an understanding that subhuman species do not possess. Of course, humans are animals, specifically primates, and thus possess many of the sensorimotor and intellectual abilities of the great apes. Without those shared abilities on which to build the uniquely human qualities, understanding would not be possible either. What abilities, shared and unique, might form the basis of the human ability to understand? Psychology and Artificial Intelligence have indirectly discussed this question, and many other disciplines, both scientific and literary, have as well. Thus I turn to some of the features and abilities that are often suggested as explanations of full human intelligence.

Understanding and learning

Intelligence and learning go hand in hand – one would not attribute intelligence to an organism that could not adapt to its environment through experience. In fact learning was the central topic of scientific (non-clinical) psychology through the first two-thirds of the 20th century. Most of this work was conducted in the *associationist* framework, in which laws of learning specified how certain behaviors ('responses') become associated with environmental situations ('stimuli') through experience. The association has a 'strength' which increases when the association is followed by a reward and decreased when it is not. Otherwise an association has no properties, that is, it is simply a connection that increases the probability that the response will follow the stimulus. One form of associationist account is *behaviorism*, which requires both stimuli and responses to be 'external' to the organism and directly observable by others. Of course, animals never see exactly the same stimulus twice. Nor do we, as Heraclites averred long ago. Therefore any associative learning must connect *classes* of stimuli and *classes* of responses if we are to account for even the most rudimentary behavior of animals. Associative learning is an important feature of intelligence. It is clear that it is an ability that is essential for adaptation in complex environments. However, since it is also found in all mammals and even in much simpler organisms, it cannot be the key to explaining uniquely human abilities, such as understanding.

Modern cognitive science, an amalgam of non-behaviorist cognitive psychology (the study of how higher organisms think) and artificial intelligence (the study of how thinking artifacts can be designed), seeks a general science of cognition applicable to all organisms and artifacts. At this stage of the science, the language in which its theories and models are stated is the language of computation. "Computation" is a general term for any manipulation of symbols, not merely numerical calculation.

It is important to note that learning theory as extended by the computational view to embrace internal symbolic states, goes significantly beyond the learning of stimulus-response associations. There is no restriction as to where the computations read their inputs or leave their outputs, that is, they could be stored 'inside' the organism. The computational view allows 'associations' to interact with one another in any computationally possible way. Thus forms of learning and adaptation could be postulated that go beyond simple associative learning, perhaps including types of learning that are beyond those available to the great apes. If so, such modes of learning could perhaps be a key feature of human level understanding, even though simple associative learning alone is not.

UNDERSTANDING UNDERSTANDING

Understanding and goal-directedness

A cockroach is able to find nourishment and avoid danger in a complex, varying environment at least long enough to reproduce in abundance. Cockroach skills can readily be described without attributing understanding or even reasoning to cockroaches. We need not assume that a cockroach goes back to the place it last ate because it thinks that food will be there. No deeper explanation of cognitive ability is required than to assume that there have been connections established in its nervous system such that, when a stimulus is perceived, a sequence of movements is triggered that takes the organism to the former feeding place. An associative explanation suffices.

However, associative explanations of skill are stretched thin as we move up the biological hierarchy. An animal, such as a rat, never engages in the *exact* same sequence or type of motor movements in search of food, nor do even simpler organisms. In fact, a rat will engage in quite different movements in achieving a goal, for example correctly swimming a newly flooded maze that it originally explored by walking.

The most natural way to describe the rat's maze-learning skill is that it is goal-oriented. That is, the rat has some concept of what will satisfy its need and an arsenal of methods for finding it. However, psychologists and other scientists have often been reluctant to attribute an explicit, conscious intentionality to the rat. The reluctance is much diminished when the maze runner is human. A man in a maze might conceivably come to believe that "a light means I will find food if I turn right," but we are not likely to attribute such a linguistically represented belief to a rat whose linguistic skills are presumably non-existent, even though the rat consistently turns right at lights. Between rat and man are many organisms that surely are goal-directed problem solvers, even though they do not exhibit human level understanding. Surely primates have goals and desires. Developmental data suggest that a chimpanzee understands some things as well as does a two-year or three-year old human, although it never advances to the depth of understanding achieved by human adults. There remains a qualitative difference between the way in which apes and humans understand and this difference cannot be accounted for by goal-directedness alone.

Understanding and knowledge

Most would say that possessing knowledge is necessary for understanding. Plato (428 – 348 BCE) argued the converse, that one *only* has knowledge if one understands. We need to characterize what knowledge is in order to determine its relation to understanding. Conventional wisdom would, I presume, hold that knowing something requires more than the possession of *information*. That is, possessing knowledge means more than recording an isolated fact, such as a phone number, in some sort of physical memory. A telephone book, though it contains information, neither knows nor understands anything.

One additional requirement of knowledge is that the whole must be greater than the sum of its parts. Information can be accumulated in computer databases and minds, but if the computer or the person does not combine it and form new information then it is not knowledge. For example, if I possess the facts that x=y and y=z, I also am aware that x=z, even though this is not one of my two initial pieces of information. A passive record such as a telephone book or a dictionary does not make such inferences. Drawing the x=z inference requires additional information about the meaning of "equals."

CHAPTER 1: UNDERSTANDING

Without that additional information and the ability to apply it, one has only the two initial facts. With that additional information and the two facts one can infer the third. The total of the two facts plus the information about equality *and how to apply it* is now more than just information.

However, that is not the whole story. There are various types of knowledge. Skills are sometimes described as knowledge, as in "He knows how to ride a horse." Skills are 'knowing how' knowledge in contrast to 'knowing that' knowledge. Another type of knowledge is sometimes described as compiled empirical experience, for example when a repairman knows that if the defective device exhibits symptoms A and B one should try to replace part X, or that many service calls are made simply because an electrical device was not plugged in. Still such knowledge need not reflect a deep understanding of electrical appliances.

In general, one may possess a great deal of such empirical experience and still not understand. One may know many facts about a subject and be able to combine these facts into other facts, and still not understand the subject. One may know how to catch a thrown ball without understanding the process (though one might). One may know how to repair televisions or automobiles without understanding either (though one might). Just as understanding is more than possessing information, understanding is more than just possessing knowledge: ". . . understanding does not depend on knowing lots of facts as such, but on having the right concepts, explanations, and theories (Deutsch (1997), page 2)." I would add that these things must also be applied by the agent said to understand. Understanding enables the use of knowledge in new and creative ways, as opposed to merely applying it to a narrow task. Mammals 'know how' to do many things. Great apes have enough productive knowledge to create and use simple tools, but yet do not understand the way humans do. Knowledge by itself does not assure understanding.

Understanding, language, and reasoning

Language is highly developed in humans, yet other forms of life obviously communicate effectively: it is well-known that bees have a sophisticated non-verbal language system, and that birds, sea mammals, and chimpanzees communicate in complex ways. There have been many long-term experiments that show that chimpanzees can be taught to use symbolic, non-verbal means of communication employing significant vocabularies even though they do not develop these spontaneously in the wild. Furthermore, even in these artificial situations chimpanzees communicate without the use of complex syntactic structure such as found in English and other natural human languages.

Life on Earth began about 4.5 billion years ago. Language is a relative newcomer to the evolutionary scene, arriving long after reproduction, metabolism, mobility, vision, flight, and the opposing thumb. Man is the only organism that possesses true linguistic ability, and he has done so for a mere 50,000–100,000 years or so, at most .002% of the history of life and .0007% of the approximately 14 billion year history of the universe.

Is understanding just language ability, and are these abilities simply equivalent to reasoning and the application of logic? Here is one standard definition of "reasoning."

7

UNDERSTANDING UNDERSTANDING

Reasoning: The drawing of inferences or conclusions from known or assumed facts. (Webster's New World Dictionary of the American language, 2nd edition, 1980, p. 1183).

Note that under this definition, one cannot divorce the notion of reasoning from the use of language. Known facts are true *statements*; assumed facts are *statements* assumed to be true; statements are linguistic representations. Conclusions are *propositions* that have truth value. Reasons themselves are universally considered to be statements of belief or fact.

If we adopt the dictionary definition of "reasoning" cited above (that is, reasoning-with-language) we must conclude that reasoning is a form of cognition limited to humans. However, not all adaptive problem solving is reasoning-with-language, nor is all thinking reasoning, even more broadly construed: subhuman species engage in sometimes quite powerful forms of non-linguistic thought. Presumably all of the non-linguistic based cognitive skills are also available to humans: not all intelligent *human* thought is reasoning-with-language.

In ordinary usage, therefore, "reasoning" has a broader definition. Most people would say that a chimpanzee who moved a box under a suspended banana and then climbed on the box to reach the banana had done reasoning, even though chimpanzees do not possess language. Given this broader definition much of thinking (including problem solving, tool use, and adaptive behavior) is reasoning, but not reasoning-with-language.

Perhaps, then, human level understanding can be explained by human language ability (reasoning-with-language), since both are possessed by all normal humans and not possessed by chimpanzees, whereas generalized reasoning is available to both. If this is the case we need to know what reasoning-with-language underwrites, and this question will be addressed in Chapter 2.

Understanding and consciousness

John Searle offers this informal, common sense definition:

> By 'consciousness' I simply mean those subjective states of sentience or awareness that begin when one awakes in the morning from a dreamless sleep and continue throughout the day until one goes to sleep at night, or falls into a coma, or dies, or otherwise becomes, as one would say, 'unconscious.' (Searle (2002), page 7).

Consciousness is difficult to analyze because it is a purely subjective matter. Presumably it corresponds to some sort of brain activity, but it almost certainly is a global property rather than a local one: there is no brain area where consciousness resides (no 'Cartesian Theater' in which we sit to view our thoughts, in the terminology of Dennett (1991)). It cannot, by any current technology, be detected objectively. It is therefore impossible to say with certainty whether any animal or person other than oneself is conscious. Nonetheless the subjective experience of consciousness is so real and important that we assume that all humans have the same experience, else it would be impossible to make sense of their behavior.

CHAPTER 1: UNDERSTANDING

We infer that some other animals are conscious as well, based upon our observations of their behavior. One major feature of consciousness is intentionality, that is, goal-directedness. Intentionality is not identical to consciousness, but it is a strongly suggestive marker of it. As discussed above, the primates, and most likely all mammals, exhibit behavior consistent with their being goal-directed. Computers also have goals, but most of us do not attribute intentionality or consciousness to them, because, first, the goals are provided externally by their designers, and second, we assume that consciousness is an emergent property of biological nervous systems. Searle asserts that by any reasonable analysis of consciousness we ought to attribute consciousness to mammals at least. I concur.

Perhaps understanding requires consciousness. However, if it is correct that other mammals are conscious but do not understand, and that humans are conscious of many things without understanding them, then consciousness by itself is not identical to understanding, and thus is not sufficient for explaining human-quality understanding of the sort with which I am concerned.

Understanding and abstract thinking

Artificial intelligence research has not created artifacts that are conscious nor artifacts that communicate with human natural language. It has, however, introduced a variety of ways to represent knowledge, goals, concepts, and ways to learn. In addition it has invented computational methods that capture a variety of important cognitive abilities that formerly were not handled or even discussed by psychological theory, and its artifacts demonstrate some cognitive abilities that exceed those of lower animals. Among the most important of these abilities are the systematic generation and search of sets of possible alternatives, the symbolic representation of facts and rules of inference, the use of variables (in addition to specific proper names) and quantification (*for all, there exists, some,* etc), and the productive generation of arbitrarily large sequences and arbitrarily long processes by iteration and recursion.

The conventional definition of computation can be expressed in a variety of equivalent ways. One is in the form of *production rules,* specifically, conditional rules that take the form "if this is the case, then make that alteration of your symbolic record." Such rules are known to be a universal way to express computations in the sense that anything that can be computed (technically, any recursive function) can be computed by a procedure that follows some set of such conditional rules. It follows that any cognitive science explanation of intelligence of the sort currently envisioned can be formulated as a rule-system.

Programs that succeed at tasks that have traditionally been considered[2] markers of human intelligence (such as chess) may in general be described as a set of rules plus a regimen for applying the rules. Will such abilities prove ultimately to be sufficient for human level understanding?

The claim that all of cognition can be described as rule-following is unpalatable for many who feel that something or some things are still missing from this deterministic,

---

[2] It has often been wryly observed by AI practitioners that once an ability has been captured in a program it is no longer considered intelligent, making AI impossible by definition.

'mechanistic' view. For example, Searle (1980) argues that even if a set of rules were discovered for a complex cognitive task such as language translation (and he does not concede that such rules *could* be discovered), these rules would still not capture the fundamental cognitive phenomenon. Searle asks us to imagine a room full of clerks none of whom understands Chinese. Indeed they need not understand English or any other natural language either. All they can do is distinguish Chinese characters one from another, and follow explicit rules that allow them to construct strings of Latin letters as a function of the sequence of Chinese characters inserted through a slot in the door of the room. Suppose their manipulations repeatedly result in the translation of arbitrary Chinese text into English. Searle's argument is that, since human translators understand both Chinese and English but the clerks do not, the rules have been able to *simulate* translation in an entirely *different way* than humans perform translation, just as Deep Blue played successful chess in an entirely different way than did Garry Kasparov. Therefore, Searle concludes, rule-based simulations cannot be veridical models of *human* intelligence *even if* they do intelligent things.

Searle's position contrasts with the well-known Turing Test. Turing (1950) suggested that to avoid disputes over how to define intelligence, we should focus only on behavior. If the intellectual abilities of an artifact could not be distinguished from those of a human through observation of behavior alone, then the artifact should be assigned the same description as a person. Specifically he suggested that if an interrogator were allowed to ask questions of both a real human and a machine pretending to be human, without observing the physical appearance of either, and if the interrogator could not distinguish the two reliably over a series of trials, then the machine should be deemed intelligent. Clearly we could make the Test as stringent as we wish by extending the range of questioning permitted and using a larger number of interrogators who are highly sophisticated in a variety of human knowledge and activities. It is important to note, however, that the Test as envisioned by Turing was not simply to see if some interrogator might erroneously take a machine to be a human, a common misreading of Turing; see Lindsay (1976). Rather, the interrogator must be put in a forced-choice situation where he knows that one choice is a human and the other a machine. If the interrogation is allowed to range over any conceivable topic, any machine thus far created will always be detected. If the topic is limited to a specific intellectual task, say chess playing, there are today computer programs that might deceive interrogators, although even there the machine's skill with natural language would probably give it away unless the discourse form, as well as content, were severely restricted.

Searle says, in effect, that even successful passing of a Turing Test would not justify the attribution of *human-like* intelligence to an artifact. In apparent agreement with the position I take, he sees understanding as the hallmark of human intelligence, and argues that it is distinct from rule-following even if the results are the same. While I am not ready to agree that understanding cannot be implemented by rules, I do concur that not all successful rule-following constitutes understanding.

There have been many objections posed to Searle's argument; see the Open Peer Commentary to his *Behavioral and Brain Sciences* article cited above for some of them. Personally, I would claim that the experiment cannot be done, that in fact there are no rules that are functions solely of the input symbols that could lead to successful translation. Rather, a translation process must have access to a much wider set of information than is found in text, no matter how extensive. In brief, it must know the non-verbal setting that provides the context of an utterance, and it must relate all of this to knowledge about the world and about human social interactions, history, and psychological attributes, such as beliefs and desires. Thus if translation can indeed be implemented as rule-described computations, its rules must make contact with much more than the physical characterization of the sets of basic symbols of the languages.

I see no in-principle reason that such rules could not be stated, but the task of finding them is enormous, and may indeed be impossible. Thus it is still an open question whether rule-based systems that have access to all of this knowledge could understand in the human sense. Searle claims not, and argues, even more strongly, that understanding (and intentionality) cannot be exhibited by digital artifacts made out of *non-biological* material.

Contextual and general information and knowledge are not only essential to the ability to translate language, but are also relevant to many other cognitive tasks, in fact probably all of any complexity. To be sure, one can perform certain simple cognitive tasks – such as crossing out the odd integers in a series of numerals – without bringing to bear one's entire history and experience. Such activities, however, are the exception in our daily lives, and certainly are the least interesting to a science of cognition. Although we may sometimes think that the majority of us during the majority of our time move zombie-like through a series of rote tasks (such as watching TV or microwaving dinner), that is not an accurate picture. Certainly introspectively we feel that we at all times understand where we are, who we are with, what we are doing, and so forth in a way that transcends simply the ability to go through the motions. One might argue that this sense of understanding is merely an epi-phenomenon, something that accompanies our actions but is not essential to them. My view is that understanding is at the very core of all aspects of our intelligence and humanity. We have goals and we understand how our actions relate to achieving our goals. We may frequently be at a loss to actually achieve our goals, or to articulate our deepest psychic needs, but our cognition nonetheless moves in a world of goals, of problem solving, of directed actions, of understanding.

While this description will seem obvious to the non-scientist, it is a position which theoretical psychologists have not taken as central. If understanding is essential for human cognitive activity, essentially all psychological and artificial intelligence experiments and theories to date have missed the mark. To the extent that they have not moved us closer to understanding understanding, and I feel that for the most part they have not, they have been of limited value.

4. Understanding Understanding

Having examined some abilities that may be necessary, but not sufficient, to account for human level understanding, I will conclude this chapter with some general features that a theory of understanding should address.

Understanding and truth

Understanding is not about truth. Rather, understanding provides a means by which humans achieve a number of psychological and cognitive benefits. For example, psychologist Don Norman observes:

UNDERSTANDING UNDERSTANDING

> My studies convince me that even the most difficult of things becomes easy when users feel they are in control, that they know what to do, when to do it, and what to expect from the device whenever they perform an operation: in other words, when they have acquired understanding. What makes something understandable? Technical knowledge is not required, just functional. What is critical is to have a good conceptual understanding of the device. Few of us understand the technologies of the automobile, radio, or television, yet we feel comfortable with these devices because each control has a known function, we can tell when the device is working properly, and we know what to do when there are problems. We feel uncomfortable when we are out of control, when we do not know how to respond, or when our actions do not lead to the results we expect. (*The invisible computer*, 1998, MIT Press, pp. 173-174.)

Nothing in the description of understanding that I will develop implies that people always understand *correctly*, or even that they usually do. Explanations that are embraced are not thereby guaranteed to be correct, and often they are not. For example, many people understand a simple furnace thermostat as working in the way a water faucet works: turning it up increases the rate of flow (of heat rather than water). The usual thermostat and furnace do not operate this way. The furnace is either on or off, and its state depends on whether the temperature being controlled is above or below the set point. A person holding the faucet model will place the set point to a high value, believing that the house will warm faster. Obviously it would be easy to test this explanation and show it to be wrong, but for most people the need to test does not arise and there is no immediate reason to reject the hypothesis. The incorrect understanding suffices for warming the house.

It is said that if one has a hammer, everything looks like a nail. This tendency applies at all levels of humans' attempts to understand. Once a new explanation has been found useful, attempts are made to apply it more widely, sometimes with success, sometimes without. In science, these generalized views are called paradigms. Physics often attempts to describe new phenomena with differential equations, psychology with associationist concepts, artificial intelligence with rule-based models. While such attempts lead to understanding commensurate with their success, they may well be found ultimately to be blind alleys. Furthermore, finding one explanation often blinds us to the recognition of other, even better ones that comport more fully with important facts, as is often the case in criminal trials, particularly those that are media events.

In fact, it is probable that the overwhelming proportion of human understanding and belief is either false, that is, it conflicts with empirical evidence, or is in principle untestable, such as religious beliefs. Science has much higher standards of hypothesis testing than do individual people, and thus science is less subject to simple errors. However, science has generated and continues to generate false hypotheses, and scientists may resist negative evidence and new hypotheses as strongly as non-scientists.

Thus human understanding may be, and often is, a form of self-deception. Nonetheless, our ability to understand is a very powerful adaptation that allows us to succeed in a complex and mysterious universe to an extent impossible without it. Therefore, while I believe that attempting to understand is the central aspect of human cognition, I do not offer it as a way to find the truth, nor as a normative theory. Rather it will be a psychological theory: this is how the human mind works, for better or worse

Degrees of understanding

Introspectively, understanding something and not understanding it are often two quite distinct phenomenological states. We can recognize cases where we understand something – an event, an idea, a passage of prose, for example – and cases where we do not. This phenomenological clarity does not establish that understanding is *always* all-or-none; it is probably not. For complex subjects one can achieve a partial understanding. Thus there are often degrees, or depths, of understanding. For example, I understand physics to a degree, but certainly not as fully as, say, Richard Feynman did. This suggests the question: is there such a thing as full understanding (of some prescribed area) or can one always acquire ever greater amounts of understanding?

I believe that understanding is a quest. *There is no upper bound to understanding*: one can continue to gain greater understanding by covering ever more of one's knowledge under fewer conceptual umbrellas. Furthermore, on the analysis of understanding I will offer, there is no one single, correct understanding of anything; rather there are many ways to ground one's beliefs, many reasons for seeking understanding. Therefore one's understanding can always be changed or augmented by looking at the phenomena in question 'in a different light.' In technical matters, one can view a system from a Newtonian, a relativistic, or a quantum mechanical point-of-view, and each offers certain advantages. In non-technical life one may view a social issue from a psychological, a cultural, or a religious stance; again none of these is the ultimate truth, and each stance may be analyzed in any number of ways.

Cookbook understanding

At the other side of the spectrum, not understanding something well does not necessarily mean that it is totally unknown or foreign. Indeed, one may exhibit a productive knowledge of some topic and be able to answer questions about or solve problems in it – even hold down a job requiring such performance – without understanding the topic in the sense that I am concerned with here.

I would not say that I understand cooking very well, but I can follow a recipe with satisfactory results. My knowledge of cooking is, well, 'cookbook' knowledge. I know the basic context of the problem – what food is, why we eat, what tastes exist, what many of the conventional ingredients and procedures are – and can follow explicit directions that presuppose such knowledge and thus produce an edible product. This cooking-related knowledge is embedded in a larger context of knowledge about the physical world, about heat and temperature, about liquids and solids, and so forth. I can draw an inference, for example, that using a higher stove temperature will shorten cooking time. When I say I do not *understand* cooking I mean that I do not have a coherent idea of the relations among the various ingredients and techniques of the sort that enables a proficient cook to achieve consistently superior results, to depart from a recipe and still consistently produce a good product, and to invent entirely new recipes.

When engaged in my annual battle with the Internal Revenue Service requirements I am often frustrated by their cookbook directions ("compare line 13a with line 4 and copy the larger to line 17, unless it is less than zero" and so forth); I want to know what the intent of the law is and why following the IRS recipe implements this intent, something that IRS forms and instructions treat either as a secret or as irrelevant to the task of the taxpayer. Of course, with care and attention to detail one can successfully fill out the forms without understanding the intent of the law. However, to understand the intent one must read other sources, and this effort must be embedded in an extensive context of knowledge of the purpose of taxation, contemporary concepts of fairness, and so forth.

Similarly, students can know how to plug numbers into a formula and turn the arithmetical crank to obtain the correct answer without understanding why the formula works or exactly what is being computed. Such limited understanding is also cookbook understanding. There are AI programs called Expert Systems (Barr & Feigenbaum (1982), Chapter 7) that encode empirical association knowledge as rules and use an 'inference engine' to systematically apply these rules to solve problems, often technical problems that human experts find difficult. These programs are archetypes of (often very good) cookbook understanding for they have no explicit theory or explanation of their subject matter.

Understanding the formula for the solution to the general quadratic equation $ax^2 + bx + c = 0$ may result from having been able to follow or discover the sequence of algebraic transformations that – applied to the general equation – yields the formula

$$x = [-b \pm \sqrt{(b^2 - 4ac)}]/2a$$

Note that even following this derivation presupposes understanding what an equation is, what a solution of an equation is, what a solution in general is, what a variable is, what rules of algebraic manipulation are, and so forth. Building on this body of understanding, the final step of understanding that the above formula for x is a general solution requires nothing more than following the derivation. On the other hand, a student with very little grasp of these concepts may simply be given the formula and still be able to find solutions to certain specific equations by applying the formula cookbook style, without understanding. Similarly a computer could be programmed to solve quadratic equations with this formula but it would be inappropriate to claim that the computer understood what it was doing.

Subhuman species presumably have an absolute zero understanding of tax law, cooking and algebra, and of almost all other human endeavors that require higher cognition in addition to the sensory processes, memory, and perceptual-motor skills that they share with us. Is there a qualitative difference between this subhuman level of understanding and cookbook understanding, or does one smoothly blend into the other?

I believe *there is a qualitative difference between no understanding at all and some understanding (such as cookbook understanding)*. Thus subhuman primates can learn generalized empirical associations that allow them to deal successfully with their world, but still not understand it in the abstract, symbolic way that permits humans to systematically follow rules cookbook style. If so, what separates understanding by empirical associations (and their statistical regularities), such as subhuman primates use, from cookbook understanding is the ability to handle abstract concepts and their logical relations.

CHAPTER 1: UNDERSTANDING

Structural understanding

Might there be another qualitative difference at a higher level, between cookbook and real understanding, another joint at which Nature should be carved?

I believe *there is an important qualitative difference between cookbook understanding and real understanding*, which is based on the recognition of the structure of the subject and seeing its similarity to previously understood subjects. It is this demarcation that I will primarily explore in this essay.

I will argue that understanding requires the development of a coherent *model* of the topic. In engineering, a model is often a physical structure that is similar in important aspects to another (usually larger) system, such as a model airplane, or a model of the solar system. In biology, a model is often a simpler species that is studied in lieu of human experimentation. In science more generally a model may take abstract forms, such as a set of mathematical equations or a computer program. Whatever its form, a coherent model must, at least, show the essential relations among various components of the topic, and must enable one to explore variations of the model's behavior through physical action, mathematical analysis, computer program execution, or thought experiments. *Models encode the structure of a body of knowledge, and this is a key concept in my analysis.*

Understanding as reduction

Understanding and knowledge are hierarchically organized. Any one level builds on lower levels. This is related to the phenomenon of *chunking*, as revealed by human memory experiments, as well as to important properties of language. For example, a single word can be used in a sentence that relates its referent to the referents of other words in the sentence. The meaning of the word can be unpacked (as philosophers say) or unchunked (as psychologists might say) if and when it is necessary to do so. When it is not necessary to do so the word provides a succinct encoding for its bundled concept, allowing our limited attention to grasp it and its relations to other concepts.[3] The ability to learn, compose, and unpack the meanings of words is a ubiquitous human cognitive ability and has been the subject of extensive investigation in psychology at least since George Miller's classic paper on "The magical number seven, plus or minus two" (Miller (1956)).

As a more specific example of chunking, in the field of mathematics one can be taught the rules for manipulating algebraic expressions, for example that from "a = b" one can conclude "b = a." The rules of algebra eventually become accepted and indeed applied in a seemingly automatic fashion (as in "of course if a=b then b=a, why bother even pointing it out"). In this case it is not a rule name that is remembered as a package, it is the truth-preserving manipulation that can be triggered by the mere presence of the expression. Algebra teaches the student how truth-preserving sequences of these rule applications can make large compound alterations. The important macro rules, or theorems, thus created are eventually accepted as names of or proxies for rule sequences,

---

[3] For example, "7,429 is a prime number" may simply provide us with a new fact, but if we wish, we can unpack the meaning of "prime number" and "7,429" and see if the claim is true.

each of whose components has previously been accepted and understood. At that point, we could say that the macro rule or theorem is understood in the sense that it can be applied as a single rule with full justification, without actually breaking it down into its explicit steps. The SOAR model of human cognition (Newell (1990)) makes quite explicit one way in which this chunking process might work.

I will argue that understanding understanding requires a hierarchical approach, the same as does understanding anything else. Thus while rules are a universal language for describing computations, and while computations *may* be a universal language for describing cognition, we will still fail to understand understanding unless we are able to construct appropriate layers of analysis on top of the rules, just as we cannot understand biology directly in terms of the fundamental physical constructs, quarks and leptons (or superstrings and p-branes). To understand biology we must construct a host of *bridging structures* including atoms, molecules, cells, membranes and organs, together with ancillary explanatory concepts such as thermodynamics, statistics, information theory and evolution. At each level, new descriptive concepts emerge, concepts that often depend on the aggregation of concepts from lower levels, and are simply not present at the lower levels. Atoms are not wet; water is. A single bird cannot flock. See Holland (1999). *To understand understanding we must create levels of organization on top of the concept of rule.*

5. What Abilities Underlie Understanding?

If understanding is more than associative learning, goal-directedness, possessing knowledge, reasoning, consciousness, symbolic abstraction, and rule-following, then what more is it? If understanding is a *special kind* of rule-following, then what is its special nature that carries it beyond the AI programs of today?

Chapter 2 examines:

Biological abilities possessed by all mammals, including humans.

Cognitive abilities unique to all humans and not available to subhumans or machines.

Chapter 3 examines:

Computational abilities available to current computing artifacts and some humans.

Chapters 4, 5, and 6 examine:

Uniquely human achievements, in particular mathematical understanding, the understanding of diagrams, and the ability to discern and exploit the structure of knowledge through analogy, metaphor, and theory.

Human understanding requires all four of these types of abilities. Thus to understand understanding in a way that accounts for uniquely human activities such as language, literature, art, science, mathematics, and religion, as well as special cases of these, including diagrammatic reasoning, we must know the relevant animal abilities and the relevant machine abilities, as well as uniquely human abilities.

In the cases of deepest understanding there must be established a relationship between a coherent model and some previously understood coherent model, which is in turn is understood at yet a deeper level. Ultimately, *these models must be grounded in inherent biological capacities*, such as those of our perceptual-motor system, which have developed over evolutionary time and permit our successful adaptation to the natural world. This grounding is provided by our perceptual-motor connection with the world, a connection we share with other mammals.

2 NATURAL INTELLIGENCE

There can be no doubt that the difference between the
mind of the lowest man and that of the highest animal is
immense. Nevertheless the difference, great as it is,
certainly is one of degree and not of kind.
                              – Charles Darwin (1809–1882)

1. Introduction

Since Darwin, the idea that there is a continuity of cognitive abilities among the animals
has dominated psychological thinking. Differences between, say, chimpanzees and
humans were considered matters of degree, with humans having the same cognitive
abilities, greatly perfected. It is possible, however, that humans have evolved certain
cognitive abilities that subhuman primates simply do not have in *any* degree. The
continuity-discontinuity question is still open.

Another seemingly Darwinian view that is popular in the lay mind, but which does not
follow from Darwin's thinking, is that there is a single dimension of intelligence along
which all animals can be arrayed, with humans at the highest extreme. In fact,
evolutionary theory suggests that this is not the case. Abilities do not form a simply
ordered set. Although evolution in general builds new features on top of the old, it
follows many different paths corresponding to the available environmental niches to
which various organisms adapt. Thus dogs do not swim like fish nor fly like birds, rather
they have adapted to a terrestrial form of locomotion. This does not mean dogs are
more, or less, successful at self-propelled motion than fish or birds, only that they are
different. Dogs, fish, and birds all exist today so all are 'successful.' The same is true of
cognition and perception.

There are many kinds of eyes and ears, and we lack some senses that other species
(such as bats) have perfected. There are many other kinds of adaptations. We humans
have some kinds that we either do not share with any other organisms, or possess to such
an extreme degree that they are *de facto* unique.

Even without human-unique abilities, many animals, particularly the sub-human
primates, are able to succeed at many complex cognitive tasks, including way-finding,

problem-solving, and learning. Since humans are capable of additional, extremely important achievements, it is appropriate to ask what additional cognitive capacities we have that are not shared by our nearest relatives. It is not easy to sort out and precisely characterize cognitive abilities, and there is not complete agreement on just how we differ from other species (Byrne (2000)). However, there clearly are qualitative differences, even in cases where chimpanzees, the other apes, and monkeys have the rudiments of a human ability.

The genomes of humans and of the modern chimpanzee differ by two to five percent, making these two species genetically closer than the horse and zebra, for example. The greater estimate of difference is derived by comparisons of whole genomes, using indirect chemical methods ((Diamond (1992)), the lesser on more recent evidence based on DNA sequencing (Britten (2002)). Recently, both the chimpanzee and the human genome have been sequenced, so more detailed comparisons will be forthcoming. Mammalian genomes include large amounts (estimated at over 90%) of non-coding DNA, that is, sequences that do not get translated into proteins or RNA products and thus, presumably, have no effect. Many of the human/chimpanzee DNA differences may be in this non-coding part. Thus the above percentage could mis-estimate the similarity with our nearest biological neighbor one way or the other depending on how the differences are split between coding and non-coding portions. At the moment it is not known how many functional genes our genome has, but the current estimates are 30,000–40,000 [Claverie (2001); Venter & others (2001)]. Thus we might guess that on the order of 1000 genes differ between chimpanzee and human. These must account for the seemingly huge cognitive differences between the species, as well as the physical differences. Given the complexity of interaction of genes (one must not think that one gene = one trait), this could easily be enough to bring about the differences between humans and chimpanzees, including the cognitive differences. It would appear that four billion years of evolution set the stage for the rapid human leap forward, a process that took only a small fraction of that history.

The most obvious cognitive ability humans possess that other animals do not is language. This seems to have arisen in fairly rapid fashion by evolutionary standards, about 50,000-100,000 years ago. This one change could possibly account for the enormous cognitive differences between humans and chimpanzees. It may be the case, however, that it was preceded by or combined with other major differences. Tomasello (1999a) and many others argue that humans have another essential ability not possessed by other species, namely the ability to understand others, as well as oneself, as intentional creatures. That is, we are able to imagine ourselves in someone else's place, imagine that person's goals, and predict that person's behavior based on his presumed goals. This is sometimes called having a *Theory of Mind*, that is, a theory that understands our own minds as intentional decision makers and projects this model onto others. It appears not to be present in monkeys, and the extent to which it is present in chimpanzees is still a matter of debate (Byrne, 2002). It is not a single ability, but a collection of them, including experiencing emotions, intentions, beliefs, knowledge and other mental states; attributing each of these to others (including other humans, animals, and inanimate 'agents'), experiencing false beliefs and attributing such to others, imitation of goal achievement by others (as opposed to rote action following), pretending, fantasy play, deception, and the ability to simulate the mental states of others.

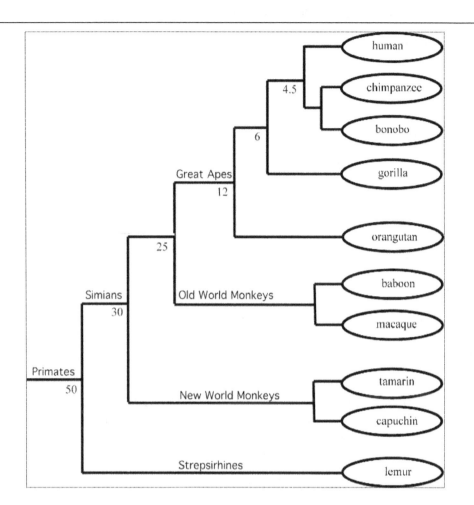

Figure 1
Primate Phylogeny
The numbers indicate approximate dates of divergence in millions of years. From R. W. Byrne, Evolution of primate cognition, *Cognitive Science*, 2000, 24(3), Figure 1, page 547. © 2000 The Cognitive Science Society, used with permission and with permission of the author.

Tomasello argues that Theory of Mind is essential for the development of culture. While it is not clear how this ability is related to language, whether one preceded and enabled the other, or whether they developed as two aspects of a common underlying ability, it is clear that both are necessary for higher cognitive processes and the accumulation of knowledge through cultural transmission. Thus over historical time an enormous gap has arisen between human and sub-human species in the ability to control and dominate the environment, even though most of evolutionary time was needed to get all primates to their present biologically very similar positions.

2. Shared Mammalian Abilities

Goal-directed perceptual motor skills
Of dogs and men

My German Shepherd, Zwei, and I are on the beach. I hold a Frisbee. Zwei waits about twenty yards from me, forelegs bent causing her head to be lower than her hindquarters. Her eyes are focused on the Frisbee. As she waits her eyes occasionally dart to my face, then back to the Frisbee. I flick my wrist but retain the Frisbee. She immediately turns left but then returns to face me, crouching again. If I hold longer she barks and wags her tail, her forepaws doing a quick dance in the sand. I bend my elbow and bring the Frisbee close to my body, then fling it into the air. Zwei immediately dashes away from me following the Frisbee's flight. The device curves slowly in the air. Zwei is running away from me, the Frisbee is now returning as it descends. A gust of wind lifts it above its path of descent. Zwei smoothly leaves the sand, tucking her legs under her. Her mouth opens and closes full of Frisbee. She extends her legs and lands, turns and trots toward me. I grasp the Frisbee but she growls and does not release it, shaking her head as she resists my pull. Finally she releases it, runs away about twenty yards, turns to face me and once again crouches, her eyes on the disk in my hand.

The center fielder leans over, hands on his knees, his gaze directed toward the infield. The pitcher goes into his motion and throws the ball toward home plate. The center fielder sees the motion of the pitcher's arm and sees the batter swing. A fraction of a second later after the bat has completed its swing he hears a sharp crack of ball colliding with bat. He begins to move toward his right. He sees the white ball ascend into the sky. He moves slowly and deliberately in a gently curved path. As the ball descends he continues to move. When the ball is fifteen feet above the ground the center fielder raises his gloved hand and continues his fluid running. His glove intercepts the ball and closes around it. The fielder's other hand is moving upward. The gloved hand moves smoothly downward until the two hands meet. The ungloved hand removes the ball, moves backward in a smooth arc. The center fielder's gaze is now again on the infield, directed toward the shortstop who has moved in his direction. The fielder's upper arm holding the ball moves forward in a smooth arc, the hand holding the ball behind the elbow and toward the fielder's body. The upper arm slows its progress and the forearm accelerates until the hand is in front of the body and coming in a downward arc. The fingers release the ball which sails in an arc toward the shortstop who is watching it. The shortstop remains motionless, then raises his gloved hand just in time to receive the ball.

We would say that the dog and the outfielder are each demonstrating a perceptual motor skill, using coordination of eye and hand (or mouth), and so forth. Clearly the skills are not identical and indeed the dog cannot throw a baseball, and the man would have difficulty catching a Frisbee with his mouth. However, it is sensible and useful to describe these two skills as variations of an underlying ability. How are they the same? How are they different?

One striking and important common feature of these two behaviors is that each operates in real time. One cannot catch a ball or a Frisbee if it takes longer to decide where it will land than it takes the projectile to get there. One could, *in principle*, compute the object's point of impact from the laws of physics, given perfect information of the initial values of the relevant variables of location and momentum when it leaves the hand or bat, and given perfect information about the winds, temperature, air density, etc. along its path. *In fact*, one could not do so with unlimited precision because such precise knowledge of initial conditions is unavailable. Such things can never be known precisely under the best of conditions, so even the human outfielder can know them only very imprecisely.

Sometimes we see evidence that confirms the belief that outfielders make accurate predictions. A classic case is Willie Mays' famous catch in the 1954 World Series. Mr. Mays turned at the crack of the bat, raced away from the infield without looking at the ball, turned at the last instant and intercepted the ball with his glove. Such extreme examples of fielding performance are rare. What seems a better description for the general case – better than an outfielder (much less a dog) who makes measurements of physical quantities and solves differential equations – is that each has representations of space and mechanics sufficient to make short range predictions from perceptual data. These predictions are continually updated as new information arrives, a procedure known as dynamic programming. Of course the predictions need to be accurate enough for the skill to succeed, at least sometimes. They appear to be. Are these predictions and the representations on which they are based conscious? The outfielder (ourselves included) would say they are not. Zwei does not say.

McBeath, Shaffer & Kaiser (1995) proposed an explanation of how a fielder performs his task. In this model, the fielder follows the ball visually and moves in such a way that the path of the ball appears to be a straight line. See Figure 2: Catching a Baseball. This results in an interception. The model makes some interesting predictions. It should be more difficult to catch balls hit directly toward the fielder. Ball players report this to be the case, and often move to one side when the ball is hit directly toward them. Also, the model predicts that the fielder's path will be curved and not of constant velocity, even though it might seem that such trajectories are more difficult to compute. These predictions also are borne out by observation.

Demonstrating that this strategy will work is not trivial, and we should not assume that the fielder has discovered this procedure by mathematical analysis. Nonetheless the method is computationally reasonable, that is, it seems to be something that people can do in real time, employing perceptual processes that are easy, such as detecting straight paths. The method, which requires constant monitoring and error correction, also works when the path of the ball departs from an ideal parabola, due to wind, spin, or other factors. Although Frisbee flight is more complex, some similar perceptual constancy-preserving algorithm might well be available for dog or man *qua* Frisbee catcher.

Although differing in detail as noted, these two examples of skilled behavior by dog and man are remarkably similar, so much so that it seems unlikely that they are accomplished in entirely different ways, by entirely different computational processes and entirely different neural structures. In fact given that both dog and man are mammals and are known to share large amounts of sensory, biochemical, and neural structures, it seems very likely that the underlying processes are quite similar. Nature – evolution – does not as a rule throw things away, but rather builds on successful solutions.

Clearly, however, dogs and ballplayers differ in their *understanding* of their actions. The ballplayer has concepts of athletic competition, score-keeping, turn-taking, rule-following and so forth that we should not attribute to dogs. It is not clear just what the dog's con-

Figure 2
Catching a Baseball
By running so that the ball seems to rise in a straight line, a fielder will intercept the path of the ball. From B. A. Cipra, Catching fly balls: A new model steps up to the plate. *Science*, 268 (April 1995), page 502, redrawn from M. K. McBeath, D. M. Shaffer, and M. K. Kaiser, How baseball outfielders determine where to run to catch fly balls, same issue, pages 569-573. Reprinted with permission from American Association for the Advancement of Science.

ception of the activity might be. We are apt to think that she is enjoying the play, and predict that she will repeat it for a while. Does she have a model of me that attributes similar experiences of fun and enjoyment to her playmate? There is no evidence for this, and reason to believe otherwise (Tomasello (1999a)). Certainly such an assumption is not necessary to explain the behavior we observe.

Of course one major difference between dog and man is that man has language and dog does not. We attribute knowledge of games and scores to the man because we recognize them as predicative knowledge in our own minds and because other people describe their mental contents in similar terms. That dogs do not is not sufficient to prove that dogs have no such predicative knowledge, but since they lack language in which to express it, it is difficult to imagine how else it might be recorded in their brains or bodies.

Of cats and boys

My cat Bones walks slowly across the lawn. Suddenly a mouse emerges from under a pile of brush in front of the cat but off to his right a bit. Bones stops and remains still. The mouse wanders about for a few seconds, getting farther from the brush pile. The cat begins to creep toward the brush pile. The mouse stops, raises his head, then dashes off across the lawn. The cat begins to run rapidly after the mouse. The mouse zigs, the cat zigs; the mouse zags, the cat zags. The cat gets closer. The mouse turns and runs toward the brush pile. He doesn't make it. The cat bites the mouse in the neck and it drops to the ground, alive but unable to move. The cat strikes it softly with his paw. The mouse twitches. This is repeated until the mouse no longer twitches. The cat picks up the mouse in his mouth and goes to the door of my house where he lives, drops it on the ground and begins to make loud noises. Eventually the cat lies down and begins to gnaw at the mouse's head. He devours most of it, leaves the entrails, and wanders back to the lawn.

A group of boys is playing tag. The one who is 'it' runs toward a group that splits into different directions. 'It' follows one group, but is unable to catch up. Suddenly he breaks off that chase to go after another nearby boy who has stopped running. That boy starts to run and the chase continues. 'It' stops, unsuccessful. 'It' feigns fatigue as he saunters toward another group. Appearing about to collapse, he suddenly breaks into a run toward the smallest boy. The group disperses. 'It' is closing on the smaller boy who dodges behind a large tree. 'It' starts to run in one direction around the tree, then reverses. The smaller boy moves oppositely, attempting to keep the tree between them.

While the dog and man could rely upon the laws of physics to remain constant during their catch play, the cat presumably has much less certain information to go on in determining the mouse's choices of direction and speed. We might imagine that the cat tacitly 'knows' a good deal of mouse psychology and biomechanics and thus can narrow the options open to it. Mice cannot fly, nor accelerate at 5 g's, though if one did the cat might simply go back to sleep, nonplussed. Nonetheless, the cat's instincts and experience have provided enough information to track the mouse simply by reacting quickly to its movements.

The boy has a similar problem and similar information about boy-mechanics. However, here again it is clear that the boy is using a much more complex model of his prey's psychology than is the cat. Strategies are involved, deception is brought to bear. While the perceptual motor task is quite similar, the conception of the situations is surely not the same, nor are the stakes. The boys understand a game is being played and although the participants may be ego-involved and quite emotional about winning and losing, they know it is just a game. The cat and mouse are of course not playing a game, and it is not necessary to assume that either knows exactly what is going on. Each may be said to be attempting to achieve a goal, powered by perceptual-motor skills. That and nothing more is needed to account for the cat-mouse activity. The human game of tag relies on additional knowledge and cognitive skills.

Cognitive abilities

Non-human animals are curious. Mammals in general have goals (desires). They communicate with conspecifics with various kinds of signals. All mammals are able to detect perceptual similarities (for example similar intensities of light) so that their responses generalize to perceptual classes of objects. In spite of lack of language, primates appear to be able not only to recognize perceptual categories but also to represent other knowledge of these categories, such as how to respond to the presence of a member of a category. Further, chimpanzees, but not monkeys, can learn *cognitive* categories based on *relations* of perceptual properties, such as the concept of *food* that includes perceptually distinct types of food. While all animals discriminate food from non-food, only chimpanzees (and humans) are able to *represent* the class of food objects, that is, they can treat all members of the class in a similar manner. However, even chimpanzees appear to need first to be taught, by humans, a symbolic communication system in order to achieve relational categories of this type (Thompson & Oden (2000)). When this is done it allows captive chimpanzees to behave appropriately and successfully in a world of perceptual regularities and do so in ways that lower mammals cannot.

Many animals do dead-reckoning and orient spatially in a manner consistent with geometric knowledge (Hauser (2000)). All primates live in the same sensory-motor world of objects arrayed in space, all have problem-solving skills, and can remember locations and events in space (Tomasello & Call (1997)). Chimpanzees in the wild use found tools and create simple tools, such as spears, from found objects, but they are not able to do this competently until well into adulthood, at age eight or nine. Various primates recall and infer food locations, select efficient travel routes, anticipate the positions of moving targets, mentally rotate objects, plan object manipulation sequences, and understand some cause-effect relations between tools and goals (Call (2000)). However, even chimpanzees do not understand simple physical principles such as statics (the forces acting on stationary objects), and they balance blocks or boxes only by trial-and-error.

If an organism or mechanism is able to do a cognitive task, it presumably must internally *represent* the knowledge, skills, and so forth that the task requires. There must be many specific types of representation since some animals exhibit some but not all cognitive abilities. It may be, as seems likely, that some of these representations form a hierarchy, so that animals that have higher representations also have all those below it in the hierarchy. The theoretical concept of a cognitive representation has been widely adopted in discussions of intelligence, both artificial and natural, and it is discussed further below.

While perceptual and motor skills can in general be readily observed, discovering what goes on 'inside the head' of an animal or infant (or even an adult) requires more indirect experimental techniques, combined with theoretical assumptions, for their interpretation. The next two sections describe some of the methods and theoretical constructs that are currently in use and have proved valuable in describing and comparing cognitive abilities of animals and humans.

3. Empirical Study of Cognitive Abilities

The last few decades have seen important empirical work focused on discovering what cognitive abilities chimpanzees possess and lack, and in determining when various cognitive abilities first appear in human infants.

On the one hand, chimpanzees do remarkable things. On the other hand, many of these things can be done with fairly simple associative and conditioning mechanisms that do not involve complex symbolic representations. The field of psychology still remembers Clever Hans, a horse purported to be able to count. Hans would tap his hoof to indicate the number of objects he saw, or even the sum of two quantities. The show was very convincing, but was finally unmasked when it was noticed that Hans took his cue from subtle signals from his handler, signals of which even the handler was unaware. In other words, Hans' success was achieved through a simple conditioning process, and did not reveal any concept of number after all.

If a chimpanzee exhibits some human-like behavior it is tempting to assume, even more so than for a horse, that the basis of this behavior is the same as it is in humans. This tendency toward false-attribution is itself a human characteristic, deriving from the fact that we think with language and with an understanding that other humans are very like us. This ability to take an intentional stance toward others often runs amok: we too readily attribute motives and emotions to other animals and even to inanimate objects.

Given the tendency for false-attribution, it is important to find ways to determine when it is and when it is not appropriate to attribute an ability to another species. Since other species lack human language ability, that avenue is not available to us. Experimental psychology has invented and refined many empirical methods based on the behaviorist approach. The general technique is to present a subject with a task involving a choice and giving a reward when the 'correct' choice is made. In this way it is possible to determine if the subject is able to make a perceptual discrimination, or recognize classes of stimuli based on a variety of types of defining abstractions, to determine if the subject could run a maze of a given complexity, solve a mechanical puzzle, or cooperate with another. If after sufficient opportunities the subject was unable to succeed at better than a chance rate it is concluded that the necessary abilities are lacking in that organism at its state of development. In order to correctly characterize the subject's ability, however, one must have correctly determined what abilities are necessary and sufficient to perform the task at hand, and this is usually difficult.

Another empirical avenue exploits emotions. These techniques are particularly useful in studying social cognition – what the organism knows about others. For example, it has been shown that chimpanzees will become angry under certain conditions where they are treated 'unfairly' in comparison to others. The presence of rage, or of refusal to perform further, suggests that the animal has the related concept of fairness.

A different type of method has proved extremely useful with human infants who are not only non-verbal but also unable to perform complex motor manipulations. It turns out that if an infant is shown a situation that is expected he attends to it with his gaze for a shorter time than he attends to a situation that is unexpected. For example, if an infant sees one toy that is then obscured by a screen and then the screen is removed after a few moments to reveal either (a) that same toy or (b) two toys, he will gaze longer at (b) presumably indicating that he expected the number of toys to remain the same. This preferential looking technique has been extremely useful in the study of chimpanzees and other mammals as well.

Using these and other empirical methods, primatologists and developmental psychologists have in recent years uncovered many important facts about cognition. As research continues we will likely discover more abilities possessed by primates and young human infants, whereas the list will not likely decrease, for once an ability has been observed we would not expect it to disappear.

4. Representations of Cognitive Abilities

A representation is a putative structure in the brain/mind that encapsulates a concept, type of knowledge, or ability. It could be as simple as a memory 'trace' which leaves a record of a stimulus event that can be matched to new events and provide recognition. More generally a representation is a symbolic record that can itself be manipulated in conjunction with other symbolic records to produce 'thoughts' which may, or may not, ultimately result in action. In general it is not known how representations are recorded in brains, but the assumption is that there is some sort of alteration of structure, connectivity, or activity that corresponds to that which is represented, and that different classes of concepts require different representation substrates. If an organism cannot represent a particular type of concept then it cannot 'think' about it, that is, it will not notice instances of it, solve problems that require it as part of the solution, and so forth.

Note that any representation is a non-directly observable theoretical construct, that is, something the theorist defines and relates to other theoretical constructs in an attempt to describe and explain cognition. It is also generally something attributed to the organism in question. That is, a representation is something the organism is said to 'have,' presumably somehow present in the organism's body or, perhaps, mind. Similarly an electron is a theoretical construct, with properties such as mass and charge, used to describe matter within a system of other theoretical constructs; but an electron is also assumed to be something that atoms 'have' in the sense that there are physical embodiments of electrons within the physical world of atoms. Comparisons of the cognitive capabilities of animals, humans, and artifacts largely amount to determining (or constructing, in the case of artifacts) the kinds of representations each entity can use.

Behaviorist accounts permitted only descriptions of the relation between stimulus and response, each of which must be directly observable events external to the organism. Behaviorist accounts eschewed any mention of intermediate concepts, mental contents or brain states that connect stimulus and response. The contemporary notion of a representation does not accept this restriction. However, if we consider a simple association of stimulus and response to be a minimal form of mental record, then even associationist accounts would be said to embrace the notion of representation. Since even strictly 'behaviorist' associations are not between unique stimuli and unique responses, but between perceptual classes and response classes (acts) the association already must do considerable computational work.

Clearly the ability to form associations on the basis of experiencing events is an essential cognitive activity, but it is not sufficient to account for all complex activity. Therefore modern psychological theory asserts that goals must have representations that are more complex than simple stimulus-response associations, because goals include not just specific physical goal-objects that can be reached by a 'response,' but also desires that can be fulfilled by a variety of actions that are functionally, but perhaps not physically, similar. More complex representations are needed, and it is important to know their functional roles, even though we do not at present know how they are realized in nervous systems. Knowledge of the functional role of a representation means, first of all, knowing what kinds of information/knowledge/events it records and how it is employed in the activities of the organism.

All mammals also have emotions, although these emotions may be expressed in different ways. Even lower animals exhibit rage and fear, for example, through facial expressions and motor activity, but only humans blush and cry tears. There is general agreement that emotion and thinking are intertwined, so ultimately a theory of cognition must explain this relation, and a complete theory of cognition must also represent emotional states.

5. Core Human Cognitive Abilities

Some contemporary cognitive and developmental psychologists have introduced the concept of *core knowledge* [Spelke, Breinlinger, Macomber & Jacobson (1992); Carey & Spelke (1996); Hauser & Carey (1998), Byrne (2000); Tomasello (2000)], knowledge that is *common and unique* to all normal humans, and that must thus be representable in human minds but not the minds of other species. Such knowledge must be innate, although not in the narrow sense that each of us possesses this knowledge at birth, but rather that each of us has the inherent ability to develop such knowledge through normal maturation and normal experiences in the world. Cognitive neuroscientists and those who use analogs of neural networks to model intelligence tend not to embrace the core knowledge concept, and the existence and boundaries of such knowledge are still in dispute. My position is that the notion is important, and if the abilities underlying the acquisition and use of such knowledge could be given precise, computational descriptions (that is, if they could be reduced to physical processes) this would be a major advance in the study of all forms of cognition.

There has also been a debate on cognitive *modularity* (Fodor (1983)), roughly whether abilities are packaged psychologically and neurologically in separable, un-analyzable units. Clearly the idea of core knowledge is in harmony with the concept of modularity, but neither entails the other, and I will not address the modular mind debate further.

I will examine the following putative core abilities: language, number, object recognition and mechanics, causality, intention and theory of mind, abduction (thinking hypothetically), and pedagogy/social knowledge.

Language

One example of core knowledge is the knowledge underlying natural language. Language, of course, is not necessarily a single ability, and it could be the case that one may have some of the components of linguistic ability necessary to achieve understanding without having full language ability.

The Language Acquisition Device postulated by Chomsky (1965) is the clearest example of a form of core knowledge, and the linguistic knowledge that it engenders almost surely is related to many uniquely human cognitive abilities, whether as cause or effect or, more likely, through some elaborate intertwining. Chomsky argued that humans must have an innate ability to acquire the syntax of a natural language. This is trivially true, since all humans acquire language, absent some severe accident or bizarre, non-social environment, while other species do not. The force of the argument, however, comes from the fact that experience with *linguistic utterances alone* does not provide enough information for a child to infer his language's syntax, hence he must come predisposed to consider only certain patterns of grammatical rules and/or make extensive use of non-linguistic information. This was proved mathematically by Gold (1967).

Many empirical investigations of chimpanzee behavior have been devoted to attempts to determine if they have at least the rudiments of natural language. Although chimpanzees lack the flexible vocal tract that humans use for our highly articulated speech, chimpanzees have been successfully taught to communicate by using plastic tokens, by touching symbols on a computer screen, and by using hand signs. However, it takes extensive and focused training for a chimpanzee to learn to use symbols or hand signs to communicate with a human. It is significant that chimpanzees reared in the wild without human intervention never develop anything like human natural language, even though they are adept communicators of some things, such as alarms and emotional state.

Nonetheless, *with training* chimpanzees are able to learn hundreds or even thousands of different symbols that function as single word utterances. A more difficult and important question is whether they are able to combine these symbols into sentences that display a rudimentary use of syntax, and to use symbols in novel situations for which they have received no explicit prior training. Early studies suggested that they can. For example, one chimpanzee who had learned signs for "water" and "bird" spontaneously signed "water-bird" upon seeing a swan. If one observed a child doing this it would be perfectly reasonable to attribute a rudimentary syntax to the child, since clearly the child will eventually achieve full language ability. However, if we reign in our tendency to attribute human abilities to animals, we might well ask if the chimpanzee was simply responding independently to two stimuli, a bird and water, to which it had extensive prior training that associated these referents with signs. While "water-bird" is more suggestive than "bird-water," perhaps the chimpanzee only got the word order 'right' by chance.

Early enthusiasm for chimpanzee-language was dashed by Terrace, Petitto, Sanders & Bever) who carefully examined over 22,000 chimpanzee utterances and concluded that all of them, including some that were longer that two symbols, could be accounted for as simple conditioned responses to their trainers. Shades of Clever Hans. Terrace further concluded that all chimpanzee utterances were imperatives (such as "give me food") and chimpanzees never made a declarative statement (such as "that is a water-bird").

Chimpanzees, even after extensive training in captivity by humans, do not use phrase embeddings or other forms of complex, recursive syntax (Hauser, Chomsky & Fitch (2002)), have limited notions of reference, do not use pronouns, variables, and quantifiers in a general way, do not understand either truth or logical validity, and do not communicate about their intentions. They are not able by any means to symbolize complex situations or events or abstractions. Chimpanzee communication with other chimpanzees in the wild is much more limited than their communication in captivity with humans. In their natural habitats they do not share attention with conspecifics by pointing or gesturing to distal objects or events, they do not hold up objects for others to see, they do not bring others to locations to observe what is there, and do not offer objects to others (Tomasello (2000)). There is some evidence, however, that they share attention by noticing the gaze of others (Premack & Premack (2003)).

There is still much to be learned about the exact mechanisms underlying chimpanzee communication, but it is safe to say that even after extensive training they come nowhere near human-level language use. If it is 'merely' a difference in degree, the degree is so large as indeed to constitute a *de facto* difference in kind.

Number

Chimpanzees and even lower animals understand number to the extent that they can individuate objects (not necessarily of the same kinds). Some species, including chimpanzees, can distinguish small numerosities up to 3 or 4 but greater quantities are not discriminated: the typical chimpanzee counts *1, 2, 3, large*. Chimpanzees can grasp simple additions and subtractions (1+1 = 2, 3 − 2 = 1, etc., but not 2 + 3 = 5) as demonstrated by preferential looking at the situations contrived to present the wrong answers (Hauser (2000)). They can also discriminate between large numerosities, provided the differences are substantial. Both chimpanzees and young children can be taught to assign symbols (including Arabic numerals) to small integers *i.e.*, they use symbolic reference. Monkeys as well as chimpanzees can learn an ordering of arbitrary pictures or numerals and apply a concept of order to novel instances, up to at least 9 items [Brannon & Terrace (1998); Terrace, Son & Brannon (2003); Matsuzawa (2001); Boysen (1993)]. However, they do not have a general concept of integers: no chimpanzee but all human children (by age 4 or so) understand that the list of positive integers (the natural numbers) is unending, and new ones can be created by a recursive process, as with language [Dehaene (1997); Carey & Spelke (unpublished manuscript), Carey (in press)]. This core knowledge of number as a *productive* concept goes beyond the capacity of all other animals. For additional discussion see Wynn (1992).

However, the full concept of number goes well beyond even the productive understanding of integers and integer addition and subtraction. Numbers comprise a structured system of objects closed under arithmetic operations, *i.e.*, all sums, differences, etc. are numbers. The concept extends to the classes of real numbers, complex numbers and transfinite numbers as described in later sections. However, these abstract and rich concepts are the products of culture, produced gradually by a relatively small number of human individuals over many centuries and passed on to a larger portion of the population through extensive education. The majority of humans are unaware of these numerical concepts. Core human knowledge lies somewhere between subhuman primate knowledge of simple numerosity, arithmetic, and order on the one hand, and a full mathematically formal understanding of the structure of the number system on the other.

Object recognition and mechanics

Children as young as 3 months have developed knowledge of physical objects (Baillargeon & DeVos (1991)). The ability to individuate objects depends upon specific properties of physical objects, *viz.*, continuity of motion, cohesiveness (objects stay connected, and contact causes motion). Interestingly, these are not merely the perceptually apparent properties, such as color [Spelke (1994); Spelke et al. (1992); Spelke,

Phillips & Woodward (1995)]. In fact, infants and children understand and use these properties *in preference* to perceptually obvious features. Furthermore, these properties of physical objects are not the essential properties of other domains of knowledge. For example, people can be caused to move by social contact without physical contact.

While chimpanzees successfully deal with objects in space, human infants, unlike even adult chimpanzees, can represent situations that they cannot see. In preferential attending experiments, infants have been shown object motions that, after they are begun, are occluded by a screen. After the screen is removed, if the object configuration (artificially contrived behind the screen by the experimenter) is inconsistent with principles of continuity and cohesiveness, infants as young as 4 months attend longer than they do to the revelation of consistent configurations. The conclusion is that infants must be able to represent the continuation of events that they are no longer perceiving. However, infants do not reason correctly about the effects of gravity and inertia. They show no preferential interest in situations involving violation of the effects of gravity or inertia until about one year of age, and this knowledge appears to be learned in a piecemeal fashion (Spelke et al. (1992)). Knowledge of these and other physical regularities is gained later, probably through experiencing perceptual constancies.

Infants and children do not always *reason* correctly about the motion of objects in space, however. Again this is revealed by preferential looking studies. Interestingly, adults often reason on the basis of presumed principles of motion, for example concluding that a stone swung in a circle on a rope will continue in a circular motion if the rope breaks [McCloskey, Caramazza & Green (1980); McCloskey & Kohl (1983); McCloskey, Washburn & Felch (1983)]. Such mistakes are obviously not based on perceptual experiences, but must reflect informal theories about object motion.

If chimpanzees do not exhibit similar abilities, and I do not believe that any evidence that they do has yet been published, then such knowledge of object mechanics would be core human knowledge.

Causality

Human infants understand the concept of physical connections among objects underwriting a causal connection between the motion of the objects [Sperber, Premack & Premack (1995); Baillargeon (1994)]. While adult chimpanzees exhibit seemingly highly sophisticated behavior, evidence from careful experiments suggests that their abilities are based only on highly sophisticated associative and perceptual learning rather than a deeper understanding of causality of the sort even human infants possess, and surely far from the concept of causality of human adults.

This conclusion is supported by experiments on chimpanzee tool use. Chimpanzees in the wild employ found tools and even construct and modify simple tools. This suggests not only an ability to reason spatially, but a deeper understanding as well. For example, chimpanzees can learn to crack nuts by placing them on a rock and hitting them with another rock, or to capture ants and termites (for food) by dipping a thin stick into nests. However, these skills are acquired very slowly by extensive observation over months or years, and without any attempt by others to explicitly teach them (Matsuzawa (2001)). Only in captivity with extensive human instruction are chimpanzees able to use a variety of presented tools appropriately and to occasionally make modifications of tools to suit a particular task, *e.g.*, sharpening a stick to use as a spear.

CHAPTER 2: NATURAL INTELLIGENCE

Kohler (1927) reported a now classic early study of 'insight' in chimpanzees. His chimpanzee Sultan was able, for example, to stack boxes to reach a reward attached to the ceiling. Povinelli (2000) has questioned whether Sultan's performance rises to the level of 'insight,' and apparently Kohler himself made claims that are much more reserved than secondary sources report. Povinelli and colleagues employed extensive tests of several chimpanzees to determine whether chimpanzee performance reflected 'high-level' understanding of physical situations and tools, or merely a 'low-level' use of (very good) perceptual-associative skills. They conclude the latter (the terminology is theirs).

Povinelli's tests involved a variety of puzzles that humans would readily solve immediately by observation. For example, food was placed in a horizontal tube open at both ends and could be pushed out by a stick inserted in one end. If pushed in the wrong direction it would fall through a hole in the bottom of the tube and be lost. Chimpanzees learned only a simple rule (insert the stick in the end farthest from the food) but failed to apprehend the significance of this rule; for example they followed it blindly even when the hole was at the top of the tube. In tool-use experiments chimpanzees were given a choice between retrieving food placed outside their cage by pulling on a rope tied to the food, or using rakes or other implements. Chimpanzees were often successful, but again seemed to respond only to simple relations between tool and object (such as contact), not whether there was a potential causal connection (for example, they did not distinguish between a rope tied to food or merely draped on top of it).

Here is Povinelli's general conclusion:

> Initially, our apes performed as if they had no understanding of the relevant folk physics of the problem at hand. However, with additional opportunities for learning, their performances improved, and indeed, in some cases there is evidence that the apes detected and used the same relevant perceptual features of the task as humans. However, in each case, transfer experiments revealed that this knowledge did not transfer easily to perceptually novel, but conceptually similar tasks. In contrast, research with children as young as two years of age suggests rapid transfer of learning in simple tool-using situations (e.g. Brown, 1990) (Povinelli, Bering & Giambrone (2000), page 172).

Povinelli summarizes chimpanzee understanding of causality: "the chimpanzee's reasoning about both physical objects and social beings appears restricted to concepts, ideas, and procedures that are linked to the world of tangible things (Povinelli, et al. (2000), p. 338)."

Intention and theory of mind

There is an important class of physical objects – namely agents – whose behavior violates many of the constraints obeyed by insensate objects. Agents exhibit self-propelled movement and may follow irregular paths, for example. Agents cannot be understood solely on the basis of the mechanical theories described above.

Dennett (1987) argued that humans should be viewed from an *intentional stance*, by which he meant that another's behavior and cognitive abilities could best be explained by assuming that he has beliefs and desires, and uses these in attempting to achieve goals. To take the intentional stance means not only that we have our own intentions, but that we recognize them in others, and assume they work in similar causative ways for them (*i.e.*, we have a Theory of Mind). Earlier, Premack & Woodruff (1978) asked whether chimpanzees see other chimpanzees (or people) as intentional beings. Can they put themselves in another's place and figure out what the other knows and what his goals are? The question of intentionality in chimpanzees has led to a number of empirical attempts to answer it. There is still dispute over whether chimpanzees do or do not have a Theory of Mind. No one doubts that humans do.

All primates not only have goals but know they have goals, which they can mentally represent and seek to achieve. What evidence might suggest that they not only have a mental representation of themselves as a individual agents, but that they also *know* they are agents? One ability that might bear on this is the ability of mirror self-recognition. Chimpanzees react to images of themselves in mirrors [Gallup (1970), Povinelli (2000)]; most mammals do not. If a chimpanzee sees an unexpected mark on the image of himself, he will reach directly and appropriately to the corresponding spot on his body. Humans possess this ability at an early age. Oddly, gorillas seem not to have this ability, although they are genetically closer to chimpanzees than are orangutans, which do. Monkeys do not have the ability, although an early unsubstantiated report claimed that tamarins, a New World monkey, do: Hauser, Kralik, Botto-Mahan, Garrett & Oser (1995). There are some reports that dolphins and elephants (and even some birds) may have this ability as well. Thus the distribution of the ability for mirror self-recognition is not clear. In spite of the interpretation suggested above, it is not clear what role it plays as part of a Theory of Mind.

Chimpanzees follow the gaze of another, and captive chimpanzees look in the direction that a human (but not another chimpanzee) points with a finger (as do, ocassionally, dogs), but they do not understand the significance of the other's attention or what the other is seeing. These gestures are for them imperatives, not declaratives. That is, they simply use gestures as a stimulus for altering behavior, not to share attention with others [Tomasello (1999a), pages 76-77; Povinelli & Bering (2002)]. Chimpanzees do not distinguish intentional behavior from accidental behavior that is perceptually the same (for example, they do not differentially prefer a trainer who deprives them of their dinner by accidentally spilling it, from one who intentionally spills it). They do not understand what another chimpanzee needs to know in order to engage in a cooperative task, even though they at times successfully work together, especially with humans. For example, under some conditions they will cooperate with chimpanzees to get a food reward. They will enlist the help of a human, but not another chimpanzee, to move a heavy object, and they will retrieve an object for a human who has dropped it. In general, chimpanzees appear to learn with help and example from humans, but not from other chimpanzees.

Simple introspection informs each of us that adult humans have and extensively use a sophisticated Theory of Mind. There is also much evidence that shows the course of development of this system of knowledge beginning in early infancy. Human infants as young as three months follow the general direction of the eye gaze of others. By nine months of age human infants understand others as intentional agents (with attention and goals). Johnson, Slaughter & Carey (1998) have shown that infants from about 12 months appear to be driven to gaze-following by non-human objects (such as cartoons) that have features that signal human intentionality (such as possessing a face and eyes), and not solely by motion or shape or other simple perceptual features. As early as twelve months, human infants show evidence of adopting an intentional stance (Gergely, Nadasdy,

CHAPTER 2: NATURAL INTELLIGENCE

Gergely & Biro (1995)). By four years of age they understand others as mental agents (with beliefs, plans, and desires) (Tomasello (1999a), page 180).

Thus about age four children understand that others may not know all that the child himself knows. For example, if a child and another person watch while something is hidden in box A but the object is moved to box B after the other person leaves the room, a three year-old child will believe that the absent person knows the object is in box B, as does the child. After age four the child recognizes that the person will think the object is still in box A [Wimmer & Perner (1983), Perner, Leekam & Wimmer (1987), Wellman (1990)].

A variety of similar experiments have been done with children and with chimpanzees. The general conclusion, though still not fully confirmed, is that chimpanzees have a severely limited understanding of the belief states of others. The original experiments of Premack & Woodruff (1978) suggested this conclusion. Cheney & Seyfarth (1990) concluded that monkeys do not have a Theory of Mind, and Heyes (1998) concluded that all the experimental evidence supporting the claim for a Theory of Mind in nonhuman primates could be interpreted as the product of associative learning. Hauser (2000) also concludes that the current consensus is that chimpanzees do not have the essential elements of a Theory of Mind, although other evidence leaves the issue still in doubt. Thus the consensus is that only humans, and only after age five or six, attain a full psychological view of others, including reasoning about their knowledge and belief states, understanding their emotional and perceptual perspectives, being able to engage in psychologically coherent play and fantasy, and being able to exploit this knowledge through deception and persuasion.

Povinelli *et al.* (2000) suggest that the human's propensity to attribute a mind to others perhaps underlies the ease with which evidence has been found to support a non-existent theory of mind in chimpanzees, as we noted earlier. By contrast, Gopnik & Melzoff (1997) and Leslie (1994) provide evidence and cogent argument for the central role in *human* cognition of the ability to construct theories of all sorts, of which Theory of Mind is one important type.

Theory of Mind is so important for normal human adaptation that when it is not present or is impaired, as has frequently been suggested of autistic people, *e.g.*, Frith (1989), it results in very unusual behavior, though interestingly in autism it may be accompanied by astounding cognitive abilities, suggesting that theory formation in autism is only hampered for the special case of Theory of Mind.

Wellman (2002) concludes that there is now clear consensus that for humans, "[T]heory of mind knowledge: (1) is rapidly acquired in the normal case, (2) is acquired in an extended series of developmental accomplishments, (3) encompasses several basic insights that are acquired world-wide on a roughly similar trajectory, (4) requires considerable learning and development based on an infantile set of prepared abilities to attend to and represent persons, (5) manifests an important fusion of first and third person perspective that allows us to use our own experiences to consider the nature of others' minds, and (6) is severely impaired in autism (page 33 of manuscript)."

This brings us to the next important core ability.

Abduction: thinking hypothetically

Theory of Mind is an example of the ability to think hypothetically, that is, to hypothesize a structured explanation. C. S. Peirce introduced the term *abduction* for this form of thinking. Wikipedia offers this definition of *abduction*:

> **Abduction**, or **inference to the best explanation**, is a method of reasoning in which one chooses the hypothesis that would, if true, best explain the relevant evidence. Abductive reasoning starts from a set of accepted facts and infers their most likely, or best, explanations. The term *abduction* is also sometimes used to just mean the generation of hypotheses to explain observations or conclusions, but the former definition is more common both in philosophy and computing.

Clearly humans do this extensively. Hypotheses *can* be explored mentally and evidence *may* be sought to support of refute the hypotheses. However, such hypothesis exploration and testing are not always done, and negative evidence is often ignored. Thus while abductive thinking is a powerful form of cognition, it may often lead to a focus on incorrect explanations and a failure to consider alternatives. Often the hypotheses generated involve the mental states of others, but they need not. That is, the same ability underlying Theory of Mind can be used to reason about other things, such as physical situations. Or diagrams, as I will argue in a later section.

A full ability to create and think theoretically, including a full Theory of Mind, requires the ability to create meta-representations, that is, representations of representations. To understand that another agent has mental states like one's own requires understanding (representing) mental states so that one can reason about them, not just use them. In order to know about bananas *I* must have a mental representation of bananas. In order to know that *you* know about bananas *I* must know that *you* have a mental representation of bananas.

Which came first, Theory of Mind or general abduction? This chicken and egg question might go either way. Clearly abduction leading to successful (adaptive) tool use would be selected for, and could then have been applied to understanding others. Conversely, understanding others could have led to complex social structure that also provided an adaptive edge; the mental capacities thus honed could then have been transferred to tool use and other non-social skills. Perhaps more likely is that cognitive computational skills arose to serve both ends over the same evolutionary period.

What is necessary for the more general of these theory formation skills, namely abduction? Many of the cognitive skills present in non-human primates are essential, such as the ability to form perceptual categories, to represent perceptual concepts mentally, to have intentions. In addition, mental representations must be extended to non-perceptual categories, and must be able to denote things not present here and now. From this it is presumably another significant step to the representation of abstractions, things that are nowhere.

However, for abduction it is also necessary to be able to form new relations among objects and to form larger structures of these representations, such as hierarchies. Thought must also become productive, that is, it must combine elements of a finite set into unbounded larger structures in a variety of ways. One must be able to understand generative classes, to see for example that one can construct an endless set of integers or sentences. One must somehow come to the concept of structure, which I will discuss at length later. One must be able to apply this concept of structure, and the constrained cognitive simulations that it permits, to generatively produce and explore structured models that serve as hypotheses. Only humans do these things.

Pedagogy and social knowledge

Chimpanzees have no writing system, and therefore the knowledge of one generation cannot be preserved for posterity. Nor does it accumulate. Each chimpanzee must learn anew each important fact and procedure of its life. Furthermore, chimpanzees do not teach each other (Premack & Premack (2003)). Chimpanzees learn through imitation, but not fully in the sense that humans do. By watching another chimpanzee or a human, they learn to respond in a similar way to a similar stimulus. However, they imitate the *actions* of others, not their goal seeking *method* (Tomasello (1999a)). Even their learning by imitation is severely limited. Again, each individual must discover everything essentially by itself, just as lower animals do.

This is not because chimpanzees are not social. They share many social traits with humans, including sexual and friendship bonds, group cohesiveness, and tribal organization, complete with intergroup violence. The reason chimpanzees do not have a cumulative culture appears to be that they do not have the cognitive capacities necessary for representing, communicating, and recording the products of culture, even the limited ones (such as simple tool use) that they are capable of discovering *ab initio* with each generation. Further, the chimpanzee's lack of a Theory of Mind is a major obstacle to the social accumulation of knowledge through pedagogy, which could in principle be attained even without written language. Thus culture may not be an additional type of core knowledge, but rather a derivative of the other human-unique features, particularly but not exclusively language.

6. Summary of Cognitive Abilities of Animals

Table 1: Cognitive Abilities of Animals summarizes current best evidence for a variety of cognitive abilities that have been studied in mammals, chimpanzees, and humans. The abilities are (only) roughly grouped as basic primate abilities, social interactions, psychological knowledge, language abilities, mathematical abilities, and human cultural knowledge and activities. Human infants are included in the Table because developmental sequence can suggest the interdependence of abilities. However, the essential message for the purpose of this essay is that adult humans possess important cognitive abilities that subhumans lack.

This table is illustrative but not definitive. The animal categories are broad and the abilities are not precisely defined. Research is actively being pursued and additional abilities, particularly with chimpanzees and human infants, are being noted and finer distinctions are being made. For example, chimpanzees at times point to share attention with humans but not with other chimpanzees; this distinction is not captured in the Table. No distinction is made between chimpanzees and bonobos, yet some researchers believe that chimpanzee aggressiveness may mask certain cooperative abilities they possess, because these abilities are clear in bonobos, a cognitively very similar but less aggressive species. An entry of "?" is used when data are not available but there is reason to believe that ability is present.

Notes for Table 1

Typical Mammals entries indicate abilities, and their lack, that generally but not universally are available, or not, to mammals   For example, dogs, which have been selectively bred for abilities that make them companionable to humans, understand pointing as attention focusing, whereas this ability is not generally found in other mammals, and so is not indicated in the Table. Similarly there is evidence that some birds are capable of mirror self-recognition, but this entry is blank since it is not true of typical mammals.

Non-Enculturated Chimpanzees refers to animals confined to laboratories or zoos who may perhaps be employed in experimental tasks, but are not embedded in a human culture.

Enculturated Chimpanzees are animals that live in close interaction with humans and are generally trained in certain activities, such as communication with humans.

Human Infants express new abilities rapidly with age. The age range of 12-15 months is pre-linguistic but by this age many skills have developed that are not present in very young infants. Since the empirical data are not complete, no attempt has been made to make finer age categories. An entry of "–" is used to indicate that an ability may not be present in most 15 month old infants but will be shortly.

Awareness of Other's Beliefs is distinct from 'merely' *Possessing Beliefs* on the basis of direct perceptual evidence, but includes knowing that beliefs can be false as well as true.

Theory of Mind includes many abilities not all of which are included in the table. An X is meant to indicate that that the group has all of these abilities.

Table 1

Part 1

	Consciousness	Goals/desires	Expectations	Physical object/mechanics	Space/navigation	Concept of animate object (agent)	Association of sensory events	Direct physical causality	Perceptual causality	Perceptual classes based on features	Perceptual classes based on function	Found tool use	Simple tool construction	POSSESS Beliefs	Mirror images	Shared attention though gaze	Mirror self-recognition	Declarative pointing	Imperative pointing	Shared visual field	Knowledge of what others see	Shared goals with conspecifics	Cooperation with conspecifics	Shared attention through pointing	Enlisting conspecific help	Awareness of others emotional states	Awareness of others intentional states	Concept of fairness	Learning by imitation of actions	Deception	Awareness of others' beliefs	Learning by conspecific instruction	Learning by human instruction	Instructing others (pedagogy)	Social causality (pedagogy)	Understanding 'make believe'	Theory of Mind 'make believe'	Metarepresentation	Abduction/Hypotheticals (Other's TOM)	Gedanken simulations
Typical Mammals	X	X	X	X	X	X	X	X	X	X	X	X	?	X	X	X										X	X	?												
Wild Chimpanzees	X	X	X	X	X	X	X	X	X	X	X	X	?	X	X	X	X		X	X	X	X	X		X	X	X	?		X										
Non-Enculturated Chimpanzees	X	X	X	X	X	X	X	X	X	X	X	X	?	X	X	X	X		X	X	X	X	X		X	X	X	?		X										
Young Enculturated Chimpanzees	X	X	X	X	X	X	X	X	X	X	X	X	X	X	X	X	X	-	X	X	X	X	X	X	X	X	X	X	?	X	-	X	X	X						
Adult Enculturated Chimpanzees	X	X	X	X	X	X	X	X	X	X	X	X	X	X	X	X	X	-	X	X	X	X	X	X	X	X	X	X	X	X	-	X	X	X						
Human Infants (12-15 mo.)	X	X	X	X	X	X	X	-	-	-	-	-	-	-	X	X	X	-	X	X	X	-	-	-	X	X	X	X	X	-	-	-	-	-	-	X	-	-	X	X
Human Adults	X	X	X	X	X	X	X	X	X	X	X	X	X	X	X	X	X	X	X	X	X	X	X	X	X	X	X	X	X	X	X	X	X	X	X	X	X	X	X	X
Most Modern Human Adults	X	X	X	X	X	X	X	X	X	X	X	X	X	X	X	X	X	X	X	X	X	X	X	X	X	X	X	X	X	X	X	X	X	X	X	X	X	X	X	X
Some Human Adults	X	X	X	X	X	X	X	X	X	X	X	X	X	X	X	X	X	X	X	X	X	X	X	X	X	X	X	X	X	X	X	X	X	X	X	X	X	X	X	X

Part 2

	Symbols for perceptual referents	Symbols for relational classes	Symbols for imperatives	Symbols for declaratives	Symbols for abstract referents	Full vocabulary with abstract referents	Recursive syntax	Full natural language	Analogies and metaphors	Small integers	Gross numerosity	Simple ordering	Simple addition	Natural numbers and subtraction	Fractions	Real numbers	Algebra	Higher Mathematics	Creative mathematics	Intuitive physics	Intuitive geometry	Folk biology	Folk psychology	Folk economics	Religion	Knowledge of mortality	Art	Music	Dance	Stories	Humor	Cultural accumulation of knowledge	Writing	Creative science
Typical Mammals	X	-	X							X	X	?																						
Wild Chimpanzees	X	-	X						?	X	?	?																						
Non-Enculturated Chimpanzees	X	X	X						X	X	?	?					X																	
Young Enculturated Chimpanzees	X	X	X	X	X				X	X	X	X					X																	
Adult Enculturated Chimpanzees	X	X	X	X	X				X	X	X	X	X				X		-	X	X													
Human Infants (12-15 mo.)	X	-	X	X	-	X	X	X	X	X	X	X	X	X		-	X		-	X	X	X	X	X										
Human Adults	X	X	X	X	X	X	X	X	X	X	X	X	X	X	X	X	X	X	X	X	X	X	X	X	X	X	X	X	X	X	X	X		
Most Modern Human Adults	X	X	X	X	X	X	X	X	X	X	X	X	X	X	X	X	X	X	X	X	X	X	X	X	X	X	X	X	X	X	X	X	X	
Some Human Adults	X	X	X	X	X	X	X	X	X	X	X	X	X	X	X	X	X	X	X	X	X	X	X	X	X	X	X	X	X	X	X	X	X	X

37

3 THEORIES OF INTELLIGENCE

Imagination is more important than knowledge.
– Albert Einstein (1879–1955)

Understanding how humans understand is a bootstrapping task that may be impossible, or perhaps one that should be left to metaphorical, literary discussion. However, science has given explanations of other deep problems, such as the origin of the universe, the nature of matter and spacetime, and the structure of living things, so perhaps we should at least try. In this chapter I will give a brief history and outline of the theoretical tools science has thus far explored in efforts to understand human thinking, and will argue that more tools, and a different perspective, are needed to solve the problem I have posed in this essay.

The perspective of science as the primary source of knowledge has not been the norm for most of history, nor is it now for most contemporary people. From primitive times through the early centuries of human civilization, knowledge and wisdom were handed down by authority, especially alleged divine authority. The earliest conceptualizations of the physical and social world were based on surface, unanalyzed experience and passed down unquestioned.

The concept of science is based on a different source of knowledge: empirical verification and falsification of explanatory theories. While this concept has no certain beginning date, it was present in early Greek, Egyptian, and Babylonian thought at least. However, it did not reach full flower and wide acceptance until the Renaissance. Even today, in spite of the success this endeavor has had with the physical world and the enormous impact this success has had on technology, science is far from universally accepted or understood by the public.

Not surprisingly the penetration of the scientific conceptualization into the human realm has been even less complete than it has into the physical world. Scientific biology receives a less than enthusiastic endorsement from the public when it moves its study from plants and lower animals to humans. For example, the overwhelming empirical and conceptual support for the theory of evolution by natural selection, the centerpiece of biology, is considered unthinkable by a substantial portion of the public. There are even some non-biological scientists who question its veracity.

CHAPTER 3: THEORIES OF INTELLIGENCE

The scientific study of human *behavior* is far more suspect yet. Our clear intuition is that our wills are free. How then can there be a science of human behavior to explain its determinants if there are none? Even many physical scientists believe that human behavior and thought cannot be understood in a scientific manner the way physical and chemical systems are understood. It is probably the case that the vast majority of people believe that human thinking, and behavior more generally, can never be explained scientifically.

Of course, interest in human behavior, including human intelligence and thought, has been around a long time in literature and art, and in a number of other non-scientific forms, particularly in the work of philosophers.

1. Logic

Logic is one of the earliest attempts to describe and clarify human reasoning processes, primarily to put them on solid footing so that arguments could be judged objectively. While logic is sometimes studied as a descriptive theory of human thought, its primary thrust has been normative: how *should* thinking be done. In this capacity it has made enormous strides in developing the foundations of mathematics, showing both its strengths and limitations. Here my concern is a fuller understanding of the psychology of human thinking. How has the study of logic contributed to that enterprise?

Deductive logic

The first and most highly developed branch of logic is deductive logic. The most fully formalized deductive logic is the first-order predicate calculus (FOPC). It captures some of the expressive power of natural languages, primarily the notions of logical constants (names), predicates (which define collections of objects) logical connectives (*and, or, not,* and *imply*), variables (which reference an arbitrary item in a collection), universal quantifications (which make statements about all items in a collection) and existential quantifications (which make statements that an item of a given type exists). This is by no means all that can be expressed with language, however, and deductive logic has more recently been extended to other aspects of language, but these formalisms have not been fully standardized in the way first-order predicate calculus has been. See Section 6.6: Geometric Diagrams versus Formal Languages.

The problem with deductive logic as an explanation of human reasoning, or even as a normative theory of reasoning, is that it only addresses the problem of how one can safely get from one true statement to another. It does not explain where to start. It does not explain where knowledge originates, or why people believe the things they believe or know the things that they know. Nor does it give a complete or accurate description of how humans actually reason, argue, and become convinced.

Inductive logic

Inductive logic is an attempt to describe one way that people figure out where to start: Having encountered several true instances of a proposition, when is it safe to conclude a general principle (or when do rational people do so, or when should they)? How many black crows must one see in the absence of any white crows to sensibly conclude that all crows are black?

Inductive logic has not achieved its goals to the extent that deductive logic has, and it never can. Obviously no finite amount of evidence can yield a general conclusion with absolute certainty, for a falsifying observation may turn up at any time. Therefore inductive formalisms rely on the concept of probability in one form or another. Although in some cases people clearly generalize from examples, induction is no more a general explanation of human thought than is deduction. It is frequently held that inductive logic is the sole basis of science. Although it clearly is an essential component of scientific investigation, it is not the sole component, because theory is also essential (see Deutsch (1997)).

Abductive logic

A third form of logic is needed to explain human thinking. This is abductive logic, one of the core abilities discussed in the previous chapter. Abduction is the generation of hypotheses to give an account of an observation or belief. In *scientific* reasoning the hypotheses are then tested against further observations that could, if an hypothesis is incorrect, refute it. If the evidence does not refute an hypothesis, the hypothesis is maintained; otherwise it is modified or abandoned. In scientific reasoning, a hypothesis is vacuous if there are no *possible* observations that could refute it. In non-scientific reasoning such as the everyday thinking of most people, the hypothesis may be subjected to little or no further testing, or to non-systematic testing, and often irrefutable hypotheses are embraced. Nonetheless hypotheses serve as a form of understanding the world.

Legal trials are an example. Both the defense and the prosecution know that what sways juries is not so much evidence as it is telling a story that is convincing. The prosecution tells a story that explains why the accused had motive and opportunity to commit the crime. The defense tells a different story. Each side emphasizes the evidence that supports its story. Each juror then decides which story is more plausible.

The process of systematic testing is not rigidly followed even in scientific discourse. Often hypotheses are too vaguely stated to permit clear refutation by any single piece of evidence. More importantly, people become emotionally committed to their beliefs (including scientific hypotheses) and readily ignore counter-evidence as well as the lack of supporting evidence.

Science avoids the errors of everyday argument not because scientists are wiser or smarter than others, but because science is by agreement pursued as a slow, *cultural* process that demands that evidence be reproducible and public, and that verified empirical evidence be the final arbiter of correctness. In the short run, science entertains many false hypotheses, and these are persistently held even as evidence mounts against them, just as in the case of everyday discourse. It is only in the long run that science weeds out the errors and makes new, better-supported theories that encompass more phenomena more parsimoniously.

Abductive logic has not been formalized and may never be formalized in the manner that deductive logic has been. The theory of abductive logic, whatever form it takes, will be a psychological theory, and the most important branch of logic, but such a theory lies in the future.

CHAPTER 3: THEORIES OF INTELLIGENCE

2. Psychology

Associationism

It was not until the late 19th century that serious empirical study of human thought and behavior began. In 1879 a psychological laboratory was established by Wilhelm Wundt (1832–1920) in Leipzig. The initial attempts to develop a science of psychology introduced empirical methods and used a variety of approaches, but the theoretical view was dominated primarily by *Associationism*, which was described in Chapter 1.

In the early 20th century Behaviorism, a radical form of Associationism, was championed by John Watson (1878–1958) and his followers. This view was rooted in a philosophy known as Positivism. It held that the only true explanations were to be found by strictly eschewing any entities, such as internal mental states, that were not *directly* observable. Behaviorism limited its descriptions to relations among stimuli and responses that are physical activities observable from outside the organism, such as a blinking light and a limb movement. The Behaviorist movement was a reaction to the predominance of much loose reasoning about mental life. Specifically, Behaviorists rejected the popular method of *introspection* – asking subjects or oneself what was going on in their minds. To remedy this reliance upon non-observable and hypothetical mental contents, Watson's extreme remedy was widely adopted. Mental concepts such as thoughts and emotions were banished from study. The science was to be simply a list of empirical laws relating stimulus and response: input and output.

Until about 1960, the bulk of cognitive psychological theory, especially in the United States, was strongly based on Behaviorism. The form that held sway was championed mainly by B. F. Skinner (1904–1990); [see Skinner (1953); Skinner (1957)]. Many interesting empirical results were produced, for example, facts about how the *pattern* of 'reinforcement' (roughly, rewards) of a response affected the speed of learning and resistance to unlearning of stimulus-response associations. This information has a great deal of practical value to this day, for example in the training of animals and in understanding their behavior. However, even brain events were not to be used in explanations of behavior. A major conceptual change was needed to accept the postulation of internal states as scientifically sound practice.

Not all forms of Associationism were as extreme as Watson's; for example Clark Hull (1884–1952) proposed hidden-variable accounts of stimulus-response connections, and his theories were influential. There were other views opposing Behaviorism, such as Gestalt psychology, the developmental models of Jean Piaget (1896–1980), and the *field theories* of Kurt Lewin (1890–1947).

Associationism remains a component of psychological theory, although the radical form of Watson and Skinner is no longer dominant. Today we know that there need be nothing vague or mysterious about hidden variables, which are essential in most physical theories. It is hard to believe that strict behaviorism achieved and maintained the grip that it had on academic psychology, a subject in even greater need of sophisticated theories than the physical sciences.

Beginning in the 1950s there were efforts to introduce mathematical models into the psychology of learning and thought, allowing rigorous use of variables representing non-directly observables. By and large these models remained within the Associationist framework. The models explored stimulus-response associations with a probabilistic overlay, and predicted approximate accounts of simple performance averaged over groups of subjects. The mathematical languages used were not up to the task of giving a full account of learning. Other theoretical methods were needed.

Although almost all of the work by Behaviorists used birds and rodents as subjects, some researchers tried to apply this atheoretical theory to human behavior, though with little success. Not surprisingly, Behaviorism's seemingly mechanistic view of living organisms, particularly humans, did not win much acceptance from the general public or even the scientific community at large. Indeed, the Behaviorist model proved to be sterile when extended to any of the truly fundamental and interesting phenomena of *human* behavior, such as language and higher thought processes. This became widely appreciated with the publication of a review by Noam Chomsky of Skinner's book *Verbal Behavior*, Skinner's attempt to apply behaviorist methods to the study of human language. Seldom if ever has a book review been such an influential part of a shift in scientific paradigm, but it came at a time when other alternatives to behaviorism were becoming available, and the combination resulted in a sea change in psychology.

The cognitive revolution

The times were ready for the cognitive revolution, and as so often seems to happen, it was driven by the advent of new technology, in this case the digital computer. Although developed for entirely different reasons, *viz.* numerical calculation, the computer's potential as a cognitive model was seen by a few from the earliest days of its general availability. Here was a device that could in principle precisely describe any possible information transformation and in fact carry it out. Heretofore, psychologists were forced to choose between two flawed alternatives for stating theories. On the one hand, formal languages for which a well-developed mathematical theory was available were usually wholly inadequate to describe the complex phenomena of human thought. On the other hand, natural language, while providing richness and flexibility of expression, lacked any formal deductive and predictive methods. Computer modeling seemed to be the answer to behaviorism, for those supposedly mysterious hypothetical mental processes could now be precisely stated.

Furthermore, computer programs could be constructed to readily capture many important human cognitive skills, some of which even chimpanzees do not exhibit. I enumerated some of these in Chapter 1: symbolic representation of abstractions, the generation and search of sets of possible alternatives, the symbolic representation of facts and rules of inference, variables and quantification, iteration and recursion.

Scientific revolutions do not happen overnight. Well into the 1970s behaviorism still maintained a hold even in the psychology departments of major universities. However, the die had been cast with the first artificial intelligence programs in the mid 1950s. By the late 1970s the battle had been won, at least in academia, but still not in the hearts and minds of the public. It is not surprising that the bold plan to model human thought by computer programs has not been received with open arms, even among scientists at large. One could scarcely imagine a more mechanistic, 'de-humanizing' view of man than as a digital computer, especially the slow, room-filling, clumsily interfaced computers of that early era.

CHAPTER 3: THEORIES OF INTELLIGENCE

Limitations of psychology

There are good reasons why any quest for a scientific account of the human mind should be viewed with skepticism, but the good reasons are not always the reasons that drive skepticism. It would take a major break from the history of scientific knowledge to conclude that the human brain is beyond the realm of explanation as a lawful physical system. But such a break has always existed in the popular and even in the educated mind. For many, humans and perhaps all living things are held as occupying a world apart – the world of the spirit. While the domain of spirit has constantly shrunk over history, and at an increasing pace in the past three hundred years, according to the majority opinion the human mind remains outside the realm of the physical and the scientific. Thus no scientific explanation of the human mind, including the ability to reason, could be acceptable to most people.

Common sense supports this view. Science demonstrates that the behavior of simple physical systems is predictable: the velocity of a brick dropped in a vacuum can be predicted precisely, for example. Engineering devises complex, carefully designed systems, such as automobiles and rocket ships and computers, that behave according to plan. Computers can be programmed reliably to perform complex computations. However, as any parent will attest, no equivalent examples of exact predictability and determinate mechanism are apparent in the realm of human behavior.

While the possibility of a science of the *physical* world capable of perfect predictions had seemed assured toward the end of the nineteenth century, the next century saw a series of astonishing limitations, and these added to the skepticism about a science of human behavior. First, the determinism of classical mechanics was replaced over a few decades in the early 20th century by the fundamental and still highly non-intuitive non-determinism of quantum mechanics. It has in fact now been established that general relativity, quantum mechanics, and naive realism (the view that there is an objective world independent of observation) are not mutually compatible!

Second, in the 1930s logicians proved theorems about the limitations of logic itself. The Incompleteness Theorem of Gödel established that for logical systems of even minimal complexity there are true statements that cannot be proved. There are questions that are *undecidable*. For example, there is no mechanical procedure that can decide for all computer programs which will halt and which will run forever. This places limits on our ability to prove that a program does what we designed it to do.

More recently still, as mentioned in Chapter 1, chaos theory has shown that even purely deterministic systems are in principle unpredictable. This result applies not because of quantum indeterminacy or logical undecidability, but because of the non-linearity of the relations among physical quantities. Furthermore, like the logical limitations that apply to very simple formal systems, chaotic unpredictability applies to very simple physical systems – they need only be non-linear.

A closely related phenomenon is the *critical state* (Buchanan (2000)). Consider highly interconnected systems composed of large numbers of components, such as stresses in seismic faults or trees in a forest, in which neighbors influence one another, and disturbances (fault shifts, fires) can be propagated throughout the system. Such systems are said to be in a critical state when it is the case that a very small disturbance can have wide-spread and even catastrophic impacts. For example a small fire in a large forest might quickly die out, but on the other hand it could turn into a conflagration engulfing thousands of square miles of trees. Due to the complexity of the interconnections there is no way to determine which will be the case, or where and when a huge fire will start, even though the system is connected by deterministic laws of physics. The same applies to earthquakes, making their occurrence and intensity inherently unpredictable no matter how many sensors we place in a fault system and no matter how closely we monitor them.

How then are we able to achieve the technological sophistication and success afforded by modern engineering? Part of the answer is that we are able to construct artificial systems that are sufficiently constrained to permit only non-chaotic behavior. A larger part of the answer is that our predictions are inherently statistical. We do not predict precise time-space behavior paths, but merely average ones. For example, we make very useful weather forecasts, but not weather predictions.

Since the logical and chaotic limitations of predictability apply to all physical systems, they apply to human behavior as well, even if humans are no more than physical systems. The recourse to statistical predictions is used in psychology, although thus far with very limited success. A typical experiment will attempt to predict not one subject's precise behavior, but the average behavior of a group of subjects as measured by some grossly defined behavior category, such as pressing a button or getting the right answer to a problem. However, even these sorts of gross statistical summaries of behavior now have and probably will forever have large margins of error due to the complexity of these systems.

This suggests that we will never predict with certainty whether a given infant will grow up to be schizophrenic, or criminal, or a productive genius. This result is in clear agreement with common sense, but it is a conclusion that is reached by an entirely different route. We are unpredictable because we are complex physical systems, not because we are spiritual creatures with free will. If this is the case, psychology may yet be amenable to the methods of the physical sciences, suitably extended and with less sweeping detail, much as evolution gives an account of the diversity of life but cannot explain the history of the formation of specific species. Even so, many remain skeptical about whether *computers* can provide all of the theoretical concepts necessary for an extended account of human behavior, as the pioneers of the cognitive revolution proposed.

Natural intelligence, artificial intelligence, super intelligence, super-human intelligence

At the same time that some psychologists were trying to develop computer programs that explained *human* intelligence, some engineers (often the same people) were attempting to develop computer programs that behaved *artificially* intelligently even if they did so in ways that were quite different than those used by humans. Should this be possible it might even lead to artifacts that ultimately surpass human performance to achieve *super* intelligence. At first the machine performance might be better than humans' only in restricted domains of application, such as chess playing, but eventually it might, in the view of some, totally encompass *all* human abilities and become fully *super human intelligence,* able to solve all human problems, to converse like a human, to create original literature, art, and mathematics, and to live a fully human life of the mind.

However, while AI has already demonstrated that computers can be programmed successfully to do complex 'intellectual tasks' such as playing chess and designing electronic circuits, and while there now exist many such powerful engineering devices, they fall well short of providing even in-principle accounts of human mental life.

3. Artificial Intelligence

Where does a person's knowledge come from? It was Plato's thesis that we never truly learn anything new, rather we only become aware of what we already know. In the *Meno*, Plato, speaking through Socrates, asks a slave boy how to construct a square whose area is twice that of a given square. The slave boy professes ignorance of how this can be done. Socrates/Plato first convinces the boy that he understands there is a problem and that he knows what is required as a solution. He has him consider a particular case, a square whose sides are of length 2, which the slave boy recognizes has area 4, and that a square of twice the area would have area 8. He then asks him how long would be the side of such a square. The slave boy's first suggestion is that a square of double the area would have a side of twice the length. Socrates then draws such a square and within it four copies of the original square, convincing the slave boy that the area of this construction is 16, not 8. Within each of the contained squares, Socrates then draws a diagonal. See Figure 3: How Socrates Showed the Slave Boy What He Already Knew.

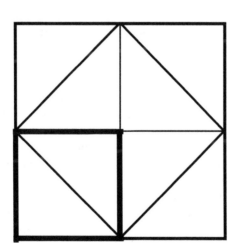

Figure 3
How Socrates Showed the Slave Boy What He Already Knew

The large square is constructed with sides twice the length of the original small bold square. It is seen to have 4 times the area of the small square. The inner oblique square is constructed from the diagonals of the small squares and is seen to be twice the area of the small square because it is composed of the sum of four halves of the small squares.

He then convinces the slave boy that each small square is thus divided in half by its diagonal. Finally, the slave boy is shown that a new square has been constructed whose sides are the length of the diagonal of the original and whose area is one half of the area of the large square, hence 8, the required solution. Thus Socrates/Plato concludes that the slave boy recognized a result that he had known all along, and needed only to be helped to retrieve that knowledge.

Today there is a straightforward reply to Plato's claim that no new knowledge can be generated by the mind. We may learn truly novel things by combining the old in new ways, just as an endless number of new compounds can be created from a finite stock of atom types, or an enormous number of new organisms can be created by new DNA combinations, or an endless number of novel sentences can be generated from a finite vocabulary and finite set of syntactic rules. Knowledge is generative. Thus all that is necessary for new knowledge is some mechanism for creating new combinations. It could be as simple as random or systematic trial and error, or as sophisticated as a deduction engine and heuristics (rules-of-thumb that reduce search). Such devices are now well understood and intuitive and should no longer present the puzzle they did for Plato. In this way Artificial Intelligence has created devices that demonstrate how new knowledge need not be just a matter of recall, but truly new knowledge can arise from the processing of old knowledge in a variety of ways.

Symbolic artificial intelligence

The Logic Theorist (LT) of Newell, Shaw & Simon (1957), a program for discovering proofs in propositional logic, lays claim to being the first artificial intelligence program, although others, such as the checker playing machine of Samuel (1963) could make similar claims. LT established a style that has been followed by much subsequent work. It manipulated sentences of propositional logic (a deductive logic without quantifiers) according to rules of deduction. In attempting to prove a theorem, that is, to show how it could arise from other statements by a sequence of logic rule applications, it generated a problem 'tree' as follows. Starting with the goal statement, the program determined what things, if proven, could establish the goal in a single rule-application. Each of these things then became a subgoal. At times a subgoal could have several clauses each of which had to be established (a conjunction), or sometimes clauses which were alternatives (a disjunction). When a subgoal was identical to an axiom or previously proved statement, that subgoal was established. The first work on automatically proving geometry theorems adopted this same problem-tree approach, applied to the manipulation of the postulates of Euclid and deductions from them.

The style of computation introduced by LT has come to be called *symbolic AI*. Seemingly it is the quintessential form of predicative or propositional, selective (heuristic) search computation. Some argue that all cognitive processes can be described in the symbolic AI computational form, mainly on the grounds that it is sufficiently powerful to define a universal computer, which can perform any possible computation. If symbolic AI is sufficient, why consider anything else? Well, sufficiency of that sort is quite easy to achieve. Universal computers need very few computational abilities.[4] Therefore there

---

[4] A *Turing machine* is one such universal computer. It consists of a device that can be in one of a finite number of states and a memory that can be accessed serially and that can

must be many other computational styles that could make the same claim about cognitive processes, if indeed any legitimately can, and some of them may be easier to develop, may lead to more perspicuous descriptions, or have other advantages.

Knowledge representation and intentionality

The concept of a representation plays a central role in artificial intelligence, just as it does in psychology. The idea is that an intelligent agent, whether a person or a computer, must have internal (nervous system or electronic) recordings that somehow correspond to external objects or abstract ideas. Cognition is the manipulation of these internal records. Ultimately these manipulations may lead to actual behavior – interactions with the physical world. However, thinking occurs even if there is no such behavioral accompaniment.

The earliest AI programs did not speak explicitly of knowledge representation, but they employed means to do so. Thus LT represented logic expressions, the coin of its ability, as lists (in the now familiar list-processing format of linked addresses and dynamic memory allocation that has become the basis of software technology). My own work (Lindsay (1961)) was perhaps the first to focus explicitly on the importance of a representation and what computational advantages and limitations it brought to a problem. Today, every cognitive model focuses centrally on how it represents the knowledge that it manipulates.

Knowledge is a concept that is not normally applied to non-mental entities, such as thermostats and automobiles. According to the analysis presented in Chapter 1, information becomes knowledge only for a goal-directed system. That is, information becomes knowledge not solely by virtue of how it is stored, but because there is a purpose for which it is used, and because of how it is used. A machine without a representation of a goal has no knowledge. Furthermore, knowledge is productive, that is, there must be means of combining chunks of information to yield additional chunks through some form of inference (perhaps, but not necessarily, logical deduction). *Knowledge, then, emerges from the productive use of information in a goal-directed activity.*

Whether we take an entity to have goals is, once again, a matter of our description, our construal, of the entity's behavior. To ascribe goals to an entity is to take the *intentional stance* (Dennett (1978)). This is advisable if and only if it allows us to better understand what is going on. For human behavior, this is almost always the case; for thermostats it is generally not a useful stance.

---

record one of a finite number of symbols in each of its discrete memory locations. The device can read one memory symbol at a time and, based on this and the machine's state, it can change that symbol and then move to an adjacent memory location. Such a device can be programmed (by specifying the rules for symbol writing and moving as a function of state and symbol read) to compute any function that is computable. Furthermore, the number of states and the number of symbols required is quite small. Thus all that is required for universal computation is the ability to distinguish symbols, to access local memory locations, to write symbols in memory locations (and, importantly, to erase the prior contents in the process), and to change state. Thus very little functionality is needed to achieve full computational ability.

One requirement for goal-directedness is that a device or a program can determine its own state, can use this information as input to a calculation, and can alter its state as a result of a calculation. However, this is not sufficient. A thermostat might be said to have a goal of temperature stabilization and to represent its set-point by a position on a dial (or the corresponding location of a contact) and to represent its controlled temperature range in similar electromechanical terms, say a gap between contacts. But this is a stretch of the concepts of goal and representation, because the thermostat itself cannot modify these representations of goals nor reason about them (such as evaluating its progress); it can only consult them. The concept of intentionality entails, at least, that the representation of the goal itself be accessible to the organism/device/program. A thermostat does not have this, although it performs a (limited) control function. It has a goal in only an impoverished sense: one would not say that the thermostat 'knows' what it is doing in the way in which this term would apply to a human who is putting logs on the fire.

It is routine to endow computer programs with goals, but still only in a limited way, namely by stating a goal and endowing the program with the ability to search for the goal, recognize it when it sees it, and perhaps alter or change its goal to another of its given set of goals. Humans clearly are goal-directed (purposeful) in this sense, although one might argue that they do not need to be supplied with goals, at least not directly. Humans are endowed with overarching goals, such as staying alive and reproducing, and they use these to generate explicit subgoals; still the higher goals do not originate with a person autonomously, but are built-in biologically through genetic structure. Perhaps computers could be constructed in the same manner.

Finally, not all agree that goals and representation of knowledge are necessary features of an intelligent system. Some AI models that seemingly have access to their internal states are nonetheless advertised as non-representational. The subsumption architecture [Brooks (1986); Brooks (1991)] is the best known. Here, components are arranged in a hierarchy, such that the behavior of one group of components simply responds to that of others in such a way that an overall goal is achieved. It is argued that the system does not 'know' what its goals are nor 'plan' on how to achieve them; it simply behaves. Powers (1973) proposed a similar architecture as the basis for all controlled behavior; see also Lindsay (1974).

Limitations of symbolic artificial intelligence

One reason given for the belief that computers *could be* sufficient models of human thought is *Church's Thesis*, the unprovable assertion that any computable function can be computed by a digital computer (idealized to have an unbounded memory, and ignoring issues of time and efficiency). The Thesis is unprovable because computability is an intuitive notion, so the Thesis cannot be stated formally. However, the Thesis is generally accepted, based on the consensus view that the mathematically precise class known as *recursive functions*[5] captures the intuitive notion of computability, combined with the formal result that a very simple mechanical device (*e. g.*, a Turing Machine) can be designed to compute any recursive function.

---

[5] The definition of recursive functions is straightforward but not important here. See Smullyan (1961).

CHAPTER 3: THEORIES OF INTELLIGENCE

One argument *against* the view that computers are sufficient as cognitive theories turns the undecidability arguments of formal systems against them. It would appear that humans can know truths that are formally unprovable. Furthermore, if we cannot even say that a program that we write does what we intend it to, nor even that it will halt as it was designed to do, then the language of computation is too limited to serve as the expression of psychological theories. This argument is weakened if we believe that humans are deterministic physical systems, in which case the same limitations surely apply to humans; if humans can know unprovable truths they must be using methods other than logical deduction that are nonetheless deterministic.

A second argument *against* the sufficiency of computational models is that many aspects of humans, such as emotional state, are not describable as computations, and yet they are intricately involved in thinking. Therefore, the argument goes, computational models cannot adequately describe human thought. While the argument that in humans thought and emotion are intricately connected is no doubt correct, there is no decisive argument that emotions are not computations. Nor, of course, is there a decisive argument that they are. Most researchers in theoretical psychology and AI simply take it as a working hypothesis that all behavior and cognitions, including emotions, can be modeled computationally. Only time will disclose the force and limitations of this view.

A third argument *against* the sufficiency thesis is that human thought is not a *digital* computation. The argument is usually based on the claim that nervous systems are not digital systems nor are they serial processes, rather they are analog and massively parallel. It is certainly true that the brain is massively parallel, and that brain signals (although all-or-none digital at the level of spike potentials) seem to code as analog signals, specifically as frequencies of spike potentials. Such arguments have enormous appeal, it seems.

For example, *connectionist (neural net)* models (Rumelhart & McClelland (1986)) caused great interest among psychologists who interpreted them as a better alternative to symbolic AI models. These models comprise (simulated) neuron-like elements connected in a network and communicating by sending signals across 'synapses' whose transmission effectiveness may alter with experience, Associationism style. To its adherents, connectionist and neural net models are superior to standard symbolic models because of their massively parallel computations. However, a close look at most of the early models developed shows that they are a step backward. These theories do not capture all the expressive power of the first-order predicate calculus, power that is certainly necessary for describing human cognition. Though putatively more 'brain-like' than symbolic AI models, they thus lack some of the abilities of symbolic models, specifically the ability to abstract through symbols and quantification. See Fodor & Pylyshyn (1988). Later research acknowledged these limitations and turned to the study of hybrid symbolic-connectionist models. It is now generally recognized that pure connectionist models are not viable. See Shastri & Ajjanagadde (1993), Estes (1988), Smolensky (1987a), Smolensky (1987b), Smolensky (1990), and Touretzky (1990), Touretzky & Hinton (1985).

Therefore connectionist models return us to the early ideas of Associationism and limit us to the simple models that predate the cognitive revolution. A network of connectionist 'neurons' that computes only by changing the strength of connections as a function of experience can compute nothing that is not based on statistical regularities of the input.

What about the claim that connectionist models are analog rather than digital and thus a better medium for modeling brain processes? This is almost to the point, but not quite. The distinction between digital and analog is that between discrete and continuous. Connectionist models as currently developed (though this is not inherent in the architecture) do employ real numbers (see Chapter 4) as connection 'weights' and real numbers (as opposed to integers or rationals) are a mathematical model of continuity. However the use of real numbers to represent quantity does not distinguish connectionist models from symbolic models, which of course also use real numbers. Certainly, symbolic models represent real numbers only as approximations, but the approximation can be as close as desired. That is, precision is unbounded when real numbers are represented as rationals rather than as 'real' continuous quantities. This of course is exactly how real numbers are represented in connectionist models as well (they are, after all, almost always modeled with digital computer programs!). Connection weights and learning models in no way depend on 'real' real numbers for any aspect of their behavior, any more than rule-based AI programs with 'degrees of belief' or 'probabilities' are based on 'real' real numbers. That is, there is nothing distinctive about this kind of continuity.

It seems to me that the real thrust of the analog argument is in the modeling of time. As long as digital models and connectionist models are synchronous, that is, state changes take place at discrete clock ticks, they fail to be analog in an important sense, as I will describe later in this Chapter.

There are now other forms of AI which have become prominent. Most of them are based on statistical approaches, as with neural nets. Many employ graphical models based on Markov and Bayesian[6] networks, graphs which connect variables to represent independence and conditional dependencies. These are powerful statistical methods, but this work is primarily focused on engineering applications rather than a scientific study of natural intelligence, and provide no account of planning or theory construction.

Expert systems and the knowledge principle

Expert systems, such as Dendral, [Buchanan & Feigenbaum (1978); Lindsay, Buchanan, Feigenbaum & Lederberg (1980); Lindsay, Buchanan, Feigenbaum & Lederberg (1993)], solve problems in a specialized area of technical expertise and use knowledge of the sort human experts in that specialty report that they employ. For example, an expert system for medical diagnosis could have the knowledge that a certain pathogen causes certain symptoms. This might be recorded as a rule, such as "If a patient is febrile and has joint pain, check for the presence of bacillus X." (Such knowledge is declarative knowledge, *knowing that*, as generally distinguished from procedural knowledge, *knowing how*. Our thermostat at best knows *how* to stabilize temperature, but it does not know *that* it is doing so.)

Expert systems have been highly successful in many applications, and their style of programming by rules has been widely adopted inside and outside of AI contexts. Feigenbaum and Buchanan in particular have characterized expert systems as 'knowledge-driven' and argued that their intelligence is dependent *primarily* on the accumulation of large amounts of knowledge which can then be processed by a very simple inference

---

[6] Bayes' Rule computes changes in probabilities resulting from the acquisition of new information.

procedure. This is called the Knowledge Principle: In the knowledge (not the inference procedure) is the power.

Doug Lenat, a former student of Feigenbaum and Buchanan, has embraced this Principle in a big way, by attempting to use rules and other symbolic forms to encode and show the interconnections of all of human knowledge in a large database he calls Cyc. After over 20 years of work, estimated to have taken well over 1,000 man-years of effort, Cyc is an enormous symbolic repository of concepts and relations among them. In 2011 it comprises about one million rules, which Lenat estimates is about three percent of what is needed for "comon sense." The hope is that it could serve as a general purpose knowledge base, although it would need to be augmented for dealing with special topics. In other words it could *become* an expert in any field of human endeavor that is knowledge intensive. Lenat also envisions that it could be the central component of a system with fully human intelligence.

One objection to the concept of knowledge representation as employed throughout symbolic AI is that such representation is merely *encodings*, that is, a simple correspondence is established between an internal symbol and an external object or event. This position is argued by Bickhard & Terveen (1995), and it applies not just to Cyc but to all classical AI symbolic programs. They raise the question of how a correspondence between representation and referent can be established without already supposing it exists. Suppose that the correspondence is established by fiat, that is, the programmer says that "Fido" corresponds to Fido. No one questions that the programmer then knows the correspondence, but in what sense does the *program* know it? "Fido" is 'in' the computer, that is, it is a physical state of the machine. But Fido is not in the computer, so what manner of association can be made between "Fido" and Fido? How can one point to the other? All the program can do is associate a symbol for the name "Fido" with another symbol for the dog Fido.

Although we now see how concepts not explicitly placed in a mind can arise from thoughts by combination, that does not answer Bickhard and Terveen because it does not explain how even a *concept* of a real object can get 'into' the mind. Bickhard and Terveen argue that the encoding problem is in fact insurmountable, that the conventional notion of representation is question-begging. Why does the same argument not apply to the programmer? Because he has sense organs that translate energy from Fido into a perception, that is, to an altered internal state (of the brain or of the mind, as you wish). The association is then made internally, between the mental percept and the mental symbol assigned to represent it. When Fido is no longer present in the programmer's visual field, some internal state may persist in the programmer's brain. There is no string or arrow from the programmer's brain to the dog any more than there is one from the computer to the dog. Both components of the association, "Fido" and the percept of Fido (or the memory of Fido), are internal in each case. Although the programmer has encoded his percept with a symbolic name, the percept itself is *grounded in experience* in a way that a simple label is not. In a sense the knowledge is represented in the structure of the world, which is tapped into by perception and memory not as an exhaustive description but in a form that can be examined as needed to provide internal knowledge, or manipulated externally so that the world performs computations (see Chapter 6).

4. Modeling Understanding

Human knowledge is grounded in experience

Could not the encoding objection in principle be addressed by giving a computer a sense organ, say a TV camera, combined with perceptual processes that can identify Fido and memory processes that store some depiction or description of the percept, thereby making a connection possible between "Fido" and the world? After all, the vision of most AI scientists is that one day we will have robots with elaborate, multichannel sensorial and effector systems that can dwell in a complex physical and social environment. We have only very limited sensory-perceptual programs today, but even within their limits, could this not satisfactorily answer the encoding objection to representation?

Adding perceptual abilities to Cyc or other symbolic AI programs still would not fully answer Bickhard and Terveens's objection to an encoding construal of representation. To give a satisfactory reply requires that we show that a symbol-percept association of the sort just described is an adequate account of human-like knowledge representation. If it is not, we need to show what sort of connection would suffice.

Simply postulating an association between "Fido" and Fido provides very little leverage for understanding human cognition. It is not that an association is not needed or not present, but that it is not enough. All of the work of understanding human cognition must be done by the computational model that combines "Fido" and "dog" and all the other mental symbols in such a way that something is discovered about Fido and dogs and allows one to interact appropriately with dogs in the world. Neither a behaviorist model, nor an associationist model (including pure connectionist or neural net models) provides a sufficiently rich computational structure to give such an account, nor does a symbolic Cyc approach.

In any case, Cyc has no perception and no experience. This is a critical problem for it: this giant network of interconnected symbols is unconnected to the world in any way. Furthermore, Cyc provides no general theory of control specifying how the data are to be used. Even a limited-domain question answering system provides no model of efficient search that would allow Cyc to effectively deal with the world in real time.

International Business Machines (IBM) has developed a system called Watson that can accept queries in unrestricted English text. Like Cyc, it has been a labor intensive project involving dozens of software engineers. For a semi-technical description of this project see Ferrucci *et al.* (2010). Unlike Cyc, it does not rely exclusively on pre-structured data bases, but rather has access to a very large amount of text documents, an amount which could be augmented indefinitely. It is not able to fully analyze a query syntactically or semantically, but does some limited analysis. For example, it is able, usually, to determine the type of response needed (say a person's name, or a date, or a location) to restrict its search. The system employs a wide variety of techniques which contribute information in ways that can be combined. The central method is to select key words and finds words associated with them in its large text database, leading to discovered connections that may be answers to or implications of the input. It is then able to evaluate the likelihood of success and compute a degree of confidence, and frame its response in a form intelligible to a human. This permits the discovery of relevant but non-obvious connections.

When appropriately tuned to a particular task, the system has proven highly robust in selecting a small number of answers that are likely to be relevant. Such a system will be far more useful than the popular Google search engine since it produces very little clutter. At the moment, however, it requires so much computing power and high-bandwidth access to memory that it could not begin to handle the load Google deals with every day. Nonetheless, the results are impressive and with continued refinement will have many applications.

It is not the case, however, that Watson understands natural language in more than a superficial way, nor that it understands either the questions put to it or its replies in a deep sense, not even why a reply is an answer to the question.

Episodic memory

Psychology has discovered two forms of memory with different functionality and different neural substrates. *Semantic memory* records factual information, such as phone numbers, and the color of bananas. *Episodic memory* records events, such as one's 16th birthday party, having spilled your coffee on your lap this morning, and driving to work.

One reason why Cyc-like and Watson-like knowledge is not human-like knowledge is that it is connected only to (at best) percepts of sensory *objects* but unconnected to *experience* in the world, the sort of things episodic memory records. Humans exist in the world. They not only have sense organs and motor organs, they experience the world as a flow of events and can recall events that they have been part of. Cyc and Watson have no such abilities, and thus they have no proper referents for their symbols. At best they have a semantic memory of knowledge, that is of facts and predications about them. Adding video and audio and tactile input channels is not sufficient. Cyc and Watson have not and cannot remember the experience of playing catch, walking, nursing, building a house of cards, using a ladder, throwing a Frisbee to a dog, changing a tire, slipping on ice, embarrassment, love, toothache, planting a flower seed, giving birth, speaking in public, a birthday party, wetness, color, friendship, orgasm, or betrayal.

Such events and their memories are the stuff of life and the stuff of literature. Consider almost any literary description. Here is one:

> Wet laundry, the snap, the yank, the wet heaviness of double and queen-sized sheets. The real sound bringing back the remembered sounds of the past when I had lain under the dripping clothes to catch water on my tongue or run in between them as if they were traffic cones through which I chased Lindsey or was chased by Lindsey back and forth. And this would be joined by the memory of our mother attempting to lecture us about the peanut butter from our hands getting on the good sheets, or the sticky lemon candy patches she had found on our father's shirts. In this way the sight and smell of the real, of the imagined, and of the remembered all came together for me. (Alice Sebold, *The Lovely Bones*, page 247.)

The examples I have given and those illustrated by the above passage of fiction of course include some instances of emotion and motor skills that have essentially been unaddressed by AI modeling. However, the issue of experience and episodic memory reaches beyond these issues into all aspects of cognition, including such 'cold' and seemingly abstract areas as diagrammatic reasoning and narrow expertise.

UNDERSTANDING UNDERSTANDING

One can readily generate a huge body of statements about any simple, common perceptual category, say trees. In the course of a few hours one can generate hundreds of facts about trees and their relations to other categories, and still the list could go on. The ease with which one can describe one's knowledge of trees leads to the misconception that all one's knowledge about trees can be written down in statements. However, no amount of symbolic coding could capture the knowledge a human has about trees that is garnered by seeing and interacting with trees as they exist in the world. Such a program of knowledge representation will fail because the process is *not reversible*: the statements cannot generate the experience.

Human episodic memory, like semantic memory, is cognitively penetrable. That is, it is not simply a super movie theater that replays impoverished records of events in a passive manner on a screen with surround sound, tactile and olfactory inputs and associated recalled emotions. What is recalled can be manipulated, altered, and recombined. Furthermore, in humans, the symbolic representational mechanism available only to humans can be brought to bear. Most likely it is an important component of the processes of abduction and simulation. Abstract representation, not sensory processes, is what underlies thinking in visual, auditory, and tactile imagery.

Earlier I discussed Searle's argument that even if a symbolic program succeeded in producing acceptable Chinese to English translations it would not do so the way humans do, a position with which I agreed (while denying that translation can be done by syntax and lexicon alone). Searle goes on to argue that computers will never be able to understand because they are not made of 'biological stuff'. While 'biological stuff' is how humans do it, it is conceivable that the same sort of understanding could be achieved with 'silicon stuff' or some other non-biological material. However, whatever stuff we use to construct truly human-like intelligent artifacts, it must be capable of roaming the world, seeing it in human-based categories, and remembering its experience in human episodic form.

The human ability to understand the world and the world of ideas requires more than the abilities of subhuman species, but there are abilities we share with those other species that are *also* essential to our ability to understand. These shared abilities include, conspicuously, our multi-channel perception intertwined with our motor and memorial abilities, and these are essential activities that allow us to live in the world. Those abilities are essential to our human knowledge as well, just as essential as our abilities to encode predications about abstracts concepts and to form inferences with logic.

Human knowledge requires human core cognitive abilities

There is yet another important fact about Cyc that will keep it from being the knowledge base that is the central component of a model of *human* intelligence. To explain my reservation, let me return to the founding source of the Knowledge Principle, Dendral. Dendral's field of expertise is the analysis of mass spectra of organic molecules. This is an important problem in organic chemistry. The properties of organic molecules depend not only on their constituents (as given in the molecule's formula, say $C_{18}H_{24}O_2$), but in how these atoms are interconnected. By bombarding a large number of identical molecules with a beam of electrons, the molecules are broken in various ways. A mass spectrometer measures the mass of each fragment and determines its prevalence in the soup of fragments. The task of the chemist is to use this information, along with other information such as the source of the sample, to infer the connectivity pattern of the atoms. Dendral consists of a structure generation algorithm that, for any given population of atoms, can list all the possible molecules (arrangements) that can be formed from the atoms subject to the laws of chemical valence. This is such a large number of possibilities that it must be sifted through, and this is the role played by 'knowledge' that has been gleaned from human experts in spectrum analysis and encoded for the program's use. Given enough knowledge, Dendral succeeds in reducing the set of plausible candidate structures to a reasonable size for some fairly complex molecules.

However, to say that the intelligence lies solely or even primarily in the rule-encoded knowledge is to ignore the role of the structure generator. Without the generator the knowledge would be useless. On the other hand, the knowledge base could be replaced in part or in whole by another that might work as well or better. The generator plays the role of a structured model, a theory, which in my analysis of understanding and intelligence is the core idea. If both Dendral's 'knowledge' and its generator are essential for its performance, we can hardly attribute its success entirely to one, nor claim that the deductions are made with a 'simple' inference engine.

Finally, even if Cyc's predications could fully encode not just semantic facts but experience as well, that would not suffice to give Cyc the equivalent of human knowledge. Cyc does not have a human's core knowledge of geometry, physics, and psychology, nor any other structured system of knowledge that underlies human intelligence and understanding. It does not have human emotions and social predispositions, nor a Theory of Mind, and without these perceptual and cognitive systems it has nothing to attach its symbols to. To Cyc, these things are 'just words' and words are not enough. Not only are Cyc's symbols ungrounded in experience, they are not organized in human cognitive terms either. As such I can see no future for Cyc as an explanation of human, as opposed to machine, intelligence, nor of super *human* intelligence.

If human knowledge and understanding are grounded in experience, how is it that we are able to understand people, things and events that we do not directly experience, events that we encounter either in fiction or in historical accounts? The human ability to think hypothetically and in an other-minds fashion is what permits such understanding. Of course one's understanding of, say, life in Ancient Rome, may well be flawed, just as all understanding may be. However, we still achieve a form of understanding in terms of our experience with present day people and institutions.

Might not a Cyc-like data base be able to pass a Turing Test by building a 'false floor' of knowledge that is not grounded in experience but appears to be? Could such a system fool the most adroit questioner? Searle, extending his Chinese Room argument, would likely say that even if such an artifact did pass a Turing Test it would not be truly human-like because it could not understand in a human way. I agree, but the jury is still out. I think the system could be unmasked not by technical questions but by those that are based on simple, common experiences.

Nonetheless, a Cyc knowledge base may well prove to be usable in many simple ways, perhaps for practical advantage in narrow domains of discourse. For example, queries in English could be translated into look-ups of information from which reasonable answers might be constructed. The answers might be understandable by a human user, but unless substantial additional power in the form of structured models is provided to Cyc, Cyc itself will not understand the answers or what it is doing even in the limited sense

Dendral understands organic molecules. Thus it will not achieve human-like performance even in restricted tasks.

Knowledge representation is not a static record

Often the term "representation" is used to refer solely to the recording – the physical state of the nervous system or computer memory. This use is misguided and misleading. If something is 'merely' a physical record, say masses and charges at particular locations, then this fact alone does not give it representational status. For "representation" to carry any functional value it must single out those physical records that are useful from those that are simply passive recordings. There is no way to do this without bringing in the notion of an interpreter.

Any model that purports to be a description of human cognition, whether stated as a program, a set of equations, or in literary form, must specify processes for recording and reading information from the model. If it does not it is incomplete and no conclusions can be drawn from it about its psychological reality.

That is, the model must describe these access processes as well as the *syntax* of the representation *format*. I call the physical record the *representation-proper*. The syntax of the format specifies what counts as well-formed representations-proper. That is, the syntactic rules define the format of the recording, and they must be fully specified in a complete formal model of a representation. I call the access processes *construction and retrieval processes*. The former are those that create the representation-proper. The latter are the processes that retrieve information from the representation-proper. Construction and retrieval processes are intertwined, calling upon one-another frequently, just as a person's behavior intertwines perception and action, including perceiving one's actions and creating new perceptions.

A computer model for the use of maps to compare routes would thus need to specify how, say, a video image of the map was examined to determine routes or distances, and while this is a process that for a human is so automatic as to seem unproblematic, it is by no means trivial. Similarly, for a human to view a scene and describe it in sentences is so straightforward that it seems there is little to explain. Thus a person can readily produce descriptions of pictures and diagrams that are seen as accurate and complete. In fact, however, accomplishing these translations is not simple nor are the translations ever complete. For the case of more general classes of pictures, the processes of fully human-like machine vision have never been successfully written. However, reading inferences from a diagram seems so straightforward to us that it is easy to overlook the extent of the processing involved. Thus, an advocate of pictorial representations might point to a map, claiming it to be a representation of distance information and noting how convenient it is to, for example, compare two distances, or to note how the distance between *a* and *b* and between *b* and *c* relate to the distance between *a* and *c*. However it is only easy and efficient to make these observations if one has the visual and cognitive apparatus of a human. Thus to say that a map is a better representation than a table of distances is not only incoherent, but also when fleshed out in the obvious way is probably wrong if the interpreter is a computer.

A similar error is made by some who argue that first-order logic is obviously a powerful method of representation for, say, robot planning. Again, first-order logic by itself is not a cognitive representation for the reasons discussed above. To become one, it must specify how knowledge is extracted from the robot's observations and turned into first-order logic expressions, and how logic expressions are turned into behavior. This problem has not been solved in general, and indeed is much more complex and problematic than the map-reading visual processes.

Larkin & Simon (1987) discuss this idea by distinguishing representational equivalence from computational equivalence. Two systems may be able to express the same knowledge and yet one might be much more efficient than the other in actually using that knowledge. Evaluating knowledge representations must be done by treating them as complete packages and asking at what tasks they excel.

Computation and process

Although it is customary to speak of information processing when describing computational models, the theory of computation has characterized processing in a very specific way. The abstract model of a process is universally taken to be a series of state transitions, as in a Turing Machine. That is, an abstract computing device is defined as an entity that can be in one of a number of distinct states, and a computation is a series of transitions from state to state according to precisely defined rules of the form "when in state a and conditions x_i persist, change to state b while (possibly) writing symbols y_i in memory and producing symbols S_i as output."

Although such a model of computation is universal, it does not follow that it is suitable for understanding *processes*, nor, perforce, for understanding cognition if cognition is a process.

An obvious objection is that interesting computations, certainly cognitions, cannot be perspicuously seen if they are viewed to be strictly serial as the above model would have it. At the very least we need to envision computations that simultaneously follow multiple state transition paths. This is widely recognized for purposes of efficient calculation in very complex situations, and parallel computing machines are commonplace. The issue, however, is not solely one of the efficiency achieved by doing several independent things at the same time to save real clock time. The issue is also one of making cognitive models that reflect phenomenological and empirical facts of human behavior and thought.

Even parallel models of computation by state transition do not fully capture the informal notion of a process. Outside of computer science, most processes, whether physical or mental, are usually viewed as continuous in *time* rather than as discrete transitions between discrete physical states. Abstract models of computation, and *a fortiori*, AI models of cognition, do not capture the continuous nature of processes. (Of course there may be additional features of processes that will prove to be essential for an understanding of cognition, and even of computation more generally.) Mathematics struggled with the problem of characterizing the geometric intuition of continuity (of functions) with discrete numbers, as discussed in Chapter 4. Computer science has yet to find the proper digital characterization of the intuitive notion of continuous process.

Bickhard and Terveen suggest an 'interactionist' answer to their encoding problem. By this they mean that what is represented is "the potentialities of interaction between the agent and the world." Although they fail to make precise how this can be accomplished, the key insight is I think consonant with my analysis. My interpretation of their suggestion is that the computations performed on a representation must permit *hypothetical* manipulations of the symbols that reflect the behavior of the represented object/event/situation. That is, the representation permits inferences that run mental experiments, in effect plans or projections. In that sense they can examine "the potentialities of interaction between the agent and the world." Bickhard and Terveen might have other things in mind, but I assume that their proposal must at least include this ability to do mental experiments. On this view, items of information are used productively to create knowledge in a special way, as predictions of events in the world under hypothetical conditions. Others as well, *e.g.*, Tomasello (1999a) have proposed that this ability to run mental simulations is the fundamental distinction between humans and subhumans, from which language, tool use, mathematics, and Theory of Mind ensue.

A cognitively penetrable, episodic memory capable of abstract representation of real and imagined experience that can be manipulated mentally is an essential component of structured theorizing and cognitive simulation.

Research that addresses these limitations

There has been other AI research that I have not discussed in the preceding section, and it would be misleading to end without mentioning that many others have addressed the issues involved in my analysis, albeit with different emphases. Much of that work is clearly more in the spirit of my approach than the work I *have* discussed.

In fact, one of the earliest AI studies was done on modeling the solution of analogy problems by Evans (1968). There has been continuing interest in this problem in AI although it has never become the dominant problem or paradigm. Some important AI research on analogical reasoning has been done by Melanie Mitchell, Douglas Hofstadter, Deidre Gentner, and others in a variety of contexts. Analogy has often been construed narrowly, as in the paradigm A is to B as C is to D, where the analogical bases are just properties of A, B, C, and D. Structure-based analogy of the sort I am advocating depends on more complex relations. Fauconnier & Turner (2002) develop a theory they call *cognitive blending* that takes the notion of simple analogy to a more abstract level more in keeping with the complex ways in which analogy (and metaphor) are recognized, generated, and used in thinking.

In psychology the work on mental models by Phillip Johnson-Laird and others is related to the views expressed in this essay, although his mental models are more limited than those I envision. Perhaps the most extensive work similar to that advocated here is the analysis of metaphor by the linguist George Lakoff. Lakoff's concept of metaphor is closely related to the notion of structure that I will advance, and he and his colleagues Mark Johnson and Raphael Nunez [Lakoff & Johnson (1980), Lakoff & Nunez (2001)] have proposed extensive examples of metaphors that underlie human cognition. This work has been extended into a more detailed analysis of how metaphors are applied, with particular emphasis on their use in mathematical reasoning. One important example is called the Basic Metaphor of Infinity, which underlies human understanding of many important concepts, including the recursive definition of the integers and the concept of a limit. The Basic Metaphor of Infinity would on this view be a component of core human knowledge. It is grounded in our experience of the physical world.

This is merely a sample of important existing work that is worth looking into for inspiration on understanding understanding. In spite of some promising beginnings, however, new conceptualizations and theoretical forms will be necessary to make progress on this very difficult problem. In the next Chapter, I turn to how humans understand mathematics by using diagrams as representations of their experience and intuitions of space. The purpose of discussing mathematics in the context of this essay on understanding is threefold. First I wish to illustrate the substantial role that geometric diagrams have played in the development of symbolic reasoning. Second I wish to introduce the fundamental concept of structure upon which I will base my analysis of understanding and diagrammatic reasoning. Third I wish to show the relationship between numerical and geometric concepts that justifies the use of numerical calculation to explain geometric conceptual reasoning even though the latter is unlikely to be implemented numerically in human minds.

4 MATHEMATICS

This, therefore, is mathematics:
she reminds you of the invisible form of the soul;
she gives light to her own discoveries;
she awakens the mind and purifies the intellect;
she brings light to our intrinsic ideas;
she abolishes oblivion and ignorance which are ours by birth.
–Proclus Diadochus (411–485 CE), Quoted in M. Kline,
Mathematical Thought from Ancient to Modern Times

Mathematics is the most clearly analyzed of the uniquely human abilities and so is an appropriate example for a discussion of human understanding. Furthermore, my subsequent analysis of diagrammatic reasoning (another uniquely human activity) and its role in understanding requires that I introduce a fundamental notion – *structure* – that has been developed most fully through the creation of mathematics. Therefore, I will describe the important role that diagrammatic reasoning has played in the very development of mathematics throughout history, serving both to introduce the concept of structure and to underscore the importance of such diagrammatic reasoning in cognition.

The quintessential formal, language-based reasoning exemplar is mathematics. Mathematics was not always so obviously linguistic. Pythagoras (estimated 580 – 500 BCE) and Euclid (circa 300 BCE) are among the earliest mathematicians of whom we have records. The mathematics of each dealt with geometry, among other subjects, and the reasoning was about objects that had clear counterparts in the world, such as areas of fields and musical pitch.

Euclid is properly credited with introducing the notion of proof into mathematics. This included the use of what are today called axioms: initial assumed-to-be-true propositions. He also introduced definitions of terms and rules for making proper deduction. However, he did not state these in a formal language as is done in mathematics today, and his axioms and definitions contain much of the vagueness of natural languages, as will be discussed in Section 5.6: Euclidean Geometry. While Euclid's degree of rigor surpassed previous styles of argument, his 'proofs' and indeed all proofs right up through Newton and well beyond, were based on largely informal verbal arguments: "Even Isaac Newton ... did not actually prove [the] fundamental theorems. ... Had you asked him to justify them, he would likely have presented an argument that, though compelling, was loose and depended heavily on pictures (Rival (1987), page 43)."

Sometimes subtle errors were present in mathematical argumentation, although most of this early mathematics has survived the test of time and eventually been put on sounder footing. As mathematics developed further so did the notion of proof, a means of insuring the soundness of inferences. This became necessary with the introduction of more complex concepts such as the calculus of continuous functions, which required new foundations. Proof became gradually more and more closely tied to formal linguistic representations, that is, to sentences composed of strings of characters whose relation to referents was arbitrary and abstract. This conception of mathematics as *proof within a formal system* reached its full modern flower with the work of Hilbert (1862–1943) at the beginning of the twentieth century, and subsequently with the introduction of fully formalized and mechanizable proof procedures stated as computer programs. In the interim between Hilbert and the computer revolution certain fundamental limitations of this approach were discovered, but that has not obviated its power, elegance, or application.

1. The Co-Development of Geometry and Arithmetic

The major branches of classical mathematics are arithmetic and geometry. Each goes back to antiquity.

The development of the mathematics of arithmetic through algebra, calculus and complex variables, and the evolution of geometry through differential and non-Euclidean geometries are highly intertwined. It is now understood that arithmetic and geometry are intimately related, indeed embody in different forms many of the same basic ideas, best illustrated by the mapping of geometry onto algebra, beginning with the seminal work of Descartes (1596 – 1650).

The modern concept of number took many centuries to evolve. The history of the concept is a clear illustration that mathematical thinking did not develop solely through the application of formal proof methods since those were only introduced later and took many centuries to reach their current state. Today, arithmetic and algebra are the most fully formalized branches of mathematics, but the formalizations never came easily or solely by formal methods themselves. The literature of the history of mathematics suggests that each new numerical concept was resisted until some model, usually a geometric model, was put forth to aid its understanding.

Compared to primitive man every modern school child has a highly refined conception of number and of space and time. The modern mathematician and physicist conceptualize number and spacetime in even more abstract terms that have permitted amazing advances in human understanding and control of the natural world, but these conceptualizations are not part of common culture. This is an important point, because it indicates that *mathematics is a cultural product.*

The body of mathematics grows incrementally as a few individuals add to it and pass it on through cultural rather than biological mechanisms. Without such cultural accumulation and transmission, the majority of individuals would possess only very primitive calculation abilities, although beyond those of the modern chimpanzee. A few individuals would be able to go beyond this knowledge for their own purposes, for example being able to understand general but simple propositions about numbers and space. However, in the absence of language these would need to be discovered anew by each individual. The cultural accumulation of knowledge is lacking in subhuman primates. However, *individual* humans must be capable of creating and describing mathematical concepts and results, and these abilities are distinct from cultural transmission.

Cultural development of mathematics

Some primitive human cultures have extended mathematical concepts only a little beyond the chimpanzee. For example, some cultures are limited in their ability to count by a system that uses physical referents, such as body parts, for integers (Rauff (2003)). Thus the head might denote one, the eyes 2 and 3, nose 4, shoulders 5 and 6, and so forth. Of course even in modern industrial cultures people occasionally count on fingers and toes. Such systems lack a generative notation and thus limit discourse about numbers to a finite set of integers, even though members of such cultures may understand that 'in principle' the set of integers is unending. Having a good notational system is often a key ingredient in developing a mathematical concept, and body-part counting is insufficiently rich.

The earliest record of what is presumably a numerical accounting system is 10,000 years old, the Ishango bone. This is a bone with a series of similar marks cut into it, presumably recording events, much as the gunslingers of modern times notched their guns for each man killed. Such markings, one tick per item, are the first notational systems for recording numbers.

The natural numbers (*i.e.*, the positive integers 1, 2, 3, . . .) and the operations of addition, subtraction, multiplication, and division were known to the ancients, as revealed by artifacts found from every known ancient civilization, beginning with the Babylonian (Babylonia was roughly coextensive with modern-day Iraq), approximately 3700 years ago. In contrast, agriculture dates to about 10,000 years. All ancient civilizations of which we have records understood the concept of counting, and had invented numerals, that is, a written system to record numbers. A variety of methods arose. The notational system in Babylonia used a base-10 grouping, with different symbols for 1-9, for 10, 20, to 90, for 100, 200, to 900, and so forth. This permits a more compact representation of large numbers than afforded by tick marks. Other civilizations used different number bases, for example 60. All of these civilizations had methods to perform the four basic arithmetic operations plus squares and square roots, and were able to solve special cases of what today are called linear and quadratic equations.

As noted, this mathematical knowledge and these skills were not available to the general population, but only to a select group of practitioners. Doubtless the average citizen could count sufficiently well for his own commercial purposes, but beyond that was not likely to possess any mathematical skills. This supports the view that mathematics is a cultural product like written language, not one inherited as a universal mental capacity the way spoken language is. The ability *to acquire* these concepts through experience, invention, and education, however, is a fundamental ability of humans and apparently no other species, as Tomasello (1999b) emphasizes.

CHAPTER 4: MATHEMATICS

The Babylonians also were aware of important elementary geometric relations. For example, a table of 'Pythagorean' Numbers has been discovered (see Table 2: Babylonian-Table of 'Pythagorean' Numbers, where $x^2+y^2=d^2$). The table is presented here in modern notation and the "y" column has been added. No explanation of the source of this information was found, but it appears that it surely was derived from a consideration of right triangles. The table is organized by increasing $(d/y)^2$. If d is taken as the length of the hypotenuse and y is the length of a leg, then $(d/y)^2 = 2$ corresponds to a 45 degree right triangle, and decreasing values correspond to decreasing angles. The table ends at $(d/y)^2 = 1.39$ corresponding to almost a 30°-60° right triangle. Apparently the Babylonians had developed a sophisticated method of calculation, and had applied it to geometric problems.

Table 2
Babylonian Table of 'Pythagorean' Numbers

Modern reproduction of the Babylonian tablet labeled Plimpton 322 which dates from approximately 1700 BCE. The extant tablet consists of the four columns on the right. If x denotes "width" and d denotes "diagonal" then $d^2 - x^2$ is in each case a perfect square, whose roots are reconstructed in the leftmost column. The x, y, and d form Pythagorean triples. From Katz, Victor J. A History of Mathematics, 2nd, ©1998. Printed and electronically reproduced by permission of Pearson Education, Inc., Upper Saddle River, New Jersey.

y	$(d/y)^2$	x	d	#
120	1.9834028	119	169	1
3456	1.9491586	3367	4825	2
4800	1.9188021	4601	6649	3
13,500	1.8862479	12,709	18,541	4
72	1.8150077	65	97	5
360	1.7851929	319	481	6
2700	1.7199837	2291	3541	7
960	1.6845877	799	1249	8
600	1.6426694	481	769	9
6480	1.5861226	4961	8161	10
60	1.5625000	45	75	11
2400	1.4894168	1679	2929	12
240	1.4500174	161	289	13
2700	1.4302388	1771	3229	14
90	1.3871605	106	106	15

UNDERSTANDING UNDERSTANDING

The Babylonians presumably developed their mathematical skills for practical reasons, such as commerce and surveying, with no emphasis on theoretical understanding of the sort the Greeks prized. Babylonian texts describe not theorems but 'methods' for solving problems. Their methods were algorithms that specified the order of performing operations, and these were generally illustrated with specific examples. They were not accompanied by explanation or justification, although surely their creators must have discovered them through some sort of understanding of what they were about.

It is important to note that the problems addressed generally arose from geometric questions. For example, one class of simultaneous quadratic equations for which methods were developed was this set of equations, again in modern notation: (1) $x + y = a$ and (2) $xy = b$. Here a and b have the obvious interpretation of semi-perimeter and area of a rectangle. The 'method' given for solving these equations has a simple geometric analog as well (Katz (1998), pages 35-39). See Figure 4: A Babylonian Method for Solving Equations. Other equations have similar geometric interpretations.

The Babylonians also were interested in the area of circles, the simplest non-linear figure of geometry. The Babylonians used 3-1/5 as the value of the ratio of circumference to diameter, probably computed from careful measurement on many specific examples. They were also aware that this proportionality constant was the same as the ratio of area to squared radius, a remarkable but not obvious fact. Thus they were able to compute areas of circles to good approximation. The Egyptians later computed an excellent approximation to π at 3.1604 (the correct value to 5 digits is 3.1416).

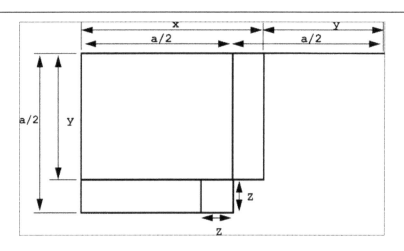

Figure 4
A Babylonian Method for Solving Equations
A geometric procedure for solving the system $x + y = a$ and $xy = b$. By observation the area b of the rectangle xy and the area $(a/2)^2$ of the large square, differ by z^2, that is, $(a/2)^2 = b + z^2$. From Katz, Victor J. A History of Mathematics, 2nd, ©1998. Printed and electronically reproduced by permission of Pearson Education, Inc., Upper Saddle River, New Jersey.

2. The Concept of Number

Natural numbers

It was not until much later, however, that the full structure of the number system was understood. Today, *number theory* refers to the theory of the natural numbers: 1, 2, 3, . . . and all numbers derived from them.

One basic property that natural numbers have is order. This is also intuitively grasped as a geometric concept; when one moves about there is an order to the intermediate places on the route. A geometric model of the natural numbers is a straight line, beginning at 1 and proceeding to 2 and so forth. By today's convention, this line is generally drawn horizontally and 1 is at the left. Perhaps there is something about this convention that is natural to the human mind, but more likely is a product of cultural convention. The line could just as well be conceived as right to left, down to up, and at any other orientation; the only requirement is that it capture the notion of order. Today we also understand about equality of intervals, and represent this by evenly spacing the numerals along the number line. This equal distance property of numbers is an additional property of integers beyond that of order. Thus the integers can be used only to denote distinct objects (a nominal scale), or to specify an ordering of distinct objects (an ordinal scale), or to compare *differences* among ordered objects (an interval scale).

The basic arithmetic operations are defined on the natural numbers. Although this structure seems to be transparently simple, number theory is a remarkably deep and beautiful subject with many simply stated conjectures (for example: every even number is the sum of two prime numbers) still unproven after centuries of effort by many great minds. Still, the natural numbers cannot provide adequate models for geometry, and from the earliest times extensions to the set of natural numbers have been made to address problems arising both from arithmetic and geometry.

In the development of arithmetic, the basic arithmetic operation of addition of integers is valuable and natural. It has a clear interpretation in terms of actions in the real world: If I have three goats and you give me four goats I will have seven goats. Multiplication (multiple additions) of integers was also clear by extension and also has clear models in terms of physical objects. However, if I give you four of my ten goats, how many do I have left? From such problems arises the concept of subtraction, the inverse of addition, and of division, the inverse of multiplication. These introduce new puzzles.

Zero

The concept of nothing doubtless was available very early in history. Even a chimpanzee can distinguish one banana from none. However, representing this concept and recognizing that that representation could be seen as a number on the same footing with the natural numbers was not immediate even to humans. It took many centuries to associate the concept of nothing with a number. Indeed to see that 'nothing' is a number requires understanding at some level that numbers are a class of objects, defined by their interrelations. This is a fundamental idea, again one that is accessible only to humans and not immediately obvious even to us.

One suggestion is that the connection between nothing and the number system arose during the development of positional notation (Kaplan (1999)). As extensive written representations of numbers became necessary for accounting in commerce, the early cuneiform notations, with a distinct symbol for each integer, soon became cumbersome. A positional notation avoids a proliferation of symbols by making each symbol's meaning depend on context, allowing a single symbol to do multiple duty: "7" can mean seven or seventy or seven hundred, depending on where it occurs within a numeral. Without a separate symbol for zero, however, ambiguity arose between, say (in modern notation) 47 and 407. At first, the correct choice of an ambiguous notation was simply determined by context (I know we must be talking about forty-seven sheep, not four hundred and seven sheep). However, soon the problem arose too often, the story goes, and the numeral zero arose as a place holder in positional notation.

Zero, the number, not just a place-holder, arose in the East. The notion that there was a number zero was not readily accepted, particularly in the Western civilizations, for example Greece, where it did not have a natural philosophical home: the Greeks did not believe that 'nothing' had an actual existence. Even today our conventions, derived mostly from Western civilization, reflect the strange regard in which zero was held. Our telephone keypads and computer keyboards have 0 not where it ought to be, before 1, but after 9, which reflects only its placeholder role, not its order in the number system. Since our calendar is based on Western ideas, it considers that the birth of Christ was not at time zero, but in the year 1, so that Christ was one year old in year 2. This confusion is reflected in current disagreement over whether the new millennium started January 1, 2000 or January 1, 2001.

'Nothing' also arises from subtraction, and this also supports the need for a representation of nothingness.

Negative numbers

When one subtracts a larger number from a smaller one, what do we have, and is it a number?

Every school child today is comfortable with the concept of negative numbers, although the extended history of the development of these concepts makes clear again that they are cultural products, not innate concepts. The Italian algebraists (1400-1700), who developed methods for solving many polynomial equations, avoided negative numbers. Equations were stated only with positive coefficients and any non-positive solution was ignored. The great English mathematician John Wallis (1616-1703) published the following argument, astonishing to us today: "Since $a/0$ with a positive is positive infinity, and since a/b with b negative is a negative number, then that negative number must be greater than positive infinity because the denominator b of a/b is less than the denominator 0 of $a/0$ (Nahin (1998), page 14)."

The common geometric model for the integers (positive, negative and zero) is a straight line, almost always horizontal, with a special place, 0, marked. Positive integers are arranged in order to the right of zero, negatives to the left. With this geometric interpretation negative integers and zero are readily understood. Addition is 'moving right' and subtraction is 'moving left.' It is this geometric interpretation – or another physical system of ordered objects – that gives the integers (positive, negative, and zero) an understandable structure that supports the formal definitions of addition and subtraction.

Rational numbers

Division of integers can lead to non-integers (fractions). Are fractions numbers? If so we must extend the definitions of the arithmetic operations so that they apply to all such 'new' numbers as well. We must be able to add and multiply fractions and get numbers, or else our conceptual landscape becomes strewn with meaningless quantities that arise here and there and must be ignored as embarrassments. The problem becomes even more troublesome when one recognizes that one can get natural numbers by arithmetic operations on fractions: $1/2 + 1/2 = 1$.

Today fractions are of course accepted as numbers, with natural numbers recognized as a special type of fraction. The complete set of 'fractions' is called the rationals since they are all ratios of integers. Furthermore, division of rationals only leads to other rationals, so no new set of questionable objects arises in this manner.

Generally it was not until geometric interpretations of numerical anomalies were achieved that they became accepted as meaningful. The fractions can be found on the same line that models the natural numbers, but not in a simple way. Rational numbers are dense, meaning that between any two of them there exists another (to find one of these, simply add the two and divide the result by 2). This means that they are (geometrically) 'close together,' which can be expressed by saying that no matter how small a non-zero difference one chooses, there exists a pair of rational numbers that are closer still. Clearly we cannot mark all such points on our line model; *the model must now be used in an abstract sense*, where we can *imagine* an interpretation of any given number, but cannot actually depict it. *This step from exact physical model to abstract mental model is another great cognitive leap that was achieved sometime in human history and is not accessible to other primates or lower animals.* There is no explanation as to how this cognitive leap is accomplished, say how it is embodied in neural circuits, nor how *the process* of abstraction as opposed to the number concept itself can be characterized precisely.

With this geometric interpretation providing intuitive understanding, the set of rational numbers is *closed* under addition and subtraction, that is, any entity arising from the addition or subtraction of two rational numbers is also a rational number, with an intuitive geometric interpretation as a place on the number line. This makes it possible to maintain the simple and elegant structure of the number system.

The Babylonians and all other ancient civilizations developed the concept of rational number and incorporated it into problem solving methods. The Greeks, beginning with Thales (ca. 634 – 546 BCE), and proceeding through Pythagoras of Samos, Plato's academy, and Euclid, understood and developed the concept of ratios of natural numbers. Euclid, especially in Book II of his "Elements," extensively considered problems of similarity and proportions of geometric figures. Book II is basically an algebraic text, although clearly dealing with geometry-inspired problems.

With zero and the positive and negative rationals it would seem that finally all the numbers had been discovered, since they now included everything on the number line with a distinguished zero point. However, denseness does *not* capture the intuitive notion of continuity that the concept of space, as embodied in the number line, possesses. Thus the model has more properties than what it models.

Irrational numbers

Pythagoras and his school of philosopher-mathematicians believed that "number is the substance of all things," that is, that all physical phenomena could be measured and expressed as numbers. According to Katz (1998) the "central goal of Greek mathematics was geometrical problem solving." They introduced the idea of proof and ". . . gradually came to the realization that the world around them was knowable, that they could discover its characteristics by rational inquiry (page 47)." Many modern day computer scientists and artificial intelligence researchers hold a view similar to the Pythagoreans – that all knowledge can be expressed with numbers.

However, our concept of number is not the same as that of the Pythagoreans, who by numbers meant only the rational numbers. When the Greeks discovered that one can produce non-rational entities by application of the basic arithmetic operations, it was an enormous shock, sometimes called the Rational Scandal.

It is possible to prove the existence of an irrational number by algebraic argument.[7] However, a geometric model of root-2 is easily constructed with the simple tools of geometry (the length of the hypotenuse of a 45-degree right triangle with legs of length 1 is $\sqrt{2}$). So here is a 'thing' that could not be represented by a 'number' in the Pythagorean (rational) sense, and yet it can readily be constructed with compass and straightedge.

In modern notation, irrational numbers, expressed as decimals, are those for which the representation never repeats, either as an endless string of 0's or any other pattern.

Geometric models of irrational numbers

The discovery of irrational numbers posed a fundamental problem for Greek philosophy, one which was not to be overcome for many years. 'Where' are irrational numbers on our model of numbers, the number line? If the rationals are densely packed, where are there places for the irrationals to squeeze in? Without knowing where they were, that is, how they fit into the model of numbers, they were not understood. Again

---

[7] Every positive integer can be expressed as the product of primes. Some of the prime factors can be repeated, so in general every positive integer can be expressed in the form $2^{n2}3^{n3}5^{n5}7^{n7}11^{n11}13^{n13}\ldots$, where each ni is an integer. The ordered set of exponents is a unique characterization of one and only one integer. For example, $2000 = 2^4 5^3$ is uniquely characterized as {4, 0, 3}. Now assume there exist two integers N and M whose ratio is the square root of 2. Then $N^2 = 2M^2$. Let the 2-power of the prime decomposition of N = k and the 2 power of the prime decomposition of M = t. Then the 2 power of the prime decompositions of N^2 is 2k and the two power of the prime decomposition of M^2 is 2t. N^2 and $2M^2$ must also have identical prime decompositions, since they are equal. Replacing N^2 and M^2 by their prime decompositions and canceling all but the powers of 2 from this equation yields $2^{2k} = 2 \times 2^{2t} = 2^{(2t+1)}$. However, this is a contradiction since 2k is even and 2t + 1 is odd. Therefore our original assumption is wrong and there cannot be any integers whose ratio is the square root of 2. Therefore root-2 must be 'irrational.'

we must treat our geometric model abstractly in order for it to encompass these entities: we 'know' they are there and we know 'where' they are, but we cannot 'see' them. *Geometric models are not literally perceptual objects!*

Kant (1724–1804) discussed this issue. He wished to distinguish cognition from perception, and to distinguish their roles in thought. He used the German word "*Anschauung*" (intuition, or more literally, visualization) to denote the product of abstract cognition. In contrast, "*Anschaulichkeit*" (visualizability) refers to what is immediately given to perception. *Anschaulichkeit* is thus less abstract than *Anschauung*. The proper role of these two concepts in the philosophy of science, particularly physics, was extensively debated in the last century; Miller (1998). A remarkable and unique feature of human cognition is that it is capable of the abstract reasoning of *Anschauung*, yet *Anschaulichkeit* is essential to it. The history of mathematics, in particular of the number theory and elementary geometry relevant to this essay, can be seen as the development and refinement of *Anschauung*. Discussions of diagrammatic reasoning often founder by failing to recognize that diagrams are not understood simply as perceptual objects.

Algebraic numbers

The concept of algebraic number arose with the development of algebra and its theory of equations. This development freed mathematics from the limiting concepts of Greek number theory and came to legitimize the concept of numbers of the types we have discussed, including the irrationals. An algebraic number is the solution to an algebraic equation that involves only the fundamental operations of addition, subtraction, multiplication (including exponentiation and its inverse, roots), and division. Since in the Middle Ages these operations represented all the operations that could be done on numbers, it was natural to assume that there was no need to expand the concept of number beyond that of algebraic number.

The theory of equations and of algebraic numbers was a major intellectual landmark, introducing to mathematics the concepts of variable and equations, concepts that are available in natural language but which required centuries to be abstracted and formally understood in mathematical thought. The theory was developed by many mathematicians over several centuries, with the first formal publications attributed to al-Khwarizmi (c. 780-850) in the eighth century CE, (for a modern reference see Karpinski (1915)).

The construction tools of geometry – straight edge and compass – are sufficient to construct geometric analogs of the algebraic numbers. I have noted that it is possible to construct a line whose length is the square root of 2 using these construction tools, by constructing a 45 degree right triangle. The equivalent algebraic operation is the solution of the Pythagorean relation.

Ultimately, all of the algebraic numbers had a geometric meaning and this finally led to their acceptance as numbers rather than bizarre oddities. Once again, the expanded category of number maintained a coherent structure under the basic arithmetic operations and could be understood through geometric models, even though one cannot physically place each algebraic number on the number line but must again resort to imagery and abstraction, moving beyond perception. Any actual finite sized 'mark' we place on a drawn line for √2 will 'cover' many rational numbers as well. Accepting that they nonetheless were meaningful is thus a triumph of the abstract concept of mathematical structure. *Algebraic numbers are understood through the existence of a conceptual model based on physical intuitions but lacking physical existence.*

Transcendental numbers

The concept of algebraic numbers, including rationals and irrationals, would seem finally to capture the notion of continuity that is basic to the intuitive structure of space, and so once again it was thought that arithmetic was complete. However, even though the irrationals and all the other algebraic numbers are squeezed into the spaces between the dense rationals, it may still be possible that there are other 'gaps' in the number line. This is again a physically counterintuitive notion: if they are packed as tightly as possible, how can there be room for anything else? Indeed something was still missing, and this was the source of several puzzles for ancient geometry, such as the problem of squaring the circle.

There exist numbers that are not algebraic, that is, are neither rational nor irrational. They are called transcendental numbers, of which π is the most famous. π is not the solution to any algebraic equation, although it can be computed by iterative numerical calculation to any precision desired. It might seem that drawing a circle of diameter 1 'constructs' π geometrically. But this does not constitute a construction because there is no way to measure the circumference of a circle: distance is defined as the length of a *straight* line. Measuring the length of a curved line requires definitions and methods that transcend algebra.

This is the difficulty underlying the classical problem of squaring the circle, that is, constructing a square whose area exactly equals that of a given circle. This is equivalent to solving the equation $\pi = (L/R)^2$, where L is the length of the side of the square and R is the radius of the given circle. This cannot be done algebraically; it also cannot be done with compass and straightedge.

An interesting aside is that it was reported by Hippocrates (5th century BCE) that one can square a lune (Dunham (1990)). A lune is the crescent moon shaped object produced by two intersecting circles of different diameters. See Figure 5: Lune. Somehow the area of the lune, it seemed, does not depend on π, which 'cancels out' of the equation in some subtle way since there are two circular arcs involved. It was later discovered, however, that the proof offered by Hippocrates held only for a particular class of lunes, not for all of them, so even the 'canceling out' is not a general phenomenon.

The Greeks were especially concerned with three classic problems: squaring the circle as just described, doubling the cube (constructing a cube with double the volume of a given cube, and trisecting an angle. As it happens, none of these problems can be solved by the standard constructions of Euclidean plane geometry. They can be solved, however, by the construction of curves (conic sections) that are algebraically well defined (Brett, Feldman & Sentlowitz (1974)). With those additional methods, then, the equivalent of constructing transcendental numbers is available and they receive geometric interpretations.

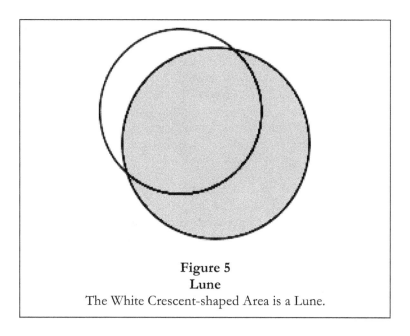

Figure 5
Lune
The White Crescent-shaped Area is a Lune.

Real numbers

With the transcendental numbers added, the set of *real* numbers was now complete. The geometric intuition of continuity is captured by the real numbers: every real number has a place on the number line, and every point on the number line represents a real number. The real numbers, unlike the merely dense rationals, are continuous in the intuitive sense that space is continuous: there are no 'gaps' between them for something else to fit in. The real numbers have evolved into a formal system that captures the intuitive abstract geometric notion of a straight line – ordered, dense, straight, and continuous. And indeed an infinite summation of ever smaller fractions could (sometimes) add up to a whole number!

Nonetheless the notion of continuity is puzzling, as shown by Xeno's famous paradoxes, *e.g.,* how could Achilles ever catch a hare if it takes a finite time for each halving of the distance between them? It required the development of *analysis*, beginning with the calculus of Newton (1643 – 1727) and Leibniz (1646 – 1716), to succeed in defining real numbers and continuity and to show that the resulting theory was consistent. This development, however, was a long road that did not end until the 19th century (see below).

Vectors

Geometric intuition of course embraces more than straight lines. What about two dimensional space, for example a plane? Where are all the numbers corresponding to these 'extra' points? These are accommodated by representing them as *ordered pairs* of numbers: the first number of a pair denotes a distance along the number line, the second a distance along a second number line perpendicular to the first. This strategy clearly can be extended to three dimensions: a point in 3-space is represented by an ordered triple of numbers. Indeed it is possible to imagine spaces of even higher dimensions, spaces that presumably don't exist in our intuition, but can be described by extending the number of items (dimensions) of the ordered list. An ordered set of numbers is called a *vector* because it is also a numerical way to represent the directed line segment from the origin (the point where the number lines – axes – intersect) to the point whose coordinates the vector comprises. There are numerical operations that can be performed on vectors and *matrices* ('two-dimensional' vectors, that is, rectangular arrays of numbers) that allow geometric-like computations on higher-dimensional objects.

Non-real numbers

Still, if one took seriously the idea of algebraic structure, that is, that the set of numbers must be the algebraic closure of the natural numbers under arithmetic operations, another puzzle remained. Combined with the square root operation, negative numbers yield $i = \sqrt{(-1)}$. Thus, to maintain the coherent structure of the numbers, i had to be a number. Once again this was universally dismissed as impossible and fatuous and continued to puzzle outstanding geniuses such as Descartes and Leibniz. Euler (1707–1783), in his 1770 text *Algebra,* wrote "All such expressions as $\sqrt{(-1)}$, $\sqrt{(-2)}$ etc. are consequently impossible or imaginary numbers, since they represent roots of negative quantities; and of such numbers we may truly assert that they are neither nothing, nor greater than nothing, nor less than nothing; which necessarily constitutes them imaginary or impossible. (Nahin (1998), page 31)". In other words, all 'numbers' must be in a strict ordering, as along a single line.

If there are no 'gaps' in the real line, where are the imaginaries? If they are not on the real line they must not be numbers, even though they arise from arithmetic operations on real numbers. There remained a mismatch between number theory and geometric models of numbers if we were to embrace the entire closure of the reals.

Complex numbers are those of the form $a + ib$ where a and b are real numbers and i is the square root of -1. Real numbers are a subset of the complex numbers, those for which $b = 0$.

Geometric models of complex numbers

It was not until it was proposed that complex numbers could be interpreted as points in a *plane*, rather than on a single line, with the imaginary number axis perpendicular to the real axis, that the puzzle was broken and imaginaries were accepted. See Figure 6: The Complex Plane. Thus again the acceptance of these strange quantities into the class of numbers resulted from a geometric interpretation. The concept of the complex plane was developed by Caspar Wessel (1745-1818) while he thought about certain specific problems from a new point of view. Wessel's discovery doubtless was derived from geometric thinking; he was, in fact, a surveyor. Wessel's geometric representation of a complex number $a + bi$ is the point in the two-dimensional coordinate system where the x-axis represents the real component, a, and the y-axis represents the imaginary component, b. The square of the length of the vector from the origin to (a, b) is the product of the number and its *complex conjugate*, $a - bi$. That product is $a^2 + b^2$.

CHAPTER 4: MATHEMATICS

Wessel's representation of complex numbers leads to clear geometric interpretations of arithmetic operations on them. For example, multiplying a complex number by i rotates its vector counterclockwise by 90 degrees. Other arithmetic operations also have clear diagrammatic counterparts.

Complex numbers are more than consistent oddities. They are powerful tools that offer algebraic manipulations that would be profoundly more difficult if applied only to real numbers. They have proven to provide enormous computational power especially in engineering applications. Once again, although all of the manipulations could be done in a fully formal one-dimensional linguistic manner, no engineer or mathematician can truly say that the geometric concept of the complex plane is ignored in practice.

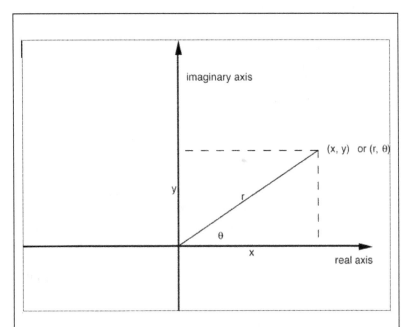

Figure 6
The Complex Plane

The complex number $x + iy$ is located on the complex plane above, with $x = r\cos\Theta$ and $y = r\sin\Theta$, and $r^2 = x^2 + y^2$. The real number 1 lies on the real axis at $x = 1$. Any point can also be represented in polar coordinates as (r, Θ). Every point has an infinite number of polar coordinate designations. For example, 1 = $(1, k\pi)$ for any even integer k, since $\cos\Theta = 0$ for all such values of Θ. Similarly $-1 = (1, -k\pi)$ for any odd integer k. i is the point that lies on the imaginary axis at $r = 1$ with $\Theta = (2k + 1) \pi/2$. -1 has polar coordinates $r = 1$ and $\Theta = (2k +1)(3\pi/2)$ for any $k > 0$.

The complex plane is essential for understanding complex numbers. Today every mathematician is fully comfortable with such facts as $i^i = e^{-\pi/2} = 0.2078 \ldots$ which is a real number! Before the discovery of the model of the complex plane such claims would have been considered beyond meaning.

We now have a very clear picture and a completely formal, algebraic interpretation of the set of complex numbers, including its subsets the imaginaries, the transcendentals, the reals, the rationals, the integers, and the natural numbers. The algebraic interpretation is that there is a set of objects upon which certain operators are defined and that the system obeys very specific axioms of closure and so forth. Arithmetic is now autonomously defined and in principle free from geometric or other interpretations despite its origins, and can transcend its origins to higher dimensional spaces. It could in principle have arisen from other roots and be applied without consideration of geometry, but it did not and is not, at least by human beings on planet Earth.

Transfinite numbers

The most recent development of arithmetic, *transfinite* numbers ('infinities'), uses the methods of formal analysis to push us beyond the intuitive, geometric underpinnings of the origins of arithmetic. While there is no geometric interpretation of, say, the number that is the cardinality of the set of all subsets of the real numbers, geometric diagrams still prove useful in thinking about these objects.

3. Metamathematics

Formal systems can and are treated as objects of inquiry in their own right, and theorems about them constitute the subject called Metamathematics. As fate would have it, it is impossible to prove that arithmetic is *complete*. This means that no formal theory of arithmetic can prove every true statement of arithmetic. This is a remarkable result of Metamathematics, the Incompleteness Theorem of Gödel. This theorem essentially says that the pursuit of a complete theory of arithmetic is as foolhardy as the pursuit of perpetual motion, for any theory powerful enough to express elementary arithmetic will entail true statements that cannot be proved within the theory.

Another powerful idea that developed in the 20th century is the concept of a *set-theoretic model.* A model for an axiomatic system is a set[8] of objects (each of which is itself a set) with specified properties that is consistent with the axioms. This notion had long been used less formally as a method of showing the consistency and the independence of axioms. For example, if one can construct a model of an axiom system, the system must

---

[8] Informally a *set* is any collection of entities (*members* of the set), presumably a notion so simple and primitive as to be understandable to any human mind. Set membership is the atomic relation – an entity is either a member of a given set or it is not. There may be a finite or an infinite number of members of the set. In Naïve Set Theory, membership can be defined in any way. An extraordinary episode of intellectual history from the early 20th century was triggered by Betrand Russell's observation that this 'naïve' definition of "set" permits paradoxes such as "the set of all sets that do not contain themselves." A consistent definition of "set" requires restrictions on set membership to avoid such paradoxes. Axiomatic Set Theory is the basis of modern formalized mathematics: every mathematical object (e.g., numbers, functions, and probabilities) is a set. For a clear and elementary exposition see Suppes (1960)

be consistent. If one can construct a model for an axiom system in which one of the axioms is replaced by its negation, the axiom in question must be an independent assumption.

Today, in the more abstract branches of mathematics, including the study of the logical foundations of mathematics, the concept of a geometric model in the form of a diagram has largely been replaced by the set-theoretic concept of a model. The set-theoretic model concept is itself an abstraction of the notion of a model as a geometric object, and understanding the set-theoretic model concept is afforded by this relation and history.

4. Continuity

In this chapter I have presented a thumbnail sketch of the history of the use of human intuitive geometry in its role as a grounding for arithmetical concepts, and shown how our intuitive geometry and intuitive arithmetic have interacted in support of one another, particularly as geometric intuition has supported the development of ever more sophisticated arithmetic concepts. The Cartesian relation between arithmetic and algebra has been a seminal insight in this history, but in an important sense it has been a troubled marriage.

The troubling aspect of the connection has been and continues to be the issue of continuity. Intuitive geometry conceives of space as continuous, that is, roughly, there are no gaps in it. Motion is the underlying experience that grounds this notion of continuity: an object moves through space without jumping over 'non-space' pieces ('gaps'). The number system has evolved from simple counting of discrete quantities to the complex plane. Still numbers remain a discrete, digital concept, not a continuous, analog concept, and melding discrete numbers with continuous space remains an elusive goal.

The issue re-surfaced with the development of the concept of a function. In geometry a function can be visualized as a 'curve' drawn on the Cartesian plane where for each point on the x-axis there is exactly one point on the curve. A function was considered to be continuous if the curve could be drawn without removing the 'pencil' from the paper. In arithmetic, on the other hand, functions are defined as sets of pairs of numbers that associate the x value with the function value. Continuous functions of course require that the set of pairs be infinite, but since numbers could range over everything on the number line this in itself seemed not a problem. However, this characterization of the concept of function allowed one to consider functions that had no clear geometric interpretation. Thus the Cartesian connection between geometry and arithmetic that had worked so well with 'simple' functions such as straight lines and conic sections (parabolas, circles, etc.) was to break down, and the issue was the characterization of the intuitive spatial notion of continuity with the discrete arithmetic notion of number.

Newton and Leibniz sought to define the slope of a curve in a general way. Since the curve could be as 'curvy' as one wanted and still be continuous what was need was a way to compute the slope of a function at a point, what we now call the first derivative of the function at that point. Newton arithmetized this notion by considering a geometric concept of a limit, specifically, the slope at a point was the slope of the line tangent to the curve at that point, and this could be computed as the limit ('end point') of the unending sequence of the slopes of secants (lines connecting the point on the curve with another point on the curve) as the endpoints of the secant approached one another. Since limits, at least for simple functions, could be computed algebraically the problem was solved and a complete description of a continuous function seemed at hand. (Of course for a coarsely discontinuous function, say one defined only at integer values of x, there was no problem and thus no solution was required.)

Leibniz solved the problem in a different way, by introducing the concept of infinitesimals, a quantity that is less than any number but greater than 0. One computed the differential as the slope of a secant of infinitesimal length. The problem with infinitesimals is that they cannot be numbers since they do not obey the rules of arithmetic. For example, the sum of a rational r and an infinitesimal ε is r, and further more $\varepsilon = 2\varepsilon = 3\varepsilon$, etc. The new calculus proved valuable in the modeling of physical processes, and so these arithmetic problems did not stop its use, but the issue remained conceptually puzzling, not because of the geometrical model but because of the need to add non-numbers to the arithmetic side in order to maintain the grounding.

The arithmetic conception of a function as a set of pairs of numbers allowed the definition of (and the simple algebraic representations of) functions that could not actually be drawn, nor even readily visualized. This revealed most clearly the breakdown of the geometric model of arithmetic. For example, the function y = $\sin(1/x)$ for x>0 reverses direction more and more frequently as x approaches 0 (where it is not defined), so that there are an infinite number of cycles between any positive value of x, no matter how small, and 0. Clearly this function cannot be drawn nor visualized, but can be generated for values of x arbitrarily close to 0, even though it cannot be fully written down as a set of ordered pairs. Intuitively the $\sin(1/x)$ function is continuous, and one can imagine an infinite process of 'drawing' it, even though the process cannot be completed nor can it be actually done very far with physical writing instruments (even computer screens) which have finite resolution.

How can continuity of functions be defined arithmetically without the use of infinitesimals? The modern answer was given by Weierstrass (1815–1897) who introduced the now familiar ε-δ characterization. A function is continuous if and only if the values of a function are arbitrarily close (within ε) when the values of the variable are close enough (within δ). That is, given any ε there exists a δ such that whenever one picks two values of x that are less than δ apart, the function values are less than ε apart. This characterization gives an arithmetic rule (involving only numbers) that defines continuous functions without recourse to geometric models, and yet captures the geometric intuition of continuity using only the notion of discrete numbers. In a sense, then, geometric continuity has been characterized as 'closeness' with discrete (arithmetic) concepts. This is the same way in which modern computer sciences and the digital revolution have characterized continuous processes as changes from one discrete step to another at each discrete 'tick' of a clock, recognizing that one can come arbitrarily close to continuity by making the ticks arbitrarily close in time and the changes arbitrarily small. That is, continuity can be approximated as closely as desired by digital methods, just as one can make a pixilated picture arbitrarily sharp by increasing the resolution 'enough.'

Still, this solution to the problem of continuity is an uneasy one, being tied as it is to the notion of an unending series of steps that has no last step yet has an actual 'end'– a limit. *This concept of an unending series with a limit appears to be a fundamental intuitive notion for humans, one that must be added to the list of our innate core knowledge that was outlined in Chapter 2.*

5. Geometric Intuition and Mathematical Invention

I have argued that the acceptance and promulgation of mathematical concepts, in the case of arithmetic at least, has been critically dependent on geometric models and vice versa. The invention of new concepts of all kinds depends on such model-based understanding as well. Perhaps the inventor of new ideas employs additional means, such as rigorous logic or systematic consideration of alternatives; if so these methods supplement the use of understanding through models and do not supplant it.

In certain limited areas it may be that interpretations, geometric or otherwise, may be without value or ignored. But certainly in most areas of mathematics that is not the case. For example, Wessel's discovery of the complex plane cited above was essential for the understanding of complex numbers. A complete psychological understanding of mathematical thinking will not be at hand until the connection between formal systems and their grounded interpretations is itself understood.

Particularly in the past century mathematical concepts are presented and discussed in highly formalized ways, often through a sequence of theorems and proofs. Certainly the rigor and value of mathematics depends on the fact that its statements can be proved. This should not blind us to the fact that neither the invention nor the assimilation of these concepts is based solely or even primarily on theorems and proofs.

What I have proposed is that understanding, rather than mathematical proof, is the central phenomenon in mathematical thinking; that formal analysis alone cannot give an account of mathematical understanding; that models, frequently geometric models, are essential to the *understanding* of mathematical understanding; and that both the invention and promulgation of mathematical truth require for their explanation concepts that go beyond formal analysis. In the next section I will extend this argument by generalizing the notion of geometric models to a larger class of semantic models, which are characterized by their structure and its relation to a grounding referential domain.

My reasons for believing the foregoing are not analytic but empirical: I have argued that the actual history of discovery and spread of mathematical concepts supports this conclusion.

It is important to note also what I am not claiming. I am not claiming that formal analysis plays no role in mathematical understanding. In particular I will repeatedly argue that certain properties of formal language, notably the ability to *refer* and to express *quantification* and *generalization*, are essential to understanding understanding and these cannot be achieved by a purely geometric, spatial, or imagistic theory.

6. Reciprocal Understanding

I have emphasized the historical role of geometric intuition in the development of arithmetical concepts. It seems natural that geometry is somehow more fundamental than arithmetic because intuition about space, as seen in the ability to successfully interact with a world of objects in space, is present in lower animals as well as humans, whereas the concept of counting is relatively new, and the full concept of the natural numbers is available only to humans.

However, the history of classical mathematics also shows that advances in geometric understanding often depend on advances in arithmetic understanding. The Egyptians are generally credited with the earliest developments of geometry, presumably driven by practical problems such as re-surveying agricultural lands annually flooded by the Nile. They developed numerical methods to solve these geometric problems. The Babylonian inventions of arithmetic methods to solve equations of geometric importance can also be seen as successful attempts to explain geometry in arithmetical terms.

The clearest example of the 'reduction' of geometry to arithmetic is the Pythagorean school. As noted above, Pythagoras and his followers based their world-view on numbers, specifically ratios. They discovered that certain ratios, such as those of plucked stings, led to emotionally charged harmonies while others led to unpleasant disharmonies. The golden ratio[9], 1.62 : 1, was found everywhere in nature and also seen to lead to beauty in architectural structures whose proportions obeyed it. Shape, a geometric concept, was seen as reducible to number. Perhaps this is another reason why the number zero did not find a receptive home in Greek mathematics: no shape has zero area (Seife (2000)).

Descartes' work and other work subsequent to his seminal insights have shown that there is a deep connection between arithmetic and geometry: they have the same structure, that is, arithmetic concepts have geometric counterparts and the relations among arithmetic concepts mirror the relations among geometric concepts. Understanding this relation has led to enormous advances in understanding both geometry and arithmetic, and to fundamental extensions of arithmetic to analysis and topology. It is also the basis for essentially all engineering applications.

The picture that emerges from these historical developments is one of reciprocal understanding. Beginning with concepts or skills that have arisen, new concepts of a different sort are built on them. The geometric concept of distance is understood with the arithmetic concept of number. The arithmetic concept of multiplication is understood in terms of the geometric concept of area. Over the course of the cultural evolution of mathematical ideas, arithmetic and geometry advance in a leap-frog manner, each new advance in one achieved by grounding it in prior concepts from the other. The historical course was not smooth because it took place, and continues to take place, at many places and times with many different people. These histories are not synchronized, and the borrowing not continuous but subject to the vagaries of cultural exchange, conquest, and commerce which though now much faster than in ancient days is still not instantaneous nor complete (Diamond (1997)).

On this view, understanding is achieved by seeing the relation between the structure of one conceptual architecture and that of another. That is, understanding is based on analogy and metaphor, but precisely defined in terms of a mapping of structure. The next Chapter explores the concept of structure, particularly geometric structure, and discusses how it can be exploited by non-deductive methods that are important in the use of diagrams to reason about and understand both geometric and non-geometric subjects.

---

[9] More precisely, $2/(\sqrt{5} - 1)$.

5 STRUCTURE

To see the world in a Grain of Sand
And Heaven in a Wild Flower, ...
–William Blake (1757–1827)

The previous Chapter introduced through examples the central concept of mathematics, which is *logical structure*. Since I wish to divorce this concept from its association with formal analysis, I have shortened its name to *structure*. The central point of this essay is that the importance of semantic models derives from very specific features of them, namely that the models provide structure that supports discovery and understanding.

The general concept of structure can be seen in everyday examples. Literal structures (*e.g.*, buildings and bridges) have structure: their components must be related in definite ways and cannot be related in other ways. Not every arrangement of building components will work. The construction of a building must proceed from knowledge that, for example, the roof must be supported. That is, we cannot have a building with an unsupported roof. That is part of what "structure" means, both in this informal sense and in its more technical sense.

Structure may exist in the world, ready to be discovered (that is, described), or it may be invented. There are physical objects, machines, say, that are structured in the sense that they can behave in only certain ways: a piston cannot go up and down at the same time, for example. Humans can observe and describe this structure in mathematical or other language, or they can make use of it simply by observing the constrained behavior of the machine. However, humans can also create structured abstract systems, such as mathematical entities (for example, functions) and reason about them abstractly; these abstract structures may or may not correspond to anything in the real world. Or, in the case of diagrammatic reasoning, we may observe physical structures (diagrams) and use them to draw abstract conclusions.

1. Axiomatic Characterization of Structure

There are different ways to specify structure and different ways to enforce it computationally. In formalizing a domain of mathematics, the modern approach is to define the objects of discourse (say numbers, functions, probabilities, and so forth) as sets (see footnote 8, Chapter 4). Structure is then defined with set relations (membership and derivative relations such as inclusion and intersection) that construct more complex objects, all of which are nonetheless sets.

The language of set theory is sufficiently expressive that every mathematical concept and relation can be expressed in it. For example, a relation is a set of ordered pairs, a function is a relation obeying certain restrictions, and so forth. To give just one important example, one defines the mathematical concept of a *group* (a technical term) as a (usually infinite) set of objects over which is defined an operation X (cross), usually called *multiplication* (not necessarily arithmetic multiplication), that when applied to any two members of the group yields another member of the group. A group must have other properties as well: there must be an identity element such that its product with any member of the group yields that member, and each member has an inverse such that the product of a member and its inverse is the identity element. The association law of multiplication must also hold: $(aXb)Xc = aX(bXc)$. Unlike ordinary multiplication X need not be commutative, that is aXb need not equal bXa. These properties define the structure of a group, which is an abstraction of the structure of many domains of interest. For example, the integers (positive, negative and zero) form a group with *multiplication* being ordinary addition: the 'product' (sum) of any two integers is an integer, 0 is the identity because $x + 0 = x$ for any integer x, and the inverse of x is –x, since $x - x = 0$.

A logical calculus (a formal language with a syntax and vocabulary) is employed to make statements about such concepts. The logical calculus is general in the sense that it could state any proposition about the concepts, whether true or false, coherent or incoherent. A specific set of statements, the axioms, are formulated in this logical calculus and asserted to be true; they are not proved. Inferential rules of logic may be mechanically applied to these propositions to produce logical deductions, which are products of that particular form of inference. Note that "deduction" and "inference" are not synonyms; deduction is one particular form of inference.

Without structure, that is, without definitions and axioms, there is no modern formal mathematical theory or object. Modern formal mathematics is about structure and what can be inferred about objects of discourse with a given structure. Naturally, the objects chosen to be formalized are typically ones that are thought to be important. For example, the concept of group captures the specific relations of arithmetic operations over numbers. But the structure of a group is the distillation – an abstraction – of the properties of numbers, and inferences about groups apply not only to numbers but to any other domain with the same structure. It turns out that there are many important groups, for example permutations (re-orderings of a set), and so statements that are true of all groups (collectively, group theory) have wide application.

It is possible to define the same structure with a different set of axioms, although usually one wants to keep the set small and each axiom simple and intuitive. One might instead choose to assert the truth of a certain carefully chosen set of theorems; doing so would make those 'theorems' into axioms that entail the former axioms and the other theorems as well.

Structure entails constraints on what is possible and what is not. This means that not all expressions that can be syntactically well-formed within the system of axioms and definitions are theorems. Structure is a core concept because without structural constraints nothing can be deduced in the strictly formal sense. Structure is what gives a conceptual object its value as a basis for understanding. Structure is a prerequisite for making information into knowledge, as I argued in Chapter 1.

One may think of the axioms and definitions that define structure as *constraints*. For example, every integer must have exactly one successor, no more, no less. That and the other Peano Postulates (see Table 3: Peano's Postulates) define what it means to be an integer.

Table 3

Peano's Postulates

The Peano axioms define the properties of *natural numbers*, usually represented as a set N. The first four axioms describe the equality relation.

(1) For every natural number x, $x = x$. That is, equality is reflexive.

(2) For all natural numbers x and y, if $x = y$, then $y = x$. That is, equality is symmetric.

(3) For all natural numbers x, y and z, if $x = y$ and $y = z$, then $x = z$. That is, equality is transitive.

(4) For all a and b, if a is a natural number and $a = b$, then b is also a natural number. That is, the natural numbers are closed under equality.

The remaining axioms define the properties of the natural numbers. The constant 0 is assumed to be a natural number, and the naturals are assumed to be closed under a "successor" function S.

(5) 0 is a natural number.

(6) For every natural number n, $S(n)$ is a natural number.

Axioms 5 and 6 define a unary representation of the natural numbers: the number 1 is $S(0)$, 2 is $S(S(0))$ ($= S(1)$), and, in general, any natural number n is $Sn(0)$. The next two axioms define the properties of this representation.

(7) For every natural number n, $S(n) \neq 0$. That is, there is no natural number whose successor is 0.

(8) For all natural numbers m and n, if $S(m) = S(n)$, then $m = n$.

Axioms 7 and 8 together imply that the set of natural numbers is infinite, because it contains at least the infinite subset $\{ 0, S(0), S(S(0)), \ldots \}$, each element of which differs from the rest. The final axiom, sometimes called the *axiom of induction*, is a method of reasoning about all natural numbers; it is the only second order axiom.

(9) If K is a set such that: 0 is in K, and for every natural number n, if n is in K, then $S(n)$ is in K, then K contains every natural number.

All theorems of integer arithmetic follow from them by logical deduction; none of the non-theorems do. The Postulates and their rules of interpretation, together with logical deduction, therefore constrain what can be said about a set of objects that satisfy them. If for example one knows that y is the successor of x and that z is the successor of x as well, then one knows that y is identical to z.

2. Non-Axiomatic Characterizations of Structure

Axioms and logical deduction are only one procedure for inferring true statements. There are also non-axiomatic ways to define structure. I will now examine an alternative. This alternative method of structure definition is important here because it is the primary way in which diagrams support inference.

It is often easier to enforce constraints in an indirect, non-axiomatic manner rather than by the direct use of rules of deduction, although the end result is equivalent. This method is often chosen in computer programming. It is also an efficient way to solve many 'logical' puzzles that are stated directly in terms of constraints. See Table 4: A logical puzzle solvable from constraints.

Table 4

A Logical Puzzle Solvable from Constraints

1. When the actress accepted her Oscar, Alice and Greta watched her on TV.
2. Betty, the designer and the barista once shared an apartment.
3. Greta and the designer play cribbage every Tuesday.
4. The designer has never met the actress.

	actress	barista	cellist	designer
Alice	NO			
Betty		NO		NO
Greta	NO			
Dorothy				

	actress	barista	cellist	designer
Alice	NO			
Betty	NO	NO		NO
Greta	NO			NO
Dorothy				

	actress	barista	cellist	designer
Alice	NO	NO	NO	YES
Betty	NO	NO	YES	NO
Greta	NO	YES	NO	NO
Dorothy	YES	NO	NO	NO

The first matrix is marked with NO for the possibilities eliminated by statement 1 (Betty and Greta are not the actress) and statement 2 (Betty is not the barista or the designer). The second matrix is marked to indicate the inferences from all 4 statements. Since there can be only one YES in any column and any row, a cascade of entries eventually results in the third matrix, which contains the answer to the question.

CHAPTER 5: STRUCTURE

Perhaps the simplest and most familiar example of a constraint-based representation of a structure is a spreadsheet program, such as Microsoft's Excel. The basic representation of Excel is a 'worksheet,' a two-dimensional array of cells each of which can hold a value, say a number or some text. See Table 5: A Simple Spreadsheet. It is also possible to define the contents of one cell to be a function of the contents of other cells. For example one might say that cell C1 is to hold the numerical sum of the contents of cells A1 and B1. Therefore, if one enters 2 in A1 and 3 in B1, cell C1 will contain 5, this value being supplied by the program. Of course if a non-numeric value is placed in A1 or B1, the value in C1 is undefined and this will result in an error message. The constraint represented by the function assigned to C1 is enforced by monitoring changes in A1 and B1 and performing an arithmetic operation. However, exactly how this is done is of no concern to the user, who simply needs to know that the constraint will always be enforced when it is well-defined.

Table 5

A Simple Spreadsheet

This spreadsheet automatically computes the sums of the marginal entries (Column A and Row 1) and enters them into the appropriate summation cell. Changing a marginal entry will change the value in all the cells of the corresponding row or column. Changing the value in a *summation* cell is not permitted since the Excel program cannot determine what the marginal cells should be set to, and there are an infinite number of choices that would yield the newly installed sum.

	A	B	C	D	E	F
1		3	7	19	24	0
2	6	9	13	25	30	6
3	115	118	122	134	139	115
4	33	36	40	52	57	33
5	8	11	15	27	32	8
6	11	14	18	30	35	11
7	77	80	84	96	101	77
8	2	5	9	21	26	2
9	100	103	107	119	124	100

The cells of Table 5, beginning with the second column, B, and continuing through F, contain real numbers. The cells of the first column, A, beginning with the second row, 2, and continuing through row 9, also contain real numbers. The cells of the 8x5 matrix contiguous to these entries contain functions that cause each of them to contain the sum of the two corresponding marginal numbers; for example, C3 = A3 + C1 = 115 + 7 = 122. Thus changing one of the marginal numbers will alter the values in each cell in the matrix of the same row or column.

UNDERSTANDING UNDERSTANDING

Notice that with the above program the effects in Excel are one-way. Entering a number directly in a matrix cell will not alter its marginal numbers. Indeed it will erase the function and replace it with the number entered and the structure of the worksheet will thereby be altered: the matrix cell will no longer necessarily contain the sum of marginal entries. To extend the functionality would also require that each marginal cell as well as each matrix cell contain a function relating three cells. The program would need to know which two data are given (perhaps, by convention, it could take the most recent two entries as givens) so that it could compute the third while still remembering the function associated with each cell. In this case, changing a matrix entry and its row marginal entry would cause a change of its column marginal entry. But the changes in those two marginal entries (both the given one and the computed one) would cause changes in all cells of their corresponding row and column. If any of these newly affected cells is further constrained to be fixed, then rather than change it the program would have to alter the other marginal entry. Clearly certain patterns of fixing values would lead to situations where there was no solution. Since there are so many complications that arise from trying to maintain the sum relation throughout the matrix, spreadsheet programs adopt 'one-way' causation and complain of 'circularity' if an attempt is made to have two cell values depend on one another.

Let us now entertain the possibility of using a spreadsheet to maintain interpoint distance relations in a diagram representation, as in Table 6: A Spreadsheet of Interpoint Distances. With Excel, we would need to represent each point as a pair of coordinates (x, y), and this would require two cells. Thus let us use the top two rows of the worksheet, beginning in column C, to represent the x (top row) and y (second row) coordinates of a point. Similarly we will use the first two columns, beginning in row 3, to represent the x (first column) and y (second column) coordinates of the same points in the same order. In fact, the entries in the marginal columns might be functions that simply copy the appropriate marginal row entries, for example they would set A3 to be whatever C1 is, and so forth. Each matrix cell would contain functions that compute the Euclidean distance[10] between the points defined by its marginal points. Each matrix entry would display the length of the line segment between the associated points. Since the points are given in the same order, the major diagonal (top left to bottom right) of the matrix would all be zeros as they correspond to the distance between a point and itself. We could now 'move' one point by changing its x and y coordinates; this would alter its distances from each of the other points as reflected in the new matrix entries.

Thus we see that this spreadsheet representation of points and segment lengths embodies some of the metric structure of two dimensional geometry, not by the representation of axioms and the use of logical deduction, but by algebraic relations imposed upon a representation of points by Cartesian coordinates.

---

[10] The Euclidian distance is the ordinary notion of distance applied to numbers with numerical coordinates and deriving from the Pythagorean relation. The Euclidian distance between two points (x_1,y_1) and (x_2,y_2) is the square root of $(x_1 - x_2)^2 + (y_1 - y_2)^2$. There are other concepts of distance that meet the definition of a distance metric, including 'city-block' distance, $(x_1 - x_2) + (y_1 - y_2)$, which is the length of a 'walking' path between the two points if you must stay on a rectangular grid of streets.

Table 6

A Spreadsheet of Interpoint Distances

A spreadsheet that computes distances between points whose coordinates are entered into Rows 1 and 2 beginning at Column C. These coordinates are first copied to Columns A and B, then each pair of (x,y) coordinates determines a value that is placed in the cell for that pair of points. Thus for cell D5, $[(8\text{-}4)^2 + (6 - (\text{-}5))^2]^{1/2} = 11.70$.

	A	B	C	D	E	F
1			5	8	4	-14
2			10	6	-5	-1
3	5	10	0	5	15.03	21.95
4	8	6	5	0	11.7	23.09
5	4	-5	15.03	11.7	0	18.44
6	-14	-1	21.95	23.09	18.44	0

Note that the matrix has structure in the sense that only certain patterns of entries are possible and others are not. For example, the matrix must be symmetric, that is, the value in cell ij = the value in cell ji. Also the major diagonal must contain only zeros as noted above. Furthermore, if one picks any three points *a*, *b*, and *c* and finds the corresponding distances *ab*, *bc*, and *ac*, the sum of any two will never be less than the third. This is the *triangle inequality*. Similarly, other metric relations must hold among the distance measures as well. For example, the distances among any three points that form the vertices of a right triangle will be related by the Pythagorean equation. It has been known since the time of Descartes that the algebraic structure of the Cartesian plane is equivalent to the axiomatic structure of Euclidean geometry. Of course our spreadsheet does not fully represent the Cartesian plane, which is infinite and continuous, because the spreadsheet is finite and discrete, but what it is able to represent is true of the corresponding subset of the plane.

We might attempt to capture more of the structure of the plane by extending the one-way causality, as we did in the previous example, by supplying each cell with a function that could determine its value by a computation on the entries in other cells related to it. Thus if we alter ('give' a new value for) the distance between point a and point b, some or all of the four coordinates involved would need to change, and the resulting values would cause a cascade of changes to other distances. The problem is now even more complex, however, because there are many, sometimes infinitely many, solutions. In order to select a particular one, it is necessary to add further constraints, say marking enough values as fixed to assure that the remaining values could be determined uniquely. One might even envision a yet more sophisticated system in which non-uniquely determined values are recorded in cells as symbolic functions of other values. In the general case, with an arbitrary number of points, solving this problem means finding the simultaneous solutions of n non-linear equations or showing there is no solution, and this problem is *difficult* in the technical sense of computational complexity theory: the number of calculations to solve it increases exponentially with the size of the array. For large numbers of points, then, the problem is intractable.

The spreadsheet model is therefore efficient at capturing only limited aspects of two-dimensional structure. Attempting to capture the full structure of the two-dimensional plane with the algebraic constraint definition method of spreadsheets will not work.

A physical two dimensional *diagram*, however, efficiently captures the structure of two-dimensional space. Like the spreadsheet it uses constraint-based inference since it enforces the structural constraints, but unlike the spreadsheet it does this fully and efficiently because the 'work' is done by the geometry of the physical sheet of paper. Humans are able to 'import' this physical structure into representations that capture this efficiency in abstract, mental ways.

I now turn to a discussion of reasoning about space and will show how it is related to the concept of structure and, ultimately, to understanding.

3. Spatial Structure and Spatial Cognition

Spatial structure is an important aspect of the experience of all organisms. Humans are able to deal with it abstractly as well as in the perceptual-motor mode that all animals use. Understanding space is one foundation of mathematical understanding. Indeed, perhaps all mathematical structures have roots in our spatial perception, but they have moved well beyond that through the linguistic processes of abstraction and generalization.

Space is not tangible or visible. More specifically, only energy can modulate our nervous systems and space itself is distinct from energy.[11] By observing the relations and behavior of objects we infer the concept of space as an abstract set of positions that are related in a consistent and coherent way. Not all people have an explicit understanding of the axiomatic structure of space, but each of us through a combination of biological and cultural inheritance plus experience with objects in the world comes to an implicit understanding of space on the scale in which we live (as opposed to subatomic and astronomical scales which behave quite differently, as discussed below).

Thus perception and motor activity permit us to observe, indirectly, spatial structure. Understanding space means being able to observe objects in space, to make inferences about future events involving those objects, to be able to arrange objects in space, to track them, to move relative to them, and so forth.

Spatial *reasoning* means using perception to create and draw inferences in the form of *statements* about objects in space. Thus spatial reasoning, on this definition, is the marriage of perceptual-motor abilities and linguistic abstraction. Dogs and chimpanzees have certain important knowledge about the structure of space, and they use this knowledge to seek and achieve goals, but they do not do spatial reasoning in this sense.

Our perception of course is not based solely on the locations and shapes of objects. Since what we observe and interact with are physical objects in space, our perceptions also embody the physics of mechanical systems: mass, velocity, acceleration and their relations. In fact since we live in a constant gravitational field our perceptions have evolved to embody an anisotropy reflecting it: down is a special direction. Note that

---

[11] Notwithstanding the fact that empty space 'contains' a 'vacuum energy.'

annotations on diagrams of a machine do not embody mechanics and gravity in the way the paper embodies the structure of space. Therefore inferences about mechanics can be aided by graphics only to the extent that they involve spatial relations; the mechanical structure must be added as additional conventions and abstractions on the spatial structure. Actual physical mechanical models are needed to capture force-mass mechanical structure directly.

Mathematicians have formalized the structure of space elegantly in a way that captures our implicit understanding of human-scale space and yet reveals un-intuitive properties of microscopic and astronomic spatial scales. So conceived, space is a non-countable infinite set of abstract objects (points) that have a particular structure. The structure includes dimensionality and orthogonality, adjacency, density, continuity, directionality, and so forth. Each of these spatial properties can be given a formal description, though few people are conversant with these descriptions.

Having structure, as I have been using the term, implies that certain situations (either actual physical situations or true propositions in some formal language) are not possible, just as not all patterns of numerical entries in our spreadsheet examples are permitted. Geometry entails that no negation of any of its theorems can be deduced. For example, we cannot have two triangles that are side-angle-side equal but are not congruent: we can always rigidly move one to the other in such a way that all three pairs of their vertices coincide. We cannot place three points a, b, and c in such a way that the sum of the distances between a and b and b and c is less than the distance between a and c. We cannot inscribe within a circle a 45 degree angle subtended by the ends of a diameter; any such angle must be a right angle. We cannot place three points on the same line in such a way that each of them is to the left of the other two. And so forth. These are not formal constraints, they are physical constraints. A formal system captures the physics with axioms and rules, but a physical system captures them with physics.

4. Real Geometry

This essay is not about physics, past, present, or future. It is about how we understand, sometimes through the use of our intuitive notion of the structure of space. However, our intuitive ideas of geometry, those that we use as a mechanism for understanding mathematical and other concepts, appear to be quite different and much more simple than the real geometry of the universe, and real geometry is intimately related to modern physical theory. For our purposes it is important to understand the relation between real geometry and intuitive geometry.

The *special* theory of relativity holds that there is no such thing as absolute time. For example, whether or not two events occur simultaneously depends on the state of relative motion of the observer and the frame of reference of the events. Thus space and time are not independent, but form a single structure, spacetime.

The *general* theory of relativity identifies gravitational force as a curvature of spacetime. A large amount of empirical evidence confirms both the special and the general theories of relativity, according to which the geometry of our universe is a curved four dimensional spacetime with three spatial dimensions plus time.

The other major theory of modern physics is quantum mechanics, and it too has enormous empirical support. Relativity gives us a powerful theory of large scale events, and quantum mechanics gives us a powerful theory of small scale events. Unfortunately general relativity and quantum mechanics are not compatible (Greene (2000)).

This fundamental paradox now has a promising resolution in string theory. It posits that the fundamental particles are not points, as electrons and photons for example are conceived to be in quantum mechanics. Rather elementary objects are one dimensional entities (strings) or perhaps multiple dimensional entities (p-branes); the theory is still under construction. While these new ideas may resolve the conflict between relativity and quantum mechanics, they introduce an even more bizarre conception of geometry: the universe is eleven dimensional, with ten spatial dimensions plus time. However, seven of the spatial dimensions are so radically curved that it is not within our ability to perceive them directly. Unfortunately, empirical tests for these ideas may never be at hand because observing events at such small scales requires vastly greater amounts of energy than any as yet conceived earthbound device could produce, and thus may require harnessing energy from beyond the earth or solar system.

Kant proposed that the structure of geometry was an innate idea, that is, every person simply knew how the universe is structured, namely as a flat geometry as described by Euclid, in which parallel lines never meet. When it was discovered that the real universe is not Euclidean, Kant's belief was discredited. That is, even if knowledge is just true belief, the innate idea Kant attributed to us is a false belief, and thus not knowledge at all! It is, nonetheless, a belief, or at least a working hypothesis. This is because, while an approximation, it is an approximation that works extremely well on the human scales of space and time in which we live and in which we have evolved. At the scales of time and distance commensurate with human experience, Euclidean geometry holds to a degree of accuracy that exceeds anything measurable. For example, floors of a building are treated as both level and equidistant throughout their extent, because any deviation due to the curvature of space is insignificant in comparison to construction errors, momentary changes from deformation, temperature variation, and so forth. The extremely large scales where relativistic models are needed are those of astronomical distances and times. The extremely small scales where quantum mechanical models are needed are those of subnuclear events. It is therefore both plausible and likely that nervous systems developed in such a way as to treat the world implicitly as though it were Euclidean and Newtonian. For humans, Euclidean geometry is conceptually and computationally much simpler than non-Euclidean geometry. Thus our nervous systems are able to get answers indistinguishable from the 'correct' answers with far simpler structure, and that was good enough for evolution, which only requires that we survive and reproduce, not that we have a correct understanding of astronomy and subnuclear events.

Let us take a closer look at how we should characterize the structure of the geometry of human scale that presumably underlies our use of geometric relations in the understanding of abstractions.

5. Intuitive Geometry

I don't know who discovered water, but it wasn't a fish.- Anon.

In the same spirit, dogs and cats have not discovered space, but they take to it like a fish to water. Up to some level, humans' articulations about the structure of space are clearly not necessary for an understanding of space since, as noted earlier, most higher animals

CHAPTER 5: STRUCTURE

have well-developed motor skills that are well attuned to moving about in space. Humans, however, not only deal smoothly with space but can articulate to a greater or lesser degree what space 'is.'

Each of us has an intuitive abstract conception of space. How this develops and how it is represented have long been subjects of philosophical and psychological discussion. One issue is the nature-nurture question. Kant may have been correct except for the fact that the inherent conception we have does not happen to accurately describe the real world, only the intuitive world.

Are we born with an intuitive abstract conception of space, embodied in our nervous system, or do we acquire it through experience in the world? The answer to all nature-nurture questions is "both." Clearly for any aspect of our behavior there is something inherent in our makeup that underlies it. In the case of an explicit abstract conceptualization of space our knowledge has an innate basis since other organisms in all likelihood, and inanimate objects surely, lack such conceptualizations. Of course, some experience and development are essential before we attain perceptual motor mastery and conscious awareness of space. Therefore any useful answer to the nature-nurture interaction must lie in the details, and these are not known.

As noted earlier, space is not directly accessible to our senses, which are driven solely by energy. Thus whatever we discover about space through experience (broadly conceived, either in our lifetime or in evolutionary time) comes from observation of the behavior of objects in space by vision, touch, and audition. Our intuition about space and physics is innate in the sense that evolution resulted in a nervous system primed to acquire the detailed parameters (for example, the gravitational constant for Earth) through experience.

The essential and fundamental ideas in our intuitive notion of space are the concepts of extent, distance, direction, orthogonality, dimensionality, straightness, flatness, parallelness and homogeneity. These are what need to be included in a useful characterization of intuitive geometry.

Extent. First and foremost, to conceive of space requires conceiving that there is a collection of distinct 'places.' These are variously called points, loci, and locations. A point, when conceived as a dimensionless 'object,' captures the notion of location as a unique member of a large collection of points. Each point is distinct from each other point. Points 'fill' space in the sense that (a) there are points between every pair of points, and (b) there is no non-space 'between' any points. That is, space is continuous. As discussed earlier, this is a concept that was not formalized mathematically until many centuries after the study of geometry began, but the intuitive notion that space is continuous is probably universal. Space is 'everywhere.' Furthermore, space is absolute – it does not itself move around.

Thus, space is points and nothing more. However, there are additional properties that give space further structure.

Distance. Distance is a relation between pairs of points. Intuitively, distances may be compared in magnitude: some distances are greater than others, a fact available to perception. In modern times, distances are represented as real numbers. However, even without the concept of real number, which was unavailable until quite recently and still is not part of the explicit knowledge of most people, an intuitive concept of distance has the following properties. The distance between two points is unchanging in intuitive geometry. The distance between two points is a positive quantity if they are distinct points and zero if they are identical. The distance relation is complete (it is defined for every pair of points), symmetric (the distance from point a to point b is identical to the distance from b to a); and the triangle inequality holds (the distance from a to b plus the distance from b to c is greater than or equal to the distance from a to c).

It is interesting to note that there are conflicts between these intuitive notions of space and other characteristic human beliefs. For example, we may behave, as shown in psychological experiments, as though we believe that the distance from a to b is greater than the distance from b to a. It is not clear why this is the case, though the answer could reside in ancillary matters, such as imagined travel times (going down hill is faster than going uphill, for example). These psychological factors will be important in many expositions and applications, but they do not refute the description given above of intuitive geometry, for when pressed, people will acknowledge their belief in the propositions listed above, even though their behavior belies this belief in specific cases. These matters, incidentally, differ from common mistakes of knowledge that people exhibit, such as believing that Los Angeles is farther west than Reno. These mis-beliefs are not matters that are in conflict with the tenets of intuitive geometry.

Direction. A direction is associated with each pair of distinct locations. It admits of a variety of definitions and our intuitive geometry does not correspond to any particular one. Some directions are the same as others, some are different. Same direction depends on the specific way that direction is conceived, that is, on how the direction between two points is computed. For the direction from a to b, the opposite direction is the direction from b to a.

Orthogonal direction is a special relationship that relates to the concept of dimension. Two directions are orthogonal if the are perpendicular to each other. In a two dimensional space, each direction has two directions that are orthogonal to it. In a three dimensional space each direction (say left to right) has an infinite number of directions that are orthogonal to it.

Dimensionality, straightness, and flatness. A point is zero dimensional. Since space comprises more than one point, space is at least one dimensional, that is, asserting that there are different places introduces the concept of dimension. In intuitive geometry not all points lie on a single straight line. Therefore space is at least two dimensional. A straight line is one for which the direction between every pair of points selected in the same order on it is the same. Given two dimensions introduces the possibility that lines (one dimensional objects) may be non-straight, that is, curved. Thus straightness has no meaning without at least two dimensions. A straight line and a point not on it determine a plane, which consists of all points that lie on all straight lines between points of the plane, and only those (the closure of the set, in mathematical language). Thus planes are flat. In intuitive geometry, there exists a point not on any given plane. Therefore space is at least three dimensional. Finally, intuitive space has no more than three dimensions, therefore it is exactly three dimensional.

Thus although 'real' geometry may not be three dimensional and flat, intuitive geometry – the geometry that is readily accessible to us – is. Our ability to use spatial models must thus be understood in the context of the structure of intuitive geometry, and even our ability to generalize to such concepts as higher dimensional spaces relies on intuitive geometry as a starting point.

The concepts of straightness/flatness, orthogonality, dimensionality, distance, and parallelness are intertwined. Any three points define a unique plane in space and each plane is flat. Straight lines are the shortest distance between two points, non-identical co-planar parallel lines are those that have the same direction and never meet even when extended as far as one cares to imagine (but of course cannot observe), so maintain a constant distance that is measured by the length of a perpendicular transversal. Furthermore, if one moves in a plane in a straight line to point a, makes a right angle turn in the clockwise direction, travels a distance D (> 0) to point b and makes another right angle turn in the clockwise direction then continues in a straight line, one will be traveling in the 'opposite' direction from the initial movement, one's path will never cross the initial line, and if one makes a third right angle turn in the clockwise direction at any point and travels a distance D one will return to the initial line.

Parallel. Given two distinct straight lines in the same plane, either they are parallel or they meet in exactly one point. If they are parallel then they have the same directions and there exist perpendicular transversals between the two, and each of these will have the same length, that is, parallel lines are equidistant.

Homogeneity. Our intuitive conception of space is that it is homogeneous and isotropic, that is, the properties of a volume of space are the same everywhere and in every direction, such that any geometric object in space has the same structure and properties no matter where it is located and no matter how it is oriented.

Summary of intuitive geometry. It is an hypothesis of this work that this description of intuitive space corresponds to human predisposition because the normal objects of our experience are consistent with it. The mathematical study of geometry is the long history of attempts to state this intuitive structure with logical precision. One of the most intriguing results of this endeavor is that the intuitive conception of space, that which I am asserting is the working assumption of all people, is not a correct description of the actual universe in which we live. This was revealed by the process of attempting to disentangle the several properties discussed above and to determine how they relate, that is, which entail which others, and which are separate assumptions that may or may not correspond to fact. The next three sections examine these issues in more detail. The story of course begins with Euclid.

6. Euclidean Geometry

Although important work on geometry preceded Euclid, he is generally credited with making the first attempt to characterize intuitive geometry precisely. Euclid's work of course lacked the rigor of modern logic in which all definitions and other statements are cast in the formal (syntactically well-defined) language of set theory and predicate logic. Rather, Euclid's characterization was stated in a natural language (Greek) with all the inherent vagueness and ambiguity of every natural language. Nonetheless, his was a remarkable accomplishment and a standard of clarity that was not exceeded for many centuries.

Euclid's major work, *Elements,* has been the subject of intense study continuing to this day. For the several centuries following its appearance his analysis was examined and elaborated by many scholars. Proclus (see Kline (1972)), in particular, published extensive and profound discussions of Euclid's *Elements*, and most modern writers still draw heavily on Proclus's work, as will I.

Euclid divided his characterization into three categories: definitions, postulates, and common notions (which he called axioms). These are given in Table 7: Euclid's definitions, Table 8: Euclid's postulates, and Table 9: Euclid's axioms. In modern terminology, Euclid's postulates and axioms would fall into the same category and be called axioms, or else the Common Notions would be used to define a system (with its own axioms and definitions) on which the formalism of geometry is built. From a formal point of view these two are equivalent.

Table 7
Euclid's Definitions

1. A **point** is that which has no part.
2. A **line** is breadthless length.
3. The extremities of a line are points.
4. A **straight line** is a line which lies evenly with the points on itself.
5. A **surface** is that which has length and breadth only.
6. The extremities of a surface are lines.
7. A **plane surface** is a surface which lies evenly with the straight lines on itself.
8. A **plane angle** is the inclination to one another of two lines in a plane which meet one another and do not lie in a straight line.
9. And when the lines containing the angle are straight, the angle is called **rectilinear**.
10. When a straight line set up on a straight line makes the adjacent angles equal to one another, each of the equal angles is **right**, and the straight line standing on the other is called a **perpendicular** to that on which it stands.
11. An **obtuse** angle is an angle greater than a right angle.
12. An **acute** angle is an angle less than a right angle.
13. A **boundary** is that which is an extremity of anything.
14. A **figure** is that which is contained by any boundary or boundaries.
15. A **circle** is a plane figure contained by one line such that all the straight lines falling upon it from one point among those lying within the figure are equal to one another;
16. And the point is called the **centre** of the circle.
17. A **diameter** of the circle is any straight line drawn through the centre and terminated in both directions by the circumference of the circle, and such a straight line also bisects the circle.
18. A **semicircle** is the figure contained by the diameter and the circumference cut off by it. And the centre of the semicircle is the same as that of the circle.
19. **Rectilinear figures** are those which are contained by straight lines, trilateral figures being those contained by three, quadrilateral those contained by four, and multilateral those contained by more than four straight lines.

> **Table 7 continued**
> **Euclid's Definitions**
>
> 20. Of trilateral figures, an **equilateral triangle** is that which has its three sides equal, an isosceles triangle that which has two of its sides alone equal, and a scalene triangle that which has its three sides unequal.
>
> 21. Further, of trilateral figures, a **right-angled triangle** is that which has a right angle, an obtuse-angled triangle that which has an obtuse angle, and an acute-angled triangle that which has its three angles acute.
>
> 22. Of quadrilateral figures, a **square** is that which is both equilateral and right-angled; an **oblong** that which is right-angled but not equilateral; a **rhombus** that which is equilateral but not right-angled ; and a **rhomboid** that which has its opposite sides and angles equal to one another but is nether equilateral nor right-angled. And let quadrilaterals other than these be called **trapezia**.
>
> 23. **Parallel straight lines** are straight lines which, being in the same plane and being produced indefinitely in both directions, do not meet one another in either direction.

The following are indications that Euclid's definitions *presuppose* an intuitive conception of space.

Definition 1: "A point is that which has no part." The underlying intuitive idea, elucidated above, is that a point is not a physical object but a location. Euclid's definition expresses this by reference to the part-whole relation which does not directly express the notion of 'dimensionless' that it presumably attempts to get at. On one reading of "part" one might say that a rock has no parts, if we construe the rock as homogeneous. And yet a rock is not a point because it has extent, that is, it occupies a finite volume. But to speak of volume, or its absence, presupposes the very notion of extent and point that we are trying to elucidate. The definitions 2 and 5 of a line as a breadthless length and a surface as, in effect, a heightless something (unspecified) run into similar problems. These definitions only make sense if they are understood already, that is, they suppose the reader knows what space is at the outset.

Definition 4: "A straight line is a line which lies evenly with the points on itself." This attempt to define straightness is perplexing. It is not obvious to a modern reader what 'lying evenly' might mean. One interpretation is that the line is symmetric, that it presents no irregularities or asymmetries whatsoever. Such could be detected if, Proclus suggested, one held the endpoints fixed and rotated the line along its length. This of course presupposes knowing what "holding fixed" and "rotating" are, terms that are not defined. Later interpretations have provided alternative formulations. One of the most popular is "a straight line cannot enclose an area," one implication being that there is only one line between two given points, else two together would enclose area. Again, this interpretation is based upon yet other intuitive notions, such as what area and distance are. Definition 7 of a plane surface depends on the definition of straight line and thus inherits the same problems, as do 8 (plane angle) and 9 (rectilinear).

Definition 10 introduces the terms "right angle" and "perpendicular" which are key ideas. These definitions seem straightforward (essentially, a right angle is half of a straight angle, which is implicitly defined). However, they too inherit the problems with the definitions of "straight" and "plane. " Definitions 11 and 12 (obtuse angle and acute angle) are straightforward introductions of terminology, although they presume a metric on angle size that imposes an ordering.

Definition 13 ("boundary"), like definitions 3 and 6, appeals to the undefined notion of extremity, which clearly invokes the notion of distance, among other concepts. Definitions 3 and 6 assert that extremities of lines and surfaces exist and are, respectively, points and lines. As such, these are actually unproved theorems, that is 'postulates' in Euclid's terminology, 'axioms' in modern terminology.

Definitions 15 through 18 deal with the concept of circle and clearly presuppose a concept of distance with its usual metric properties. Note that 17 asserts without proof that any diameter bisects a circle, which makes it more than a definition.

Definitions 19 to 22 mainly introduce terminology (a proper function of definitions), but again presume the concept of straight line.

Definition 23 (parallel straight lines) *defines* parallel lines as those (distinct and coplanar) straight lines that never meet no matter how far extended.

Table 8
Euclid's Postulates

1. To draw a straight line from any point to any point.
2. To produce a finite straight line continuously in a straight line.
3. To describe a circle with any centre and distance.
4. That all right angles are equal to one another.
5. That, if a straight line falling on two straight lines make the interior angles on the same side less that two right angles, the two straight lines, if produced indefinitely, meet on that side on which are the angles less that the two right angles.

The postulates are generally construed to be statements about geometry, while the axioms are statements about non-geometric concepts, such as numerical equality. Postulate 1 is generally interpreted to assert that one and only one straight line can be constructed between any two points. Postulate 2 asserts that any straight line can be extended from an end in the same direction, the combined extended line therefore also being straight, and that this can be done in only one way for a given end and distance, that is, the direction of extension is unique. Postulate 3 asserts the possibility of constructing a circle, and that the circle is unique given a center and a radius. This postulate is also generally interpreted to assert the continuity of space. It *assumes* that distance measures are continuous, as suggested earlier.

Postulate 4, asserting that all right angles are equal, seems to be un-necessary. After all, a right angle has been defined as half of a straight angle, and surely all straight angles are equal. On closer inspection, however, the issue is not so clear. "Right angle" was defined with reference to "a straight line set upon a straight line." In three dimensional space, there are infinitely many lines that can be 'set upon' another line at the same point in such a way as to bisect the (plane) angle that lies in the plane determined by the two lines. It would be necessary to prove that all such are equal, or else to assert that they are. Euclid chose to assert the equivalent with Postulate 4.

Postulate 5 is the famous Parallel Postulate. Note that Euclid defined parallel lines (Definition 23) to be straight, co-planar lines that never meet. Postulate 5 asserts that such lines have an additional property, one which is required by intuitive geometry and thus seemed unproblematic for centuries. Postulate 5 in fact was so obvious that it was long believed to be provable from the other postulates, axioms, and definitions. Perhaps the most telling testimony to Euclid's genius was that he saw that the postulate was necessary for the development of his mathematics. For over 2,000 years it was assumed that he was wrong. Many 'proofs' were advanced, all of them incorrect. As recently as 1733 Gerolamo Saccheri published such a fallacious proof in *Euclides ab omni naevo vindicatus* (Euclid freed from every flaw). It is now known that Postulate 5 is independent, and indeed can be replaced by alternatives that yield consistent but different geometries.

Table 9

Euclid's Axioms

1. Things that are equal to the same thing are also equal to one another.
2. If equals be added to equals, the wholes are equals.
3. If equals be subtracted from equals, the remainders are equal.
4. Things that coincide with one another are equal to one another.
5. The whole is greater than the part.

What is problematic about Euclid's axioms is what a *thing* is. If a thing is, in modern terms, a real number as formalized by a theory of arithmetic that defines numbers and the usual operations on them, then Axioms 1-3 and 5 are theorems of arithmetic. On the other hand, if a thing is, perhaps, a geometric figure, then the Axioms amount to definitions of the predicate 'equal' as applied to figures. Axiom 4 obviously can be interpreted as referring to figures but not to numbers. In use, all 5 axioms are applied to both numbers and figures.

The notion of "coincide" of Axiom 4 is not trivial. Presumably it means that two figures can be moved about in space until they (that is, all of their parts) lie in the same places. While this idea is part of intuitive geometry and intuitive physics, the definitions of "coincide" and "move" are not provided by Euclid. "Move" must capture the notion of rigid movement, including translations and rotations but not dilations or other distortions of form. Defining these properly is not trivial.

Many of Euclid's theorems involve the notion of congruence that depends upon the definition of "coincide." Thus the side-angle-side theorem states that two triangles with two pairs of equal length sides and equal included angle are *congruent*. This means that two such triangles could be moved about rigidly (perhaps turning one over) and made to occupy exactly the same portion of space (the same points). Thus geometry is inherently intertwined with the concept of motion, in particular of rigid motion in which certain properties and relations are maintained.

The underlying operations are the movements of a point and a line. It is assumed that any point can be 'moved' to any other point. But since a point is not an object but a location, what does "move" mean? "Move" only takes on meaning when we move a group of distinct 'points', *i.e.*, parts, such as the 'points' of a line. Movement then means that another set of (actual) points is identified and these define the new location; the points do not actually move. However, motion also intuitively entails the notion of incremental steps. The set of initial points is not merely identified with the final points, but a path exists for each of the points as the set moves. Clearly these geometric notions are intertwined with physical intuition. Rigid motion of a line means that one end can be moved to any other location, but motion of the second end is restricted to those locations that are a fixed distance from the first endpoint at all times during the motion. The theorems of geometry do not explicitly depend on continuous motion in space, however; they are concerned only that the end result of the motion obeys the constraint. Thus if lines *ab* and *cd* are of the same length, we can move point *a* to point *c* and point *b* to point *d* in a discrete jump; this is rigid motion and the result is that *ab* and *cd* coincide, hence must be 'equal,' that is, congruent. So all lines of equal length are congruent.

One may of course envision other types of movements (more precisely, of transformations). For example we may define a movement of the endpoints of a line in such a way that the end result is that the displaced points are twice as far apart as they were at the start. If we hold one point fixed – that is, it remains where it started – and require that the other end move in the same direction as the original line's orientation, we have a movement that doubles the length of the line.

Such a transformation does not correspond to the behavior of actual objects in space in the direct way that rigid motion does. It is, of course, possible to construct a stretchable rod of, say, rubber, and to stretch it to twice its length. But this operation requires careful measurement of length. If the rod is of steel, we can move it rigidly with no effort nor accurate measurement. Conceiving the underlying operations to be a *transformation* that maintains relations, wherein rigid movement is a special case of transformation, one can divorce geometry from physics, even though it is likely that the intuitive geometry derived evolutionarily and developmentally from intuitive physics. Geometry thus viewed is an abstraction from physics and this is the usual conception.

Thus *rigid transformation* is another component of intuitive and Euclidean geometry.

Notice that the notions of coincidence and transformation presume homogeneity and isotropy, two properties of intuitive geometry that are not stated explicitly in Euclidean geometry, but which follow from the axioms indirectly.

Hilbert's axiomatization of Euclidean geometry

David Hilbert was probably the greatest pure mathematician of the late 19th and early 20th centuries, although Poincaré (1854–1912) may have equal claim to that title. The thrust of Hilbert's work was the formalization of many branches of mathematics according to modern standards of rigor that he helped develop. One of his many important results was an axiomatization of Euclidean geometry that eliminated the vagueness of the subject.

One of the things that formalization makes clear is that there is no single axiomatization for any complex field of mathematics. Rather there are alternative formulations even if we restrict our consideration to equivalent ones, that is, those with identical sets of true theorems. Certain statements may be axioms in one system and theorems in another. By studying the alternative formulations one sees how the structure interacts. There may also be distinct formalizations of the same subject matter that entail different consequences, for example, weakening a system by removing an axiom or replacing it with an alternative may make it impossible to prove some statements that were true in the original. However, such weakened systems may have important set-theoretic models (recall from Section 4.3: Metamathematics) this technical sense of "model" as a set with predicates defined on it) that make them interesting in their own right. In any case, their study again reveals the structure of the system and can often lead to generalizations and other advances.

Hilbert's system, as presented in Hilbert (1930), contains many more axioms than Euclid's five. Some of these replace Euclid's definitions. Hilbert also presupposes the axiomatic structure of arithmetic. His methods of proof rely heavily on finding numerical models.

The details of the Hilbert system are not essential to the topic of this work. The essential features that Hilbert brought to Euclidean geometry are presented in Appendix A: Hilbert's Axiomatization of Euclidean Geometry.

Non-Euclidean geometry

One of Hilbert's contributions was to prove that Euclid's Parallel Postulate was an independent assumption, not derivable from the others, just as Euclid's work suggested. It was then realized that other geometries could be consistently defined using alternatives to the Parallel Postulate. This led to new consistent theories of non-Euclidean geometries.

Thus the modern mathematical conception of real space is that it is non-Euclidian, but this has not altered the human intuitive notion of space, which is in all essential aspects Euclidian. This is because the 'space' within which we spend our perceptual-motor lives cannot be distinguished by us from Euclidian, intuitive space and intuitive physics. In particular, buildings we build and diagrams we draw obey laws of physics that are consistent with our intuitive notions. Appendix B: Non-Euclidean Geometries provides additional detail.

7. Diagrams as Physical Models

As discussed above, there are ways other than formal logic to draw inferences from given assumptions. That is, there are inferences that are not deductions. Prominent among these is the use of constraint analysis. One important way in which such inferencing calculations can be done is with physical models. We might construct an actual three-dimensional physical model of something. The object modeled could be another physical situation at a different scale (a real airplane could be modeled by a model airplane) or it could be an abstract situation whose structure is reflected in the physical model (the motion of planets could be modeled by a set of differential equations).

Diagrams are a type of physical model in that they are physical objects and as such their components must obey laws of physics and geometry. Physical models in general, and diagrams in particular, can be used as methods of inference: the laws of physics do the inferencing, not by using a formal calculus but by enforcing physical constraints. Such models can do much (but not all) of the work of a formal axiomatization of space and physics. (What they cannot do directly is support general conclusions.)

Thus if a circle is to the right of a triangle, and a square is to the right of the circle, the square must be to the right of the triangle. The physics (including the geometry) of the paper enforces the ordering constraint. Of course there must be someone to notice this and to know what it means. The next Chapter explores this simple but powerful idea in more detail.

6 UNDERSTANDING AND DIAGRAMS

"What is the use of a book," thought Alice, "without pictures and conversations?"
–Lewis Carroll (1832–1898)

An important type of knowledge is knowledge of space as exhibited by all mammals through goal-directed movement. For humans this knowledge is the basis for the deeper understanding of space we exhibit through complex tool use and construction and through mathematical analysis of spatial structure. This Chapter narrows the scope of the discussion of general spatial knowledge to focus on how humans combine their mammalian knowledge of space with their ability to think abstractly in a particular realm of thinking and problem solving.

1. Diagrammatic Reasoning

Physical models are often used by engineers, architects and others to encode physical and geometric properties of the (usually) larger objects they model. Road maps and blueprints also encode, in two-dimensions, some of the spatial properties of things they model. Graphs and charts encode abstract relations among general concepts – such as money, quantity, and preferences – that are not limited to mechanical or spatial features. Mathematics makes extensive use of such representations even though they lie outside the purely formal languages of proofs.

One familiar application is in logic, where simple diagrams are used to make inferences. One method is known as Euler Circles, in which a circle is associated with the name of a set. The intended interpretation is that points lying within a circle are members of the named set. See Figure 7: All C are A, in which a circle labeled A contains a circle labeled B. According to the interpretation just given, every point within B is in the containing circle A and thus "All B are A" is represented in this way. When we add the proposition that "All C are B," this adds a circle C wholly contained in the B circle, as in Figure 7. "All C are A" follows directly from the interpretation.

Novices to logic find this picturing of the process to add intuitive support, and to enable reaching conclusions more rapidly. For them it is more difficult to use a rule such as "If all C are B and all B are A then all C are A." This is because the spatial structure is readily accessible to human spatial perceptual processes in a more direct way than is the abstract relation, which must be explicitly learned and applied.

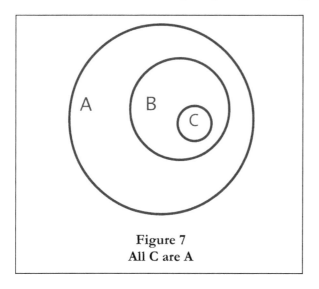

Figure 7
All C are A

It may be tempting to look upon graphs and diagrams as examples of purely perceptual representations in sharp contrast to linguistic representations. This is a mistake. Graphics are linguistic in a very central way, even if we do not use explicit annotations. What the two – language and graphical representations – have in common is an abstract referential mechanism. Hieroglyphics are an example of an intermediate mechanism.

The word "cat" refers to an animal, a cat, but the association is entirely arbitrary. The word could be another string of letters or sounds, and indeed it is, for speakers of other languages. A pencil sketch of a cat by the same token lacks the physical qualities of the animal. It is not soft, it does not move. Furthermore, an unlimited number of pencil sketches could be associated with a cat, including highly stylized ones such as cartoons or stick figures. One might imagine a continuum of cat sketches ranging from a photograph-like image to a stick figure to a blob that is merely associated with a cat by convention, that is, by saying "this represents a cat." At that end of the continuum we have reached the purely linguistic symbol, a word.

Just as no animal save man uses natural language, no animal save man draws pictures meaningful to itself and conspecifics (elephants notwithstanding; see footnote 1). The fact that two major contrasts between humans and other organisms are language and graphical representation suggests that perhaps there is a common ability underlying linguistic and graphical representations. This ability must permit representing the external world abstractly. It expresses itself in language and in drawing alike. The two come together most completely and most importantly in mathematical thinking, but also in art of all kinds.

Abstract reference is a common feature of all notational systems, not only written language and graphics, but also musical notation, physical models, choreographic notations, and so on. All of these notational devices are used by humans. None is used by non-humans. For a human, any distinguishable symbol can refer to any object or event that is within our conceptual powers, including abstractions such as *number* or *sincerity*.

The interpretation of a linguistic utterance, written or spoken, is a matter of convention. The conventions are learned by experience in a speaking community, and neither the learning mechanism nor the resulting structure of conventions of interpretation has been precisely described. Thus it is not known how we understand that "the cat is on the mat" is related to an event in the world, and yet any adult speaker of English understands the relation, can confirm or disconfirm its truth with respect to a given location, can paraphrase it, and so forth.

Similarly, the interpretation of a graphic is a matter of convention. These conventions are sometimes conveyed in part linguistically, but are acquired through other experience as well. Some graphics such as annotated scientific graphs and architectural drawings require a large amount of explanation or experience before their use is fluent and their meaning is obvious or clearly seen. Others, such as cartoons and highly representational drawings, are mastered with less effort and experience, even by young children.

There is, nonetheless, a difference in kind between fully arbitrary linguistic references and at least some aspects of graphic references. Characterizing this distinction is not easy, and to simplify the task I will restrict the following comments to two-dimensional graphic representations – marks on paper – and exclude three dimensional models, auditory representations and so forth. The distinction I wish to characterize is that *visual displays <u>when used as diagrammatic representations</u> use the spatial structure of the physical medium (e. g., paper) in a way that is analogous to the structure of the referent.*

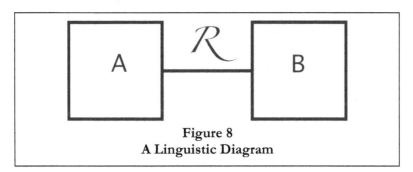

Figure 8
A Linguistic Diagram

Note that this is not always the case with every drawing or visual display. For example two boxes connected by a line may represent an abstract relation between the entities represented by the boxes. See Figure 8: A Linguistic Diagram.

When the relations are abstract, linguistic labels are typically employed both for the boxes and the line. As such, the graphic is equivalent to a purely linguistic statement such as "A is related to B in manner $\mathcal{R}$", or "$\mathcal{R}(A, B)$."

However, graphics are generally used in a spatial-code manner. For example, if the relation to be represented is the subset relation, then a graph consisting of three boxes and two lines may represent "all cats are mammals and all mammals are animals." However, the graphic representation may, by convention, be understood in such a way that one can conclude that all cats are animals by tracing (using spatial properties of connectedness, etc.) from the cat rectangle to the animal rectangle. See Figure 9: A Subset Relation Diagram.

More transparently than Figure 9, one may adopt the single convention of Euler Circles that containment denotes the subset relation, that is, we may employ a diagrammatic representation. In this case the conclusion that all cats are animals is directly represented because of the spatial containment interpretation rather than spatial connectedness of the arrows. Furthermore, the construction of the conclusion is entailed by the construction of the premises. No additional construction is necessary; the conclusion is there to be read off.

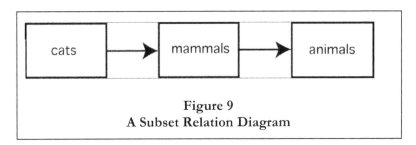

Figure 9
A Subset Relation Diagram

In these simple examples the physical fact that the paper exists in space and the marks on the paper must obey the structure of space, by virtue of physics, not logic, has allowed an interesting and powerful computational advantage, one that must be made explicit if one is to employ a linguistic representation to the same effect. For the subset relation, little is gained in computational terms by the Euler representation as opposed to augmenting the linguistic representation with rules to implement the transitivity of the set-membership relation. In more complicated cases the computational advantage is greater. However, this advantage is entirely dependent on the fact that human perceptual processes, evolved because they permitted survival in a complex and dangerous world, are extremely efficient at doing the required computations. In this case they readily determine if one simple closed curve contains another. For a computing machine or for biological organisms ill-designed for this perception there might be a loss rather than a gain.

It can hardly be denied that human visual perception (and other modalities as well, especially tactile) are efficient at dealing with the structure of space. Such processes have a clear adaptive advantage, indeed are a necessity for survival. Furthermore, they are familiar and natural to us, and this leads to a second though related advantage of graphics: graphic representation reduces knowledge and inference processes to something familiar, and hence yields a sense of understanding that is absent or difficult to achieve from abstract linguistic representations.

Diagrammatic representation, then, is powerful because (a) it is computationally efficient for human perception and (b) it grounds knowledge and inference in the familiar.

But why does it not do the same for dogs and cats, chimpanzees or chickens? Surely their perceptual processes are also efficient at observing spatial structure, and surely spatial structure is familiar to them. What is lacking is the ability to understand the concepts for which humans employ graphics and need to use them. A chimpanzee cannot understand the Pythagorean theorem, so it cannot understand a diagram depicting it. This is *not* to say that, for example, the chimpanzee cannot make use of a shortcut in its travels. In fact, several species of primates are adept at taking the shortest route possible (Garber (1989)). On the other hand, it *is* to say that chimpanzees cannot understand this notion as an abstract proposition, true of an infinite class of instances. Presumably this is because they do not have the skill that is necessary to represent and use such abstractions, one that also underlies linguistic ability, or is co-extensive with it.

2. Diagrammatic Reasoning as Physics + Language

Of sticks and numbers

Suppose I wanted to sort a list of numbers, say L = {17, 11, 16, 10, 14, 12, 10, 15, 18, 13}. To do so I will need a way of representing them and a procedure for manipulating them in a way that reveals their order. One way of representing them is with numerals, as has been done here (what I *referred* to above was numbers but I did so with the use of *numerals*, not numbers). Numerals are physical objects, ink on paper, chalk on blackboard, magnetic states in a computer memory, biochemical/brain states, or some such device. A computation, including one done by a brain, is a physical manipulation of physical representations. ('Mental' arithmetic is of course a brain process, thus it too is a physical manipulation of physical representations.) I might for example take the list of numerals L above and compare the first two; if the larger is first it is left there, otherwise interchange them. Comparing must be reduced to a physical process as well, one that defines "larger" appropriately, not as "containing more ink" but as "being the name of a number that is numerically greater." Proceeding down the list L, I compare the first numeral with the next item and again place or leave the larger at the beginning and the smaller in the other position. After one pass through the list I have computed the largest of the numerals. A second pass through the remainder of the list will compute the second largest numeral and so forth. All of this is straightforward, but note that it is a substantial cognitive achievement to actually implement the physical process that accomplishes this.

Another way to sort these numbers is to represent them a different way, not as numerals but, say, as the lengths of sticks: larger number, longer stick. Neither numerals nor sticks are numbers, but each can, by convention, be used to represent numbers. There are a variety of other ways to represent numbers as well, but they all are physical. Computation means manipulating these physical representations. See Figure 10: 'Numerals' Unsorted.

With the stick representation I can sort the numbers by holding all of the sticks loosely in my hand and letting their ends drop to a flat surface, as in Figure 11: 'Numerals' Sorted. The numbers have now been sorted and the computation was the physical process of their movement.

Figure 10
"Numerals" Unsorted
The length of each stick represents a number.

Inference by physics

Of course, the physical process is a computation only to an agent that can interpret it as such, that is, one who understands the relation of the representation to the numbers and who understands that the process results in an ordering.

A computation is an interpreted physical process.

Conversely, any physical process can be interpreted as a computation of something. To a mathematician movement of a planet around its orbit can be interpreted as a computation of that orbit, seen perhaps as a solution to a set of differential equations. To a physicist a nuclear explosion can be interpreted as a computation of an amount of energy. Of course, not all representations and computations of the same results are identical. In particular they may take more or less time and other resources to achieve, and they may be more or less easy to interpret and understand.

Figure 11
"Numerals" Sorted
The unseen device attached to the hand is an essential part
of the sorting computation.

Diagrams are physical: ink on paper, say. As such they must obey the geometry and physics of paper. But diagrams are also interpretable as abstractions. We may choose to ignore certain of their physical properties. For example, we generally do not assign meaning to their weight. We can also ignore certain of their geometric properties. We may choose for example to say that while left-to-right order is important, distance is not.

Finally, we may assign arbitrary meaning to certain geometric structures. We may say that in a graph (one kind of diagram) this direction represents temperature, and that direction represents pressure, or whatever we choose. Sub-human primates do not understand this conventional character of diagrams. To them a diagram is just a piece of paper, with all the properties of paper and bearing no relation to anything else in the world.

Most diagrams have annotations, which are fully arbitrary (linguistic) assignments of meaning to symbols. Some diagrams rely heavily on linguistic convention and make almost no representational use of the physical properties of the diagram. In that case, the representation is essentially fully linguistic because all languages make use of this structure: they are linear orderings of symbols. At the other extreme, such as in geometric diagrams, all of the two-dimensional structure of space is used. In a sense, geometric diagrams are a very special case, making maximum use of geometric structure with minimum use of linguistic structure. However, all diagrams, even geometric diagrams without labels, entail propositional understanding because they require understanding the connection between the spatial structure and the relations represented.

In these uses of diagrams, the actual physical paper does the 'inferencing' in the same way that gravity acting on sticks did the sorting calculation in my earlier example. In all such cases, however, a cognitive agent, an interpreter, is needed to make the physics into a calculation. A cognitive agent also must draw or construct the diagram in pursuit of a goal. Both the construction and the observation of a diagram involve complex interpretive processes. Of course if a teacher has provided the diagram, then the teacher must have the requisite cognitive abilities, and the student must interpret the diagram in that light.

Although some of the computation is done by physical processes outside the agent, the interpretation is done internally, presumably by the agent's nervous system. As it turns out, some of the physics part can also be done internally, by imagining changes that are not actually made in the physical world. The ability to imagine changes (an ability that is severely circumscribed) is an additional cognitive ability that humans possess, and one that is important for diagrammatic and other uniquely human reasoning processes.

3. Geometric Diagrams and Reasoning

Diagrammatic reasoning is a circumscribed, stylized form of spatial reasoning in which the phenomena of understanding are relatively clear and powerful. The extensive use of diagrams in many areas of human cognition, especially mathematics, science, and engineering, needs no documentation. For historical perspectives see Miller (1984). While diagrammatic reasoning does not encompass all of the uniquely human cognitive abilities it does require a minimal set that takes us beyond the level of the other primates as described in Chapter 2.

There are many kinds of diagrams, including scientific graphs, charts, maps, house plans, logos, cartoons and so forth. The use of diagrams to reason about – and understand – the special case of *geometric* concepts is the simplest instance of diagrammatic reasoning. Geometric diagrams generally do not involve colors, irregular shapes, or other features of arbitrary pictures, but are confined to representing geometric properties such as connectivity, containment, direction, length, perpendicularity, and so forth. Thus understanding with the aid of *geometric* diagrams is a potential 'fruit fly' of a theory of conceptual understanding[12]. For this reason, diagrammatic geometric reasoning is the focus of the more detailed models to be presented later in this essay.

In high school, Euclidean geometry is characterized as the canonical example of reasoning by means of formal methods of proof. In fact, however, the subject is invariably presented with extensive use of diagrams. Diagrams are not elements in the formal proof method. Rather, they are what the formal[13] statements are 'about.' They are what help the student understand what the formal statements are discussing. The teachers and textbooks presuppose that the diagrams are understandable *a priori*, and that what remains is to show how they relate to the verbal and symbolic descriptions of them.

Doubtless these textbook diagrams are essential for conveying the concepts of geometry to the students. Most students have had little experience with careful proof procedures, but have had experience with pictures and graphic forms of expression throughout their lives, including their pre-verbal lives. Geometric diagrams are a distillation of this rich graphic knowledge and method, and thus provide a familiar and simple instance of how we come to understand one topic through the use of pre-existing abilities and knowledge. These are the reasons that I have chosen this area of human cognitive ability as a focus of an exploration of understanding.

Geometry deals with idealized objects: dimensionless points, one-dimensional lines, two dimensional planes and other abstractions mentally composed of them. Geometric diagrams – actual physical objects such as ink on paper – while being imperfect representations of such ideal objects are intended *to be interpreted* as veridical representations of these idealizations, maintaining all of their essential properties and relations, even though they manifestly do not.

Thus an actual physical diagram of two triangles may be composed of ink on paper. Each line has a finite, not infinitesimal, width and is not perfectly straight. Indeed diagrams are often drawn freehand and the lines are distinctly not straight, perceptibly so. Nonetheless we are able to treat them 'as if' they were straight. If we are told that two segments are of the same length, we can treat them as such even if measurement or simply unaided observation reveals that they are not. However, if the departure from equal length is *too* great we cannot treat them as equal, and attempts to do so may introduce confusion and outright errors.

An example of historical significance is illustrated in Figure 12: Archimedes' Palimpsest: Idealized Sketch and Figure 13: Archimedes' Palimpsest: Actual Sketch.

---

[12] In biology the rapidly reproducing fruit fly has been an important model in the study of genetics because it embodies the essential properties of genetic inheritance and expression in a relatively simple organism.

[13] The statements and methods actually used in high-school geometry texts are far from formal in the sense that term is understood in contemporary mathematics. They do, however, contain the elements of formal argument: they are symbolic statements with a structured (if undefined) syntax that are manipulated by rules (although the rules are usually explained in a natural language such as English rather than in an artificial and precise language).

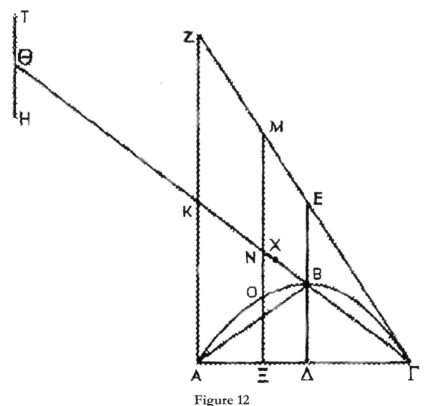

Figure 12
Archimedes's Palimpsest: Idealized Sketch

This drawing is derived from Archimedes' drawing, but is not identical to it. The figure depicts a section of a parabola. Archimedes used his 'Method' to show that the area of this parabolic section is exactly one third the area of the large triangle. Relating the area of a curvilinear figure to that of a rectilinear figure was a major achievement. ΓZ is tangent to the parabola, AZ is perpendicular to AΓ, and MΞ is an arbitrary line parallel to AZ intersecting KΓ at N. Θ is chosen so that ΘK = KΓ. Archimedes argued that a copy of OΞ placed along the segment TH centered at Θ 'balanced' the segment MΞ at fulcrum K. The argument turns on the curve being a parabola to establish that OΞ:MΞ :: AΞ:AΓ. The similarity of triangles then establishes that OΞ:MΞ :: KN:KΓ. Since MΞ is an arbitrary line, taken together all segments OΞ constitute the mass/area of the parabolic segment and all segments MΞ constitute the mass/area of the triangle. The center of mass of the triangle is at X. The OΞ segments "piled up" on TH have a center of mass at Θ; they balance the mass of the triangle centered at X, which from geometry is known to be 1/3 the distance from K to Γ (and ΘK=KΓ), establishing the result. Reprinted with permission from R. Netz, The origins of mathematical physics: New light on an old question. *Physics Today*, 53, June 2000, page 35. Copyright 2000, American Institute of Physics. With permission and permission of the author.

Archimedes established a ratio between the area of the section of a parabola and a triangle enclosing it, as illustrated in the first figure. However, the figure that Archimedes actually used is the second, in which the curvilinear figure is not a parabola but a crudely drawn circle. With this figure, Archimedes's argument does not actually work were one to check it with ruler and straightedge. But in the application of his 'Method' Archimedes actually treats the rough circle as though it were a parabola for purposes of his construction. This is a stark illustration of how diagrams are used as-if they are what they are manifestly not!

Few people in history have been as adept at diagrammatic reasoning as the great genius Archimedes. For most of us such a large departure of diagram from conception might lead to error, but all of us readily tolerate small departures.

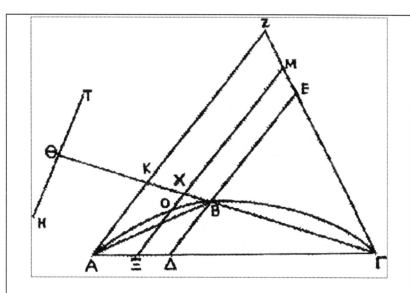

Figure 13
Archimedes's Palimpsest: Actual Sketch
This is the drawing Archimedes actually constructed to establish the area relation. The drawing is a sketch, and the curve is an approximate circle, certainly not a parabola. The line ΓZ is clearly not tangent to the curve. If one measures the critical line segments used in the argument their lengths do not satisfy the necessary proportional relations. Nonetheless, Archimedes treated this figure "as if" it were a parabola. Reprinted with permission from R. Netz, The origins of mathematical physics: New light on an old question. *Physics Today*, 53, June 2000, page 35. Copyright 2000, American Institute of Physics. With permission and permission of the author.

4. Geometric Diagrams and Unsound Conclusions

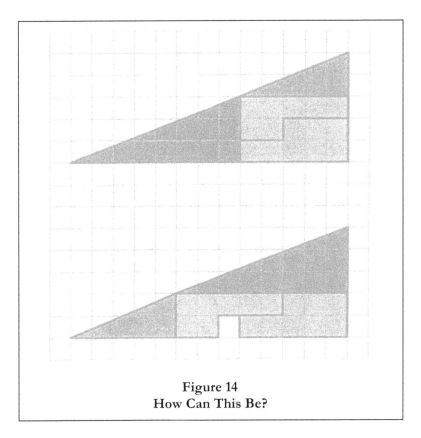

Figure 14
How Can This Be?

It is possible to create a very convincing, yet false, demonstration based on an improperly constructed diagram. While Archimedes' drawing did not hinder his reasoning, inaccurate drawings may lead to unsound conclusions. It is possible to make drawings that appear to be what they are not (a slightly bent line, two approximately equal segments) and these 'support' arguments that lead to puzzles and contradictions. See Figure 14: How can this be? In this case perception has been deceived: the slopes of the two hypotenuses look the same but are not.

Another source of error or paradox is the failure to accurately construct the diagram that corresponds to a propositional description. Figure 15: A Fallacious Proof and Figure 16: Still Fallacious illustrate an incorrect geometric 'proof' where the problem is blamed on the use of a diagram. The 'proof' is of the proposition that all triangles are isosceles. The diagram is purported to represent an arbitrary triangle, and the implicit generalization derives from the claim that it embodies no hidden assumptions.

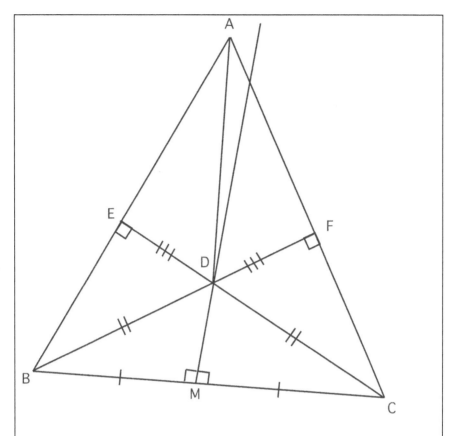

Figure 15
A Fallacious Proof

Let M be the midpoint of BC and let D be the intersection of the perpendicular bisector of BC and the angle bisector of ∠BAC. Let E be the point on AB such that AB⊥DE and let F be the point on AC such that AC⊥DF. Now BM=CM by construction, ∠BMD=∠CMD (=90 degrees) by construction and DM=DM. Therefore, triangles BMD and CMD are congruent (angle, side, angle theorem). Thus BD=CD and ∠MBD=∠MCD (corresponding parts of congruent triangles are equal). Next, DE=DF (a point on an angle bisector is equidistant from the sides) and ∠BED=∠CFD by construction. Therefore, triangles BED and CFD are congruent (two right triangles with two equal sides and equal hypotenuses are congruent – or, by the Pythagorean Theorem, the other sides are also equal and then we can use the side, angle, side, or the side, side, side theorems). Therefore, ∠DBE=∠DCF (corresponding angles of congruent triangles are equal). Thus ∠MBE=∠MCF (sums of equals are equal). This says the triangle ABC is isosceles with equal angles at B and C and thus the sides opposite these angles, AB and AC, are equal. From Harold M. Stark, *An introduction to number theory*, Figure 7.17 with caption. © 1978 Harold M. Stark, by permission of the MIT Press.

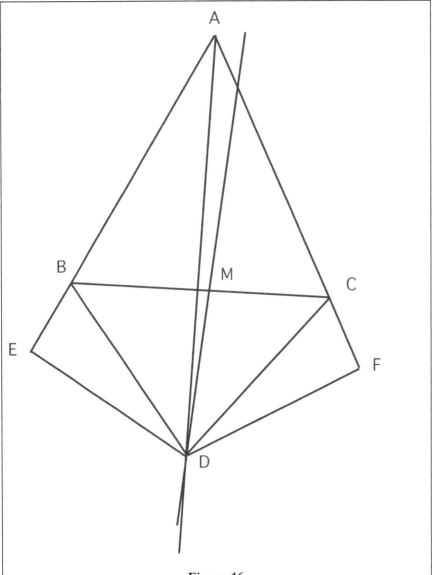

Figure 16
Still Fallacious

It is mistakenly stated that the error consists of the fact that D is drawn above BC, whereas D is actually below BC. Thus, the reader may enjoy proving that AB=AC from Figure 16 (the letters have the same meaning as before). The proof is practically identical to the one given using Figure 15. From Harold M. Stark, *An introduction to number theory*, Figure 7.17 with caption. © 1978 Harold M. Stark, by permission of the MIT Press.

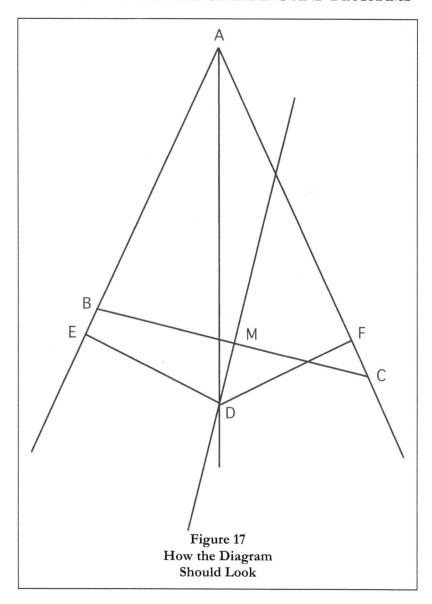

Figure 17
How the Diagram
Should Look

Here the proof went wrong when the diagram was drawn, not because of the its misperception. The instructions were not followed accurately. One common reason that wrong pictures are drawn is that we are not very good at determining from verbal descriptions on which side of a line a point must lie. A second reason is that we are not good at generating all possible alternatives; we tend to stop after finding one. These problems underlie this example. It is not obvious that points E and F must lie on opposite sides of BC for any triangle, but accurate measuring shows that they must. The first drawing puts both of them above BC from which the error follows. Interestingly the text obscures the source of error as well, suggesting that point placement is not the issue because the second diagram leads to the same error. However the two cases both have E and F on the *same* side of BC; they only differ in that in one case they are both above it, in the other they are both below it. A careful ruler and straightedge construction (See Figure 17: How the Diagram Should Look) reveals that E and F must be on opposite sides of BC. This example illustrates the need for embracing within the theory a *complete description of the perceptual processes* if one is attempting to formalize diagrammatic reasoning.

What this example illustrates is not that diagrams are misleading, but that humans are bad at translating language into diagrams. We would not fault predicative methods because a proof can be improperly stated and thus lead to an incorrect conclusion. That tolerance derives from a failure to see the limitations of predicative methods due to the conventional failure to demand a fully formal (algorithmic) account of how formal proofs are created and understood. Formal reasoning is hardly immune from the problems inherent in diagrammatic reasoning, and its difficulties are compounded by the fact that fully-detailed predicative proofs are essentially unintelligible to humans. Formal proofs can, of course, be checked by a computer algorithm, at least in principle. But given that it is impossible to prove that a program is a correct embodiment of an algorithm (in fact Turing showed that there exists no algorithm that can even decide if an arbitrary program will halt or run forever), the absolute integrity of such checking is itself suspect.

5. Geometric Diagrams and Generalization

Clearly, mathematics is about general statements, and mathematical abstraction is a means of classifying objects that differ in detail but share important properties. Models of mathematical reasoning must therefore provide a mechanism to express generalization.

Diagrammatic reasoning, even about Euclidean plane geometry, is often seen as inferior to predicative reasoning because it does not permit abstraction. Of course, as just discussed, a diagram itself is treated as an abstraction: an ink-on-paper diagram may represent the abstract concept of "triangle," for example. However, diagrams are necessarily specific in their commitments: this diagram may depict an "acute triangle" or an "obtuse triangle" but it cannot be a depiction of both.[14] This particularity is seen as a major weakness because it can lead to error by failing to consider other cases for which the conclusion under study does not hold. Thus diagrammatic reasoning can lead both to under-generalization and over-generalization.

It was a major cultural step when someone (or more likely many people independently) described *generalizations* of their observations of rigid objects in space. The Pythagorean Theorem is a classical example of this, though doubtless it was not the first. It states a general relation among the lengths of the sides of right triangles. It is a particularly powerful generalization primarily because right angles are particularly important, especially in a gravitational field.

It is undeniable that diagrams, if restricted to straightforward representations of arrangements of geometric objects without additional notation or other coding conventions, cannot *state* a general conclusion, nor can they alone logically justify the drawing of a general conclusion by a human observer.

---

[14] Strictly speaking this objection is false. Since we can assign arbitrary symbols to anything we can represent, we could say that an acute triangle is to be taken to denote all triangles, just as we could use a circle, a square, or the word "triangle" for this purpose. The above claim clearly turns on the notion that the geometric properties of the symbol are, in the case of diagrams, to be taken seriously.

Generally, however, geometric diagrams consist of more than just lines and curves. We almost always allow names to be associated with locations or objects in the diagram, and use special symbols to attribute properties to components (such as indicating that an angle is a right angle) and to mark a relation between parts (such as tick marks to indicate that two line segments are equal in length). Do these extensions address the concern about stating general conclusions? No, because these annotated diagrams generally do not employ variables and quantifiers, so they cannot state the equivalent of "for all cases of this sort, it is true that . . . ." Thus the customary use of diagrams in geometric thinking cannot be a complete description of geometric thinking, even in the restricted case of Euclidean plane geometry. It must be augmented by some form of predicative representation.[15] In short, *there is no such thing as purely diagrammatic reasoning*, for reasoning entails generalization (through linguistic devices), and standard diagrams, even conventionally annotated ones, cannot state generalizations since they do not fully use linguistic representations.

6. Geometric Diagrams versus Formal Languages

In spite of the need to idealize physical diagrams that are imperfect and inaccurate, in spite of their power to deceive, and in spite of their inability to state generalizations, diagrams are invaluable. The great mathematician David Hilbert wrote:

> In mathematics ... we find two tendencies present. On the one hand, the tendency toward abstraction seeks to crystallize the logical relations inherent in the maze of material that is being studied, and to correlate the material in a systematic and orderly manner. On the other hand, the tendency toward intuitive understanding fosters a more immediate grasp of the objects one studies, a live rapport with them, so to speak, which stresses the concrete meaning of their relations (Hilbert, quoted by Zimmerman & Cunningham (1991), page 1).

In this passage, Hilbert distinguishes abstract thinking and concrete thinking as two aspects of mathematical thought, each of importance, and suggests that formal mathematical thinking is appropriate for abstraction whereas concrete thinking is appropriate for understanding.

One motivation for the development of formal languages is to capture the expressive power of some aspects of natural language, such as being able to state propositions and predications. One well-developed standard formal language (with notational variants) is the first-order predicate calculus (FOPC), mentioned in Section 3.1: Logic. The FOPC is first-order because it does not permit quantification over variables that denote predicates, only variables that denote individuals. Thus if one uses predicates to represent properties of human thought (perhaps *rational, irrational, productive, analogical*, and so forth), one cannot then state the equivalent of "All properties of human thought are deterministic" in a first-order logic. Proposals have been made for higher-order logics but these have not been as fully studied as FOPC. Other extensions of formal languages have also been made to include concepts such as necessity and probability. There are many other

---

[15] The 'augmentation' is often implicit. For example, the scale of a diagram is implicitly recognized as irrelevant for most geometric conclusions.

aspects of natural language that have not yet been formally captured, such as vagueness and metaphor.

To this day there is debate over whether or to what extent human thought is mediated by predicative or depictional means, roughly, by words or by pictures. The debate waxes and wanes, and reverses polarity occasionally. The importance of diagrams in a psychological account of human thinking and in the development of artificial intelligence has been denied by some. Their view has accompanied the rise of predicate-calculus based reasoning systems in artificial intelligence [see e.g., McCarthy (1988) and Nilsson (1980)]. The argument is that all forms of thought can be modeled entirely with the constructs of formal symbolic reasoning, properly extended beyond FOPC. Since such processes are both rigorous and sufficient for any symbolic calculation, the use of ancillary representations such as diagrams is superfluous. Furthermore, they argue, diagrams have limitations, such as those discussed above, that predicate calculus does not; hence diagrams are not *sufficient* for reasoning.

Addressing this distinction proves problematic because it is not clear exactly what the alternative styles of cognition are. While I have referred to the styles as descriptional and depictional, other terms are also used. "Depictional" suggests visual and tactile, spatial, perceptual, parallel, and analog. "Descriptional" suggests verbal, linguistic, propositional, predicative, logical, serial, and digital. Unfortunately these terms are not well-defined in the context of cognition, and the terms within each set should not be treated as synonyms.

Depictions and imagery

Intuitively when one reasons 'depictionally,' it often seems that one is 'looking' at not an actual physical diagram, but a mental image of one. Thus the issue of diagrammatic versus formal reasoning is often conflated with the issue of mental images and their role in thinking. This aspect of the role of diagrammatic thinking flourishes primarily in the psychological literature, where the issue is not the use and value of physical diagrams, but rather the role of mental imagery. In particular, many researchers call into question the view that humans think with imagined diagrams (and other visualizations) in a way that is in important aspects the same as how they reason with actual diagrams.

Most people experience visual imagery. Close your eyes and imagine your living room. Though the image is impoverished in comparison to the perception when actually in the room, and more so for some of us than for others, it maintains certain features. Thus you can imagine moving around the room or looking in particular directions, counting the windows or recalling the shape and color of furniture and so forth. It is also true that, with the exception of cases that are easily explainable as anomalies due to developmental errors, accidents and so forth, all people have auditory images of speech.

Aristotle taught that all thought required imagery and this view persisted without substantial empirical test until the beginnings of scientific psychology. Francis Galton (1822–1911) was the first to study imagery systematically (Miller (1962)). He did so by asking people about their images, to describe them and report when they occurred, and so forth. Surprisingly some scientists seemed to have trouble doing so, whereas most others readily described images ranging from vivid to dim. Galton's main finding was that imagery varied greatly among people.

CHAPTER 6: UNDERSTANDING AND DIAGRAMS

Wundt's psychological laboratory, established in 1879[16], used introspection to study thought. Not surprisingly, people reported imagery. This supported the Aristotelian dictate that thought was based on imagery, but it hardly put the notion to a critical empirical test. The Würzburg school of psychology, in flower around the beginning of the 20th century, produced empirical evidence that certain judgments were possible without imagery, seriously calling into question the hypothesis of universal imagery underlying thought. It remained an open issue as to what role imagery did play in human thinking.

There is a second component to this argument that I have not addressed. That component is generally called the Imagery Debate: Do humans process their visual images in a manner that is basically the same as the one they use when perceiving actually present visual scenes, or are there significant differences? To assert that the processes are the same for image and percept is a strong form of the imagery argument: images are just like percepts, and are 'seen' by the 'mind's eye' in the same way and using essentially the same visual processes as those that see the world with the real eye.

This question is not the same as asking what format the representation takes, because it might be the same for images as for percepts, and yet reasoning with images may still be distinct from perception. I will return to this aspect of the discussion in Chapter 8 after introducing my model of geometric reasoning.

Predications and language

Advocates of formal models tend to think of images as purely epi-phenomena that operate solely on verbal-like *descriptions* of diagrams, while playing no essential role in the reasoning process. Advocates of mental imagery treat images as essential to the reasoning process, which they claim operates at least in part on non-verbal *depictions* of diagrams.

By "descriptions" one generally means predications in some natural or formal language. Thoughts are presumably always 'about' something. When we think 'about' an event we may be able to describe it with linguistically phrased descriptions, e.g., "the cat is on the mat." Since thoughts are complicated, the description of an event may consist of many statements. Since events unfold in time, the statements may include descriptions of when, in what temporal order, and so forth as well as of objects in the world and relations among them. Sometimes our thoughts are only a re-experiencing of an event, but the more problematic cases involve more than this, and much of thinking is conscious, productive and goal-directed. Thinking descriptionally-predicatively-verbally means doing something with language. It is not clear what that means precisely, but the modern answer is that thoughts are represented with sentences that are processed computationally, by manipulating their symbols according to specific rules that permit generating new sentences that represent other events or concepts. Two hundred years ago it was not at all clear what any of this meant (and no one said it!). Today, subsequent to the invention of formal languages beginning with Frege and continuing through Hilbert and Gödel among many others to the development of digital computers that do

---

[16] Coincidentally 1879 was the year that saw the publication of Gottlob Frege's *Begriffsschrift*, the seminal work on mathematical logic that marked the beginning of the modern era of formal logic, and also was the year that Albert Einstein was born.

symbolic manipulation and 'word processing,' it seems quite straightforward: thinking is some form of manipulating words and phrases.

One may ask if there is not more to thinking than just elaborate symbol manipulation. There is an in-principle question and an empirical question. The first asks if everything that human cognition does could be done by symbol manipulation, appropriately defined. The second asks if *in fact* that is how human thinking *is* done. It is likely that the answer to the in-principle question is "yes," because any computation can be done by symbol manipulation (the Church-Turing thesis). However, I believe that there is an important functional distinction between predicative and depictional representations even though both may be described as symbolic computations at base.

Mathematical rigor of the past century is far greater than that used for the development of mathematics for millennia. Formal languages with precise syntax have been developed for expressing mathematical statements, and specific rules of deductive inference are stated in these languages. The major theories and concepts of modern mathematics are defined with formally stated axioms.

Some conclude from this that standard diagrams are limited to a purely heuristic use, important perhaps to human mathematicians in discovering geometric truths, but not an essential part of the body of mathematics *per se*. However, mathematics developed without the contemporary conception of formal rigor because it was driven by intuitive understanding and concrete, often diagrammatic, thinking as discussed in Chapter 4. Furthermore, the absoluteness of the rigor of formal mathematics, even in its modern form, is more apparent than real, as is its supposedly clear advantage over non-formal methods. Neither diagrammatic reasoning nor formal reasoning has been *fully* characterized as *physical processes* – energy transformations on physical objects; both still require human interpretation. A recent proof of Fermat's Last Theorem runs to over 200 pages. Fully formal proofs are so long and detailed as to be essentially opaque; a proof of completeness of the classification of finite sets is over 10,000 pages in length. Mathematician Hyman Bass characterizes the role of proofs as follows: what mathematicians do is, rather than producing a proof, produce an argument that convinces mathematicians that a proof exists.

Others have responded to the challenge to the use of diagrams in argument by amending the annotated diagram system to permit the statement of general conclusions, provide a sound basis for inference, and still maintain the diagrammatic character of the representation. A variety of attempts have been made to extend the representation system in these ways and some of these will be described in more detail in Section 7.3: Diagrammatic Reasoning in Logic. Essentially each provides a notation that looks diagrammatic but is made precise and unambiguous, and permits the proof of theorems about the rigor of the revised notation. Typically these attempts force diagrams into a predicative notation, and beg the question by assuming that human perception of these notational devices is not problematic. Some do, however, maintain a true diagrammatic character because they cannot be expressed in a purely predicative form, and do make substantive use of the structure of space.

I advocate a third position about the role of diagrams in mathematical argument and understanding. It has three parts.

- First, mathematics cannot be divorced from human psychology. Understanding mathematics is the heart of the issue, and to understand mathematics as a human enterprise we must understand mathematical discovery, that is, one must model human use of diagrams as well as human use of language, not merely change the notation to fit the predicative model. The complete theory will combine standard diagram and predicative representations and each will maintain its characteristics, since each is essential for a proper scientific understanding of geometric (and mathematical) reasoning.

- Second, the in-principle autonomous sufficiency and formality of traditional accounts of predicative reasoning is an illusion.
- Third, generalizations can be discovered by diagrammatic means even though they must be represented and established in another way. (Maxwell's discovery of the laws of electromagnetism and Kekule's discovery of the structure of benzene are classical examples of this.)[17] Again, a model of human reasoning will encompass a true hybrid of methods.

Theory and fact

I now return to the broader issue of what should count as the *true* or *correct* account of a phenomenon, specifically of human reasoning and how it is implemented. The position I hold is essentially that put forth by the philosopher Immanuel Kant (1724–1804). Reality is not coextensive with some set of true facts that are independent of interpretation. According to contemporary thinking, the world presents itself to us as an energy flow in time and space. We must parse the world into entities and events in order to understand it and discuss it, with ourselves or with others. Thus all facts are embedded in theory. Any knowledge that can be verbally communicated to others is based on a theory, and there is no one-to-one mapping of theories onto reality, no correct theory, only more or less accurate ones, where accuracy means consistency with other theories, including theories of the results of empirical observations, including scientific experiments. This is particularly difficult to appreciate in cases where the 'facts' seem to be obvious and incontrovertible. Apples fall down, not up. The body contains one liver and two kidneys. But apples, down, up, liver, and kidneys are not directly observable, incontrovertible objects, things or properties. The parsing and the discussions are theories, not in and of themselves objective truth and reality.

This is not to say there is no objective reality. Kant distinguished between the *noumenal* world and the *phenomenal* world: the former is 'reality' and the latter is our experience of it. In a deep and important sense we do not know and we cannot know what reality is. All we can do is experience it and insofar as possible describe it, though our experience may never be *fully* describable. We can then see how well our putative theories are consistent with one another including reports of observations, and how well they agree with the reports of other persons, over a range of events that our theories are intended to cover. That, in brief, is the nature and the limitation of science as well as of all human knowledge. This of course manifestly does not mean that any description is as good as any other, or that all claims about the world are just opinions that are on equal footing.

---

[17] Maxwell thought about the phenomena of electricity and magnetisms by visualizing mechanical analogs. Kekule allegedly dreamed of a series of snakes eating one another's tails and this led him to considering that benzene might be a cyclical rather than a linear structure of atoms.

UNDERSTANDING UNDERSTANDING

Do the planets *obey* differential equations as they move about the sun? Yes, in the sense that the equations model the planet's motion, so that if *we* solve those equations we can predict the motions of the planets. Do *the planets* solve the equations rather than just obey them? We are inclined to say no because we do not think of planets as problem-solvers, or even as computational devices. Our reasons for doubting the cognitive computational abilities of planets derive from the context of other things we have learned about planets such as their physical structure, which shows no signs of a nervous system or other computational facility. However, if we did so describe them and if the description fit the observed facts, there is no more reason – if we limit ourselves to this narrow context – to say that they are not solving equations than there is to say that they are merely obeying them.

Is our world composed of quarks and leptons, of atoms and molecules, of proteins and DNA, of plants and animals, of emotions and cognitions, of societies and cultures? Yes. Theories, even though given in vastly different terms and different levels of description, need not be inconsistent nor incompatible. In fact as these particular classes of descriptions have been chosen to illustrate, they may be mutually supportive with the combination enhancing our understanding in ways that no single descriptive model can.

Is our world composed of good and evil, humans and gods, reality and mysticism, magic and normalcy? Yes. However, these alternative accounts are far less useful for certain tasks, such as prediction and technological advancement. Furthermore, they add to the previous accounts no further predictability nor do they underwrite further technological advances, even though they are not contradictory nor incompatible. However, for the majority of people alive up until now, at least, they offer a deeper sense of understanding than do quarks and molecules. Appeals to magic are construed by some as an *alternative* to understanding, amounting to giving up the quest. However, magic and mysticism do indeed provide most people with a sense of understanding, even if they merely attribute phenomena to the action of a mysterious power.

One might argue that the only reality of the situation is the interactions of electrons and photons, and these are properly described by quantum theory. That is, one might say that true reality is indeed captured at the level of fundamental units, currently conceived to be the elementary particles of the Standard Theory of physics. Such accounts are particularly unsatisfying, however. First of all they are unduly complex. Second they seem terribly far removed from an explanation that we can relate to. But worst of all, they are no more 'real' than any other description of equal accuracy and scope (notwithstanding that we have no such alternative accounts at the moment).

If we characterize "description" broadly, there are forms of description other than verbal by which we comprehend reality. For example, we may represent the world imagistically, using visual or non-visual perceptual modalities. We may also comprehend reality through the process of interacting with it, through perceptual and motor systems that allow us to accomplish things without verbally describing exactly what we are doing or accomplishing. These alternatives to verbal description, however, suffer the same limitation: there is no guarantee that they characterize a unique underlying reality.

Thus theory-descriptions, including verbal, imagistic, and interactive, may not be true characterizations of reality, but they are all we have. Nonetheless, not all theories are equally good: some may be wrong, that is, they might be inconsistent with our other theories or observations. Choosing an appropriate one is a matter of finding those that meet three tests. One, they must not be inconsistent with observations. Two, they must help us achieve some purpose, which in general is some form of understanding. Three, they must mesh with other successful theories of other aspects of our experience.

Is light waves or particles?

Consider a case parallel to the question of whether humans truly think in images or words. For a long time there were two theories of light, one that it consisted of particles (*corpuscles*, Newton called them) and the other that it was a wave phenomenon. The reason for the debate was that light appeared to behave in both ways as observed in different experiments. With the advent of quantum theory, light was construed as discrete packets of energy, seemingly a win for the particle view. However, these particles turned out to be quite different from the corpuscles that Newton imagined. They behave in very strange and non-particle ways. To account for all the experimental facts, one must conclude that while light sometimes behaves as particles and sometimes as waves, it is in fact neither of these things as they were classically conceived.

The quantum theory of light is now generally accepted, but that does not mean that we know it to be true. All we can say is that it is the best theory we have, it is consistent with our most careful measurements, and that both the particle and wave theories of classical physics are wrong, though still useful in certain contexts.

Do we think in images or words?

What we take to be how humans *really* think is also a matter of theory, and as pointed out above there is no such thing as the 'real' description. We might for example describe thinking phenomenologically: I am thinking about a purple cow and wondering where I could buy one. Or we might describe thinking as a sequence of brain states: activity levels pass from one neural circuit to another in a particular fashion. Or we might describe thinking behaviorally, as a sequence of actions: "yes" "no" "maybe" "yes" "twenty-seven" (in response to questions about something). Unfortunately none of these forms of description is either well-defined or coherent or explanatory.

The way to answer the images vs. words question is, as in the case of the physics of light, to employ the method of science. To wit, we hypothesize an explanation, use it to make predictions of observables, and make the corresponding observations. If observations are limited to watching people perform certain tasks, such as those commonly employed in psychological experiments, we can conclude that the explanation does or does not work, and modify it as required. However, we can never prove that the explanation must be a veridical account of what is really happening. Note that this all applies perforce to neurological explanations as well; we do not know what the brain is *really* doing (whether in chemical, electrical, or functional terms). There are only theory-descriptions of more or less adequacy; there is no real representation, *whether there is an objective reality or not.*

The debate about imaging has generally revolved around the question of what humans are really doing when they observe pictures, diagrams, and so forth. Are they dealing with these perceptual objects directly in some sense, or are they translating them into a language-like encoding, and then reasoning with those representations? In light of the preceding discussion these questions are unanswerable. They are apt to remain so even after that distant day when thoughts can be precisely related to brain events. Why?

Because brain events are not 'really' images nor 'really' predications. Brain events will almost surely be described in the language of electrical and chemical activity, couched in statistical generalizations. This is because our notion of brain must be so couched for it to continue to fit into the overall scientific model. A theory of thinking will require a non-brain-state level of analysis.

Imagery and perceptual reasoning in general are psychological-level concepts. They can only be properly described in functional terms: what computations (or other processes) are needed to account for performance. How these processes are implemented is a different question. There is, of course, a question of plausible match. If we can conceive of no way in which the putative computations could be implemented in brains, they fail at that level of description.

Since most people experience, at least, both visual and auditory images, perhaps the answer to the depictional-descriptional either-or question is *both*. This is often the answer to such either-or debates, such as nature vs. nurture and conditioning vs. cognition. There is now evidence from brain imagery studies (Dehaene (2000)) that there are two forms of short duration memory (so-called working memory) that hold information currently being processed, one a visual store, the other an auditory store, and that they reside at different locations in the brain. This is recent evidence and has not yet deeply influenced the imagery debate. Furthermore, this evidence does not address the central issues, which are what role these images (or the associated brain processes) play in thinking, and exactly how they function.

7. Representation of Geometric Diagrams

Physical diagrams are often called representations because they 'stand for' something else. Since diagrams, considered as drawings on paper, are not themselves internal to a human or computer, they are representations in a different sense than the cognitive science and AI concept of representations. When a person looks at a physical diagram he somehow forms an *internal* 'representation' of that *external* 'representation', which in turn refers to something else again.

Note furthermore that the 'recording' part of a representation may just as well reside in part in the physical world, outside of the human or computer. A diagram as defined above – an arrangement of ink on a sheet of paper – is a recording in that sense and, combined with human perception and cognition, becomes a representation. I say 'may reside in part' because commonly we assume that neither human nor computer can 'think about' the physical world without creating a corresponding internal record to manipulate.

I will distinguish three methods of representing diagrams in a computer model: pixel arithmetic, algebraic, and visual. These do not exhaust the possibilities, indeed many published models of diagrammatic reasoning have used other methods, such as semantic networks that use named labels to show how objects are spatially arranged. Such methods in general, however, only capture some of the geometric relations that are present in a diagram, whereas the three styles I will discuss can potentially fully represent the geometry of a diagram, at least to an arbitrarily close approximation.

Consider a diagram of a circle. Let us suppose that the diagram is a continuous black line on a sheet of white paper. To describe diagram processing we must have a way of referring to the elements of the diagram. Let us impose a fine pixel array on the diagram, by tessellating the sheet of paper with squares, each of which has a name (address) that we may refer to. Each pixel is either predominantly black or predominantly white and each has eight immediate neighbors. Examples of the three computational styles will now be given to illustrate their strengths and weaknesses.

Pixel arithmetic

In pixel arithmetic processing, each pixel is assigned a pair of integer coordinates. Processing may attend to any pixel by being supplied with its coordinates, that is, coordinates are arguments to perceptual processes. There is a color function from coordinates to the set {black, white, red, etc.}. Furthermore, the arithmetic properties of the coordinates may be used by the perceptual processes. Thus one can find the color of the pixel to the immediate left of a given pair of coordinates by computing the address of that pixel (subtracting 1 from the given x-coordinate and keeping the y-coordinate unchanged) and then apply the color function to the resulting coordinate pair. In similar fashion one performs other operations by doing arithmetic on coordinates. One may scan the diagram left to right by iterating through the appropriate sequence of coordinates. One may stop a scan when a certain color is encountered, or when a certain history of colors has been encountered. One may examine all of the neighbors of a black pixel and determine which are black, then move to one of them. Iterating this operation allows the tracing of a continuous black line. One may detect a closed curve by such curve following; if the sequence returns to where it started a closed curve has been detected, and the sequence of visited pixels can be retained as a record of the location of the curve. Another perceptual process could determine where two curves cross. To compute this requires tracing of connected paths (lists of pixels) and determining their commonalities by set intersection.

With pixel processing, one is using the coordinates as a proxy for spatial relations, e.g., "immediate left" means a difference of 1 of the x-coordinate. Distances between pixels can be computed from their coordinates using the Euclidean distance function. This representation assures that distances are preserved and processed in a manner that reflects accurately the spatial distances in the diagram, by vector addition. In other words, the structure of space is maintained by the structure of arithmetic *plus* the mapping of coordinate pairs onto spatial locations in the conventional Cartesian representation of analytic geometry.

Having found a closed curve, how can we find a point inside it, or equivalently, how can we determine if a particular pixel is inside, outside, or on the curve? This requires more work. One way to accomplish the task is to begin with an arbitrary point, mark it or remember its address, and examine its neighbors, but never cross the black border of the curve. When no new neighbors are encountered either the entire inside or the entire outside of the curve has been marked or otherwise remembered. If the marked area is adjacent to the edges of the paper, the original point was outside; otherwise it was inside. See Figure 18: Using Color-Spreading to Find if a Point is Inside a Closed Curve. Similar *color spreading* computations can be used to detect the overlap of closed curves, the exact decomposition of one closed curve into a finite set of areas defined by other curves, and so forth. These are described in detail later as they are used in my model of diagrammatic reasoning (see the section Observing Partitions in Section 8.6: Retrieval Processes).

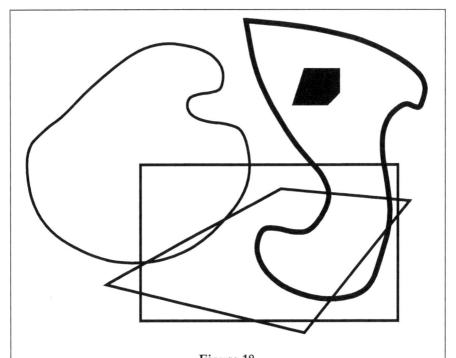

Figure 18
Using Color-Spreading to Find if a Point is Inside a Closed Curve
After marking the boundary of the right-hand figure in bold, its interior is found by starting at an interior point and marking points up to the boundary. The solid black irregular area indicates the partially completed spreading process.

Note, however, that some things are difficult to do, for example, determining that a closed curve is or is not a circle. Consider the easiest case, where there is a single closed curve in the diagram. Testing for a circle might be accomplished by first determining that the curve was closed, using a method of the sort outlined above. Then we would determine if the curve had the same curvature at each point. Since the diagram is digitized, "constant" would have to be approximated. Alternatively, a computation could determine the center pixel of the putative circle as that one midway between the leftmost and rightmost black pixel and the topmost and bottommost pixel. Again the discrete pixel representation complicates the calculation now, because midway arithmetically might fall between pixels. Ignoring that complication and assuming we have found the putative center, we could find the black pixel closest to the center in one direction along a putative diameter. Noting its coordinates we could compute where its diagonally opposite black sister should be and check for its presence. The test would proceed by producing and testing each pair of sisters. Finally, having marked or otherwise kept track of all the loci, the diagram could be scanned to make certain that there were not unaccounted-for black pixels destroying the symmetry.

CHAPTER 6: UNDERSTANDING AND DIAGRAMS

Algebraic processing

In algebraic processing, objects are represented by algebraic formulae. For example, a circle with radius r with its center at the origin is represented as $y = (r^2 - x^2)^{1/2}$. There is no pixel map, only the formula, it being understood by supplementary convention that the infinite set of pairs of real numbers (x, y) that satisfy the formula denotes the circle. With this computational style one can determine if a given pixel is on the defined locus by substituting its coordinates into the formula. The difficulties caused by the digitization of the plane in the pixel representation vanish. If there are two curves, and hence two formulas, it is easy to compute if and where they cross by solving their equations simultaneously.

On the other hand, if the curve cannot be described by a closed formula, the computations become very difficult or impossible. A list of (x, y) pairs will not suffice because the list must be infinite if the curve is continuous (or even just dense). Similarly, the detection of overlapping areas, inside-outside, and so forth are difficult even when each curve has a simple closed formula. For arbitrary curves the computations become unmanageable, or impossible if the curves defy algebraic representation.

Thus, each of these two representations, pixel and algebraic, has advantages for some kinds of perceptions and is at a disadvantage for others.

Visual processing

Visual perceptual processing is what human vision does, and of course we do not know precisely how it works. We can, however, describe some of the things it is good at, and some of the things it is not so good at. We are extremely good at making the closed curve distinction, provided the curves are not too 'curvy.' Compare Figure 19: Perception of Inside-Outside. For similarly 'simple' cases we can immediately make the inside-outside distinction, detect overlap, and detect decompositions. If the number of compartments becomes more than a few, we are not so good at enumerating them, however. See Figure 20: More Difficult Perception of Inside-Outside. Bilateral and radial symmetry are other properties of diagrams where visual computation excels. The detection of straight lines and of area congruencies (again, for sufficiently simple figures) is also rapid.

It is unlikely that brains represent and compute algebraically. The main reason for doubting this is that our facility for computing (detecting) symmetry, closed curves, inside-outside, overlap, and so forth is largely independent of the complexity (measured algebraically) of the shapes involved, again so long as they are within the scope of our ability. Secondarily, it is difficult to imagine neural structures that could do the symbolic manipulations of formulas that the computations entail; one might more readily imagine that equations are manipulated by numerical methods, but again that seems improbable.

On the other hand, serial pixel computations of the sort described above appear to be far too slow since they involve sequential computations and careful record keeping. However, since pixel computations such as color spreading lend themselves readily to parallel processing, this seems a much more plausible match. Note that pixel computations need not be literally topographically mapped onto brain structures. All that is necessary is that the properties of space are preserved by the computations. Adjacency is a primitive detectable property that may be represented physically either locally or at a distance in neural space, but locally in time. However, directions and distances must also be preserved, and this is by no means a trivial requirement for a brain architecture.

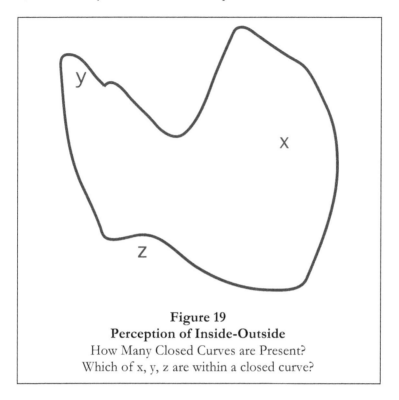

Figure 19
Perception of Inside-Outside
How Many Closed Curves are Present?
Which of x, y, z are within a closed curve?

Descriptive annotations

In addition to the three encodings for diagrams that have just been described, each can be augmented by predicative notes that provide additional description, and these may be essential for the use of the diagram in particular ways. The simplest annotation is to provide names to components of a diagram so that they can be referred to and related to other named components. More generally, one may specify constraints on the diagram that cannot be encoded otherwise. For example, one may wish to specify that two line segments must be the same length or orientation. Such information is important if the diagrams are to be altered subject to these constraints, as is the case in my reasoning model ARCHIMEDES.

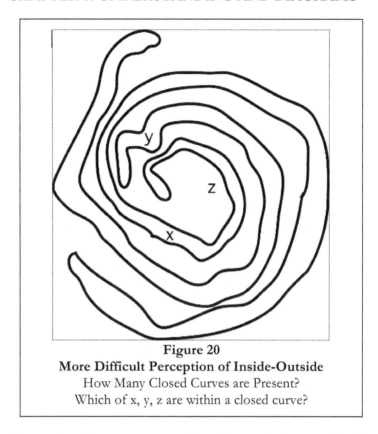

Figure 20
More Difficult Perception of Inside-Outside
How Many Closed Curves are Present?
Which of x, y, z are within a closed curve?

The next Chapter describes current research on diagrammatic reasoning done from an AI perspective. This research contrasts with my ARCHIMEDES model, presented in Chapter 8, and the discussion will serve to highlight the differences, especially that ARCHIMEDES treats diagrams as described physical models which can be 'mentally' manipulated to draw inferences and which relate a diagram to properties of space, thereby grounding understanding.

7 RESEARCH ON DIAGRAMMATIC REASONING

A picture's meaning can express ten thousand words.
– Chinese proverb

Recent decades have seen an increasing interest in exploring the role of diagrams in reasoning. Most of this research has addressed issues of formal reasoning in mathematical domains. The motivations of these projects have varied, but the major thrust of the efforts has been artificial intelligence rather than psychology, that is, they have addressed questions of how diagrams could be used by artifacts rather than how they are used by humans.

In this section I will point out some ways in which my approach is the same as the work of others, and some ways in which it differs. It is my contention that my computer model, ARCHIMEDES, treats its tasks in a way that is justifiably called diagrammatic, while much prior work that is putatively 'diagrammatic' does so in only a limited way, or not at all.

ARCHIMEDES exploits the full Euclidean geometric structure of two-dimensional space, where diagrams remain equivalent under displacements and rotations that preserve all metric properties. There are other ways to employ geometric structure. One might *augment* this structure to include constraints imposed by physical laws or even arbitrary relations. It is also possible to *relax* some of the constraints of full Euclidean geometry. For example linear and angular metrics could be ignored, so that diagrams are equivalent under stretching and shrinking (*affine*) transformations but still preserve parallels and distance ratios (squares remain squares, *e.g.*). If parallels and distance ratios are ignored, diagrams are equivalent under *projective* transformations, which preserve colinearity and betweeness while sacrificing shape properties. Finally, diagrams may be considered equivalent under any *topological* transformation so that only connectivity is maintained and used as a basis of inference.

Some diagrammatic reasoning models, including my work, have focused on geometric reasoning, especially plane geometry theorem proving. Still other work includes reasoning from diagrams of simple physical systems, especially mechanical or electrical ones. Diagrams have also long been used as pedagogical aids for students of logic, and recently some efforts have been applied to treating these methods more formally, putting them on a sound footing and extending their usefulness in teaching and problem solving.

CHAPTER 7: RESEARCH ON DIAGRAMMATIC REASONING

I will review this work selectively only to identify the similarities and differences it bears to ARCHIMEDES. Still other work studies the use of graphs and other graphical devices. I will attempt to show how all of this work relates to my thesis that diagrammatic reasoning is based on using the geometry of space.

1. Diagrammatic Reasoning in Geometry

As we know, the study of geometry both formally and informally has been going on for centuries, at least since the first historical records of human civilization. Perhaps it is thus not surprising that one of the first efforts in the field of artificial intelligence, coinciding essentially with the earliest general availability of digital computers, was an attempt to devise a computer program to prove theorems of Euclidean plane geometry. The Geometry Machine [Gelernter (1959), Gelernter, Hansen & Loveland (1960)] used a search algorithm based on formal rules. The program began with the conclusion of the theorem and developed a 'problem-tree' of statements (subproblems) from which the conclusion could be reached by a single rule-application. Subproblems for each of these were generated recursively until a path to the premises of the theorem was found. Such a problem-tree has many paths and requires extensive search. The Geometry Machine used a diagram solely as a heuristic device to prune this tree. The rule was that if a subproblem statement was not true in a diagram of the situation then no further attempt was made to prove it.

The 'diagrams' made available to the program were not automatically constructed from the theorem statement: they were provided as points with coordinates.[18] Thus the program could readily compute, say, the perimeter of a given triangle, and if that differed from the perimeter of another triangle, it would not attempt to prove the two to be congruent. The Machine pruned many false paths but left many other false paths unpruned. The heuristic reduced the search by a factor of about 600 and resulted in a system that was able to prove some non-trivial theorems in reasonable time, even on a computer that was six or seven orders of magnitude slower than present-day desktop machines.

Others, following in the tradition of Gelernter, have also coupled a heuristic search of statements and rules with a diagram representation that can be used to guide the search. The Koedinger & Anderson (1990) model embodied diagrammatic information and this substantially improved performance, while making it more similar to the problem solving strategy of human experts. They explicitly provided a set of prototypical diagrams and associated information that served as a classification of problems. This classification aided theorem proving by focusing the program's attention on the appropriate category with which specific hints were associated. As with the Geometry Machine, diagrams *per*

---

[18] Historical note: As a graduate student I had a summer job working with Eugene Gelernter and his team, Donald Loveland and James Hansen. One of my tasks was to write a program to convert the statement of a theorem into the set of coordinates used by the Geometry Machine for its diagram heuristic. I only completed the work for some cases. For the experiments published in the cited papers, the Machine was always supplied with the coordinates by a programmer, contrary to what is sometimes reported in secondary sources.

se were not available to the programs, and could not be modified or used to form new conjectures, nor were geometric constraints used to draw inferences.

A number of other projects addressing reasoning about geometrical theorems have appeared over the years. Some employ rigorous mathematical approaches and eschew any attempts to model human cognition. The work of Chou (1988), building on work of Wu (1978) and Ritt (1938) introduced a combination of diagram and algebra to produce a theorem prover of scope and power. It worked as follows. A diagram for a proposition is drawn and one point is assigned specific numerical coordinates (typically the origin) to fix the location of the diagram, and a line through that point is selected as determining the x-axis so that points on it have y-coordinates of zero, thereby fixing the orientation of the diagram. Variables are introduced for the x-coordinates of the other points on that line and for both x- and y-coordinates for those other points that can be chosen arbitrarily. Finally, other variables are introduced for point coordinates that are dependent upon the original assignments and variables. The hypotheses and conclusion of the theorem are stated as a set of simultaneous equations that relate all of these variables. An algebraic algorithm is used to determine if the system of equations has a solution; if so, the proposition is a theorem. An important side effect of this procedure is that it identifies special conditions that must hold for the theorem to be valid. Matsuyama & Nitta (1995) extended Wu's algebraic method by integrating it with logical problem graph reasoning methods to widen the scope of applicability beyond Chou's system. These methods use a diagram in a substantive way, but the algebraic inference procedures do not embody an intuitive spatial semantics that makes the deduction clear, at least to the non-algebraist.

2. Diagrammatic Reasoning in Other Mathematical Domains

Geometry is only one mathematical domain in which diagrams prove valuable for human reasoning. A number of research projects have explored the role of diagrams in the context of formal and quasi-formal reasoning.

One way to use diagrams in mathematical reasoning is to fully formalize diagrams in the style of formalized language. A number of efforts have been directed toward this goal with some success. Kaufman (1991) devised a formal theory that could represent both physical and geometric properties of some simple objects and could be used to prove such things as that a string can be used to pull but not to push. [Stenning & Oberlander (1991); Stenning & Oberlander (1992)] introduced algorithms for manipulating Venn diagrams.

Barwise & Etchemendy (1992) and Barwise & Etchemendy (1996) report a programmed system that helps students reason about both first-order logic and diagrams by integrating propositional statements and diagrams in a common system, accessible to the students by a graphical interface and based on precise rules for manipulating the representations. The system has been pedagogically useful, suggesting again the value and perhaps necessity of diagrams in the understanding of propositions. Wang (1995) has introduced a more general descriptive language for diagrams and devised a semantics for the language that maintains important logical properties such as consistency and soundness. This permits the representation of diagrams in a formal calculus, although the diagram elements are not perceptual objects. None of these theories specify precisely how objects can be recognized in a real diagram or a digitized picture, but rather work from a diagrammatic description that does not enforce geometric constraints directly by physics and geometry.

Barker-Plummer & Bailin (1992) constructed a theorem proving system for set theory that extracts information from its representation of diagrams, provides a decomposition of the theorem into lemmas, and orders them into an overall proof plan. Still other projects [Glasgow & Papadias (1992); Larkin & Simon (1987); McDougal (1993); Narayanan (1992); Novak (1977), to name a few] have employed diagrams and diagrammatic information in a variety of ways. These projects are at least in part attempts to embody in computer models some of the methods that intuitively seem to be those employed by humans, as opposed to those that seem unlikely to be. Although some empirical work has been done to test the claim of psychological validity, generally the models at present can make only limited experimental predictions.

Mateja Jamnik's DIAMOND system has been applied to propositions of number theory. It is similar to ARCHIMEDES in that both treat diagram manipulations as central features, but Jamnik additionally is interested in establishing diagrammatic methods that meet the usual standards of formal reasoning, so her work also shares similarities with work discussed in the next section.

Jamnik (2001) has primarily focused on the sort of 'Proofs without Words' that are seen in Nelsen (1993), including several examples of proofs of numerical relations. See Figure 21: $1 + 3 + 5 + \ldots + (2n - 1) = n^2$. The system provides the user with a set of diagrammatic operations that apply to a specific diagram. The Figure illustrates 'L-cuts' which are formed by one of the available operations. An example proof is a (short) finite sequence of the products of such operations. This permits the construction of a sequence of steps that is a demonstration of the relation to be proved. The heart of DIAMOND is a procedure that abstracts from this example and produces a general proof by induction. It then formally verifies that the proof is correct (if it is).

DIAMOND implicitly uses some limited features of two-dimensional space and thus it may justifiably be said to be working diagrammatically. Of course it also must use predicative operations, so it does not work 'purely diagrammatically' either. In the case of DIAMOND, the extent of spatial knowledge used is limited relative to ARCHIMEDES, and is about the same as with Bitpict and IDR, which are described below in Section 7.4: Diagrammatic Reasoning in Physics.

While all of the foregoing have used diagrammatic representations in one form or another, none of them has treated them as the central computational object the way ARCHIMEDES does. Thus, while representations are consulted, they are not manipulated in ways that preserve or employ the structure of space. This central focus in ARCHIMEDES sets it apart from these other projects.

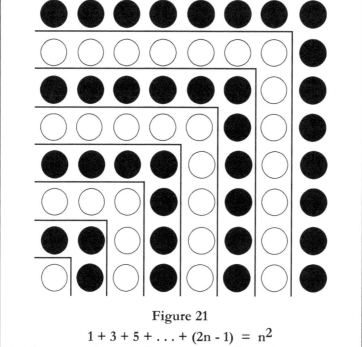

Figure 21

$$1 + 3 + 5 + \ldots + (2n - 1) = n^2$$

A diagram and symbolic statement illustrating L-cuts as produced by Jamnik's DIAMOND. From R. B. Nelsen, *Proofs without words. Exercises in visual thinking*, 1993, page 71. Copyright the Mathematical Association of America 1993. All rights reserved. Reprinted by permission.

3. Diagrammatic Reasoning in Logic

In the 1990s interest was reawakened in diagrammatic aids to specifically *logical* reasoning, resulting in several formal proofs that these methods, properly defined, meet standard criteria of logical systems. Similarly a program intending to place geometric diagrammatic reasoning on a sound formalist foundation has been undertaken by Miller (2000).

The major criteria of logical systems are soundness, completeness and consistency. *Soundness* means that no false theorem can be obtained. *Completeness* means all true theorems can be proved. *Consistency* means that no statement and its negation can both be proved. (An inconsistent system will also be unsound, because from a contradiction every statement can be proved with standard logic.)

To accomplish these goals, researchers have defined specific, formal rules for constructing and 'reading' logic diagrams. This work in essence translates diagrams into a linear, formal language which is far less familiar and 'perceptual' to the typical person than are diagrams. This work illustrates some important aspects of the issue of diagrammatic reasoning, specifically the need for dealing with construction and retrieval processes. Some of the details that are not important to my main argument, and which may be difficult to follow for those unfamiliar with formal notations, are given in appendices.

Euler circles

One well-known diagrammatic method used in logic is Euler Circles, which I discussed earlier. This is a device for representing certain classes of logical statements about the relations among sets. A circle is associated with a set by labeling the circle with a name for the set. Points within the circle represent members of the set and regions within the circle represent subsets of the set. Thus it is implicit that any point not within a circle represents something that is not a member of the set. A universal statement such as "All A are B" is represented by completely enclosing the A circle within the B circle. Thus it is perceptually automatic that any member of A (any point within the A circle) is also a member of B, that is, within the B circle. The proposition that "No C is B" is represented by constructing a circle C that does not overlap with B. Doing this construction after the one just mentioned necessarily results in the C circle not overlapping the A circle because to do so would force it to overlap the B circle which is forbidden by the rules of construction. From the result, Figure 22: Euler Circle Demonstration that No C is A, one can see that "No C is A".

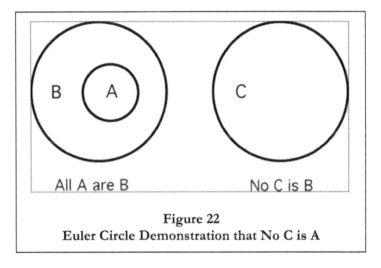

All A are B   No C is B

Figure 22
Euler Circle Demonstration that No C is A

The spatial structure exploited by Euler circles is quite limited. The rules for drawing them require, in addition to labeling, only the property of containment. Containment is a reflexive, asymmetric, transitive relation[19] and thus mirrors the structure of the subset relation. There is an *implicit* syntax in that circles are not allowed to overlap. The syntax is implicit because no ill-formed diagrams can be created if the rules are followed.

The same effect could be achieved in a linear notation by using parentheses to enclose a set label. Nested parentheses then reflect the subset relation and disjoint parentheses represent disjoint sets. The above example is thus equivalent to (B (A)) (C). The structure of sentences of the representation is partly linear in that they are merely a concatenation of symbols with no meaning given to other spatial (physical) relations. However, the representation is not strictly linear. Notice that there is an implicit syntax in this example: parentheses must come in pairs and certain arrangements are not

---

[19] A relation R is reflexive if xRx is true for all x in the domain of the relation, is asymmetric if xRy implies not yRx, and is transitive if xRy and yRz together imply xRz.

permitted.   Thus (A)) (((B) C) is ungrammatical for a number of reasons.   The parenthetic syntax is equivalent to the implicit syntax for Euler circles, but would be expressed in slightly different form by the construction and retrieval processes, making it slightly less 'diagrammatic.' On the other hand the parenthetic syntax mirrors the phrase structure of natural languages and thus is probably just as easy for a person to work with.

Even though the structure of Euler Circle notation is equivalent to that of a simple nested phrase language, the circles seem to achieve a slightly greater perspicuity. This is because adult human perception readily creates and recognizes the boundaries of simple closed curves, whereas seeing the relation between pairs of parentheses requires learning a convention, albeit a simple and fairly natural one.

Original Venn diagrams

Euler Circles are extremely limited in their expressive power and are unable to capture all elementary logical relationships. For example, there is no way to note that a circle is empty (that the set has no members) or that two circles overlap (that the sets contain some members in common but one is not necessarily a subset of the other). These limitations are overcome by an improvement called Venn Diagrams, devised by English logician John Venn (1834–1923); see Venn (1971). Venn Diagrams introduce new notations. First, circles for every pair of sets overlap. The region of overlap represents the elements common to both sets. The region not contained in any circle or other enclosed region implicitly represents all elements in the universe of discourse that are not members of any referenced set. One may consider the piece of paper on which the diagram is drawn to delimit this region. Shading a region means that the set denoted by that area is empty. This allows one to explicitly state, for example, that two sets have no intersection: their overlap is shaded.   The construction functions (rules) are also devised so that two areas denoting the same set cannot be constructed.

With these changes, Venn diagrams permit one to specify all possible relations among sets. However they still do not provide a notation for the existence of elements of a specified kind. Charles S. Peirce (1839–1914) added the convention that the presence of a symbol, an x, denotes the existence of at least one element in the smallest region containing the x.

Another limitation of the original Venn system was that existential disjunctions, for example "There exists an element either in area A or area B," could not be represented. Peirce introduced the convention that a chain of connected x's in different regions, called an x-sequence, denotes a multiple disjunction stating that an element exists in at least one of the regions. The Peirce modification of Venn's method is what is now generally called the method of Venn Diagrams in textbooks.

These modifications allow the representation of statements such as "Some As are Bs," by drawing overlapping circles A and B with an x in the overlap. "No As are Bs" is represented with overlapping circles in which the overlap is shaded. "All As are Bs" becomes two overlapping circles with shading in the portion of A not overlapping B. Some As are not Bs becomes overlapping circles with an x in the part of A that is not in the overlap with B.

The syllogism "All As are Bs, No Bs are Cs, therefore no As are Cs" is represented in Figure 23: A Venn Diagram. Since three sets are mentioned, three overlapping circles are drawn. The first premise then adds the darker shading and the second premise adds the lighter shading. The conclusion can then be 'read' from the diagram.

The x-sequence is irrelevant to this argument, but is added to illustrate the notation. It represents the proposition that "Some As are Bs", that is, there is at least one element in the intersection of A and B, but it could be in either of the subregions of that intersection. In this syllogism, "No Bs are Cs" implies that x can only exist in the higher region. In Aristotelian logic, "All As are Bs" implies "Some As are Bs." In contemporary symbolic logic this is not the case: A may be empty. The Aristotelian "Some As are Bs" proposition is irrelevant to the syllogism represented here but is included to illustrate the use of x-sequences.

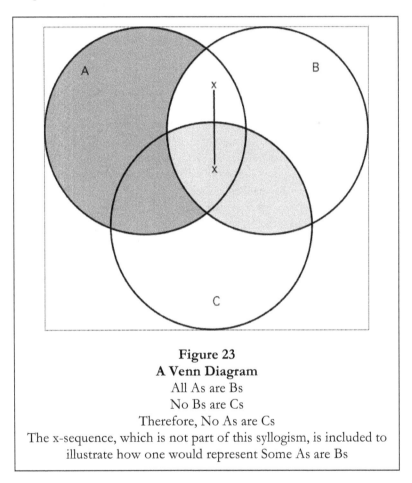

Figure 23
A Venn Diagram
All As are Bs
No Bs are Cs
Therefore, No As are Cs
The x-sequence, which is not part of this syllogism, is included to
illustrate how one would represent Some As are Bs

In simple cases the diagram is constructed from the premises and the conclusion is then retrieved from the diagram, using the obvious perceptual processes, as above. More complex deductions are possible, however, by using diagrammatic manipulations. For example, if a new circle is added that subdivides a region containing an x, then x's are added to each of the new sub-regions and they are connected into a sequence or 'spliced into' a previously existing x-sequence. This rule reflects the fact that it is known that an element exists in at least one of the sub-regions because one was known to exist in the initial region.

Are Venn diagrams, like Euler circles, equivalent to linear-hierarchical notations? We certainly can encode a simple Venn diagram as a linear string of symbols. For example, overlapping circles A and B are represented with parentheses as (A(B)). But notice that this now violates the usual rule for nesting of parentheses, for the intended groupings overlap: the first left parenthesis and the first right parenthesis are paired, while the second left parenthesis and the second right parenthesis are paired, whereas the usual rule would pair the inner and outer groups. We could solve this problem by introducing a new convention of labeled parentheses to indicate grouping pairs: [A(B]). Adding additional circles that overlap with both A and B is however not possible, and adding sequences of x's would leave a spaghetti-like mess. Thus Venn Diagrams do in fact make use of two dimensional representations, that is, they are truly diagrammatic. However, they do not use full geometric structure.

Work by Shin and others begins with the Peirce extensions of Euler-Venn diagrams, and casts them in more precise language by creating rules that replace the informal definitions given above with precise definitions of what constitutes a logic diagram. Shin's rules are given in the style of formal definitions rather than process descriptions. The rules do not use the full geometric structure of the diagrams. Rather, there are specific rules for adding and subtracting elements from diagrams without regard to metric properties. Furthermore, they are not algorithmic, that is, they do not specify precise computer programs but rely on un-formalized human perception and knowledge for their application. Finally, when a diagram has been modified appropriately (usually by simplifying it) a conclusion may be 'read' from it by the use of specific retrieval functions (rules). (Wang (1995) has introduced a more general descriptive language for diagrams and devised a semantics for the language that he is able show maintains consistency and soundness. This permits the representation of diagrams in a formal calculus, although the diagram elements are not perceptual objects. I will not describe this work further.)

Venn- I: Shin's initial formalization

Shin (1994) has re-stated the Venn-Peirce method in a system she calls Venn-I, following the formalist convention of inductively defining the set of well-formed diagrams. Her rules of diagram well-formedness are given in Table 10: Syntactic Rules for Format of Venn-I Representations. The system begins with a 'unique rectangle' that defines the universe of discourse; every Venn-I diagram includes this rectangle and all other elements lie within it. (*Region* and *minimal region* have been previously defined in the obvious ways.)

The set of recursive definitions in Table 10 produces only well-formed diagrams in Venn-I. The definitions would need to be restated in order to put them in the form of processes. While it appears that it would be straightforward to translate these into construction processes that produce only well-formed diagrams, there are some subtle difficulties that will be described presently.

The operations (rules of inference) of Venn-I are designed to preserve well-formedness and to yield only diagrams that are logical consequences of those one starts with. Shin shows that the resulting system is sound and complete. Her completeness theorem is a finite version, that is, if D is a logical consequence of a finite set of diagrams, then D is provable from that set: there exists a set of transformations on the set that will yield D.

Table 10

Syntactic Rules for Format of Venn-I Representations

From S.-J. Shin, *The logical status of diagrams*, page 57. © Cambridge University Press 1994. Reprinted with the permission of Cambridge University Press and the author.

The set of well-formed diagrams, say $\mathcal{D}$, is the smallest set satisfying the following rules:

(1) Any unique rectangle drawn in a plane is in set $\mathcal{D}$.

(2) If D is in set $\mathcal{D}$, and if D' results by adding a closed curve interior to the rectangle of D satisfying the partial-overlapping rule (described subsequently) and the avoid-x rule (described subsequently), then D' is in set $\mathcal{D}$.

Partial-overlapping rule: A new closed curve introduced into a given diagram should overlap a *proper part* of *every* existent *nonrectangular* minimal region of that diagram once and *only* once.

Avoid-x rule: A new closed curve introduced into a given diagram should avoid every x of every existing x-sequence of that diagram.

(3) If D is in set $\mathcal{D}$, and if D' results by shading some entire region of D, the D' is in set $\mathcal{D}$.

(4) If D is in set $\mathcal{D}$, and if D' results by adding an x to a minimal region of D, then D' is in set $\mathcal{D}$.

(5) If D is in set $\mathcal{D}$, and if D' results by connecting existing x's by lines (where each x is in a different region), then D' is in set $\mathcal{D}$.

Extensions of Venn models

Shin later introduced a more expressive system, Venn-II, that can represent propositions with truth-functional connectives; she then proves the soundness and finite-completeness of this system as well. Hammer & Danner (1996) use essentially the same system as Venn-I but are able to remove the finiteness restriction from the completeness proof. See Appendix C: Hammer-Danner Venn Analysis.

Peirce alpha graphs

Peirce extended the ideas of Euler and Venn in other ways to permit diagrammatic reasoning about a larger class of logical problems. Doing so, however, has reduced further the naturalness of the diagram representation. Peirce diagrams still use parts of two-dimensional geometric structure to encode logical relations, but the perceptual processes needed to read these diagrams are less familiar and thus require more training in their application. Peirce's intention was to provide visual notation that related compound structures in a way that was more perspicuous than traditional linear-hierarchical notations. In other words, he was not trying to improve the power of logic or derive new theorems, but to improve the understanding of it.

There are two classes of Peirce diagrams, which he called alpha graphs and beta graphs. In alpha graphs, set labels are again enclosed in closed curves (which Peirce called *cuts*). However, the interpretation of enclosure differs from the Euler-Venn convention: (i) a cut negates its contents, and (ii) items in the same cut represent the conjunction of the items. Figure 24: A Peirce Alpha Graph thus represents the proposition "Not (A and B and Not-C)" which is logically equivalent to "If A and B then C." Once again rules of transformation are employed to make inferences. One formulation of these rules is given in Table 11: Construction Rules for Peirce Alpha Graphs.

These rules are truth preserving. For example *insertion in odd* applied to *A(B)* can yield *A(BC)*. That is, "A or not-B" implies "A or not(B and C)." Hammer has characterized Peirce alpha graphs and their transformations and proved that the resulting system is sound and complete (Hammer (1996)).

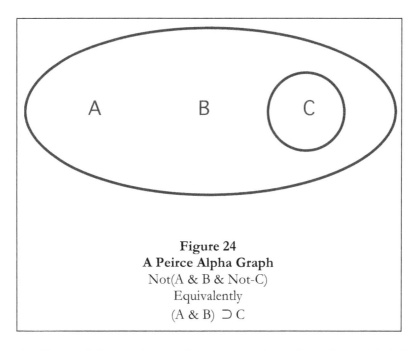

Figure 24
A Peirce Alpha Graph
Not(A & B & Not-C)
Equivalently
(A & B) ⊃ C

Clearly, Peirce alpha graphs can be rendered in a linear-hierarchical form, using parentheses according to the usual conventions. In fact, they usually are because it makes typesetting easier. Thus Figure 24 becomes (A B (C)). Again, the 'diagrammatic' notation may be more perspicuous because it employs some spatial perceptual processes rather than learned conventions, but the difference is minor. The structure of space exploited by Peirce alpha graphs is also accordingly minimal. On the other hand, by using containment to represent negation, the notation no longer neatly maps that spatial relation onto one with similar structure. The result is a mis-match that requires some effort to embrace and which provides little diagrammatic support.

Whether Peirce alpha graphs achieve the goal of increasing understanding is debatable and may come down to a matter of taste, basically meaning familiarity.

Table 11

Construction Rules for Peirce Alpha Graphs

From E. Hammer, Peircean Graphs for Propositional Logic, In G. Allwein and J. Barwise (Eds.), *Logical reasoning with diagrams, 1996,* pages 137-138. By permission of Oxford University Press, Inc.

Insertion in Odd Suppose X is a subgraph of G' falling within an odd number of cuts, and suppose G is a graph that results from G' by erasing that occurrence of X. Then one can obtain G' from G by Insertion in Odd.

Erasure in Even Suppose X is a subgraph of G falling within an even number of cuts (or else no cuts), and suppose G' is a graph that results from G by erasing that occurrence of X. Then one can obtain G' from G by Erasure in Even.

Double Cut This rule has three different parts.

1. Let X be a subgraph of G where $G = x_1 \ldots x_m X x_{m+1} \ldots x_n$. Then one can obtain $x_1 \ldots x_m ((X)) x_{m+1} \ldots x_n$ from G by double cut, and one can obtain G from $x_1 \ldots x_m((X))x_{m+1} \ldots x_n$ by double cut.

2. Similarly, if $G = x_1 \ldots x_m x_{m+1} \ldots x_n$, then one can obtain from G $x_1 \ldots x_m(())x_{m+1} \ldots x_n$ or vice versa by this rule.

3. Finally, the graph (()) consisting of two cuts is an axiom.

Iteration G' is obtainable from G by Iteration if and only if (1) there is a subgraph X of G' falling within cuts $C_1, \ldots, C_n$, (2) there is another instance of X in G' that occurs within at least the cuts $C_1, \ldots, C_n$ (and possibly others) of G', and (3) G results from G' by erasing this second, more deeply enclosed instance of X.

Deiteration G' is obtainable from G by Deiteration if and only if G is obtainable from G' by the rule of iteration.

Juxtaposition One can infer the juxtaposition of $G_1, \ldots, G_n$ from $G1, \ldots, G_n$. Conversely, one can infer any G_i, $1 \le i \le n$, from the juxtaposition of $G_1, \ldots, G_n$.

Peirce beta graphs

Neither Venn diagrams, even as augmented by Peirce, nor Peirce alpha graphs are sufficiently expressive to handle all important features that standard symbolic formalisms do. For example, while they are able to state the there is an entity with property P, they are not able to state that two entities are in relation R. Furthermore, while they are able to state negation, conjunction, and disjunction, they are not able to express universal and existential quantification. Peirce invented Beta Graphs to enable the expression of these features. More details are given in Appendix D: Peirce Beta Graphs.

Logic diagrams and perception

It is important to recall once again that all computations, including all logical deductions, are *physical processes (the interactions of physical particles)*. To be fully formalized a description of a computation must reduce it to physical processes. Conventional proofs in mathematics are not presented this way, and typically the difficulties of doing so are not appreciated. Every conventional mathematical proof assumes a human interpreter with human perceptual and cognitive abilities. It also assumes a physical world in which the interpreter and the notational systems are embedded and whose laws they must obey.

This is true of both informal arguments and standard presentations in journals, which presume an enormous amount of knowledge on the part of the reader, including the ability to understand the natural language in which the proof is embedded. However, it is also true of the most highly formalized proofs that follow as closely as possible the ideal of the formalist program. There the presumed abilities are much simpler but nonetheless not trivial. The proof assumes that the interpreter can correctly recognize all *tokens* of a formula *type* no matter what physical representation it appears in. It also assumes an ability to parse the expressions and make correct substitutions for variables. Indeed the formalist approach was constructed to make these assumptions plausible. Nonetheless they are not unproblematic. Furthermore, when one strictly adheres to the program to make the assumption plausible, the proofs grow to such complexity and opacity that they are not comprehensible to the un-aided human mind and must be verified by computer program, which process has is own difficulties, as noted earlier.

In the case of the above work that demonstrates soundness, completeness and consistency of certain logic diagram systems, the plausibility of the token representation assumption is greatly challenged. Rather than merely requiring, say, that all A's are recognized as equivalent, one must assume, among other things, that the interpreter recognizes all members of the class of closed curves.

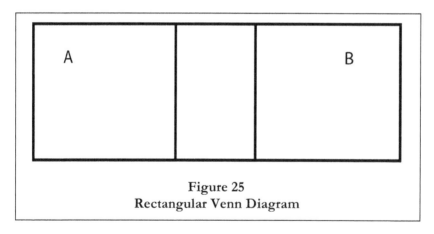

Figure 25
Rectangular Venn Diagram

In Figure 25: Rectangular Venn Diagram, rectangles rather than the usual circles have been used. In terms of the construction and retrieval rules any closed curves of any size would suffice, and this is how the Shin rules are presented. If the reader is accustomed to seeing Venn diagrams with circles, the rectangular form will be more difficult to follow. Consider drawing the diagram with rectangles having overlapping sides, as in Figure 25 as compared with circles as in Figure 26: Circular Venn Diagram.

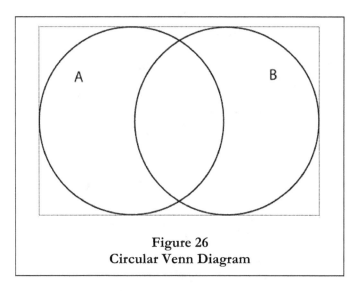

Figure 26
Circular Venn Diagram

With rectangles an ambiguity is introduced. Does the figure consist of (i) three disjoint rectangles, or (ii) two overlapping ones, or (iii) one large rectangle with a smaller one inside? To what does "A" refer? The ambiguity can be resolved by adopting the convention that all rectangles are of the same size, but this adds another step of propositional interpretation, one that cannot be done by merely examining the outlines.

Thus circles are better choices than rectangles not simply because they are familiar, but because resolving the ambiguity of the overlaps is easier. Note that a diagram such as Figure 26 could also be interpreted as consisting of three shapes sharing common boundaries. However, this interpretation is not what the diagram first suggests. This perceptual fact was recognized, though not explained, by the Gestalt principle of 'good form.'

Although any closed curve will in principle work for Venn diagrams, if one chooses arbitrary and differing shapes such as illustrated in Figure 27: Irregular Venn Diagram, the human perceptual processes become so laborious and problematic that the method loses it power. (Note that the Hammer-Shin rules do require that the intersections of shapes be a single region, but it is even difficult to determine if this rule is violated in Figure 27.)

Of course, the diagrams already have propositional conventions that must be understood for them to work. For example, it must be understood that a label such as "A" within a region refers to the interior of a region, and that the region referenced is not necessarily the minimal region delimited by the nearest boundary. The scope of x's must similarly be understood.

The Shin/Hammer-Danner rules for Venn Diagrams presuppose that shapes, including minimal regions, are readily apparent. The rules do not specify precise procedures for detecting them. As I have noted, this is also common practice in standard formal predicative descriptions: it is assumed that multiple copies of the same symbol can be identified, and so forth. *It is only because such abilities are so easy and natural for human perception that no one bothers to spell them out.*

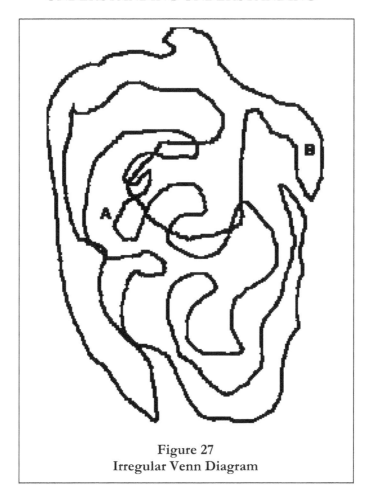

Figure 27
Irregular Venn Diagram

Of course contemporary computers avoid the problem altogether by using an input device (a keyboard). This eliminates the problem by assigning it to another part of the design process. One might do the same with Venn notation by devising an input device of an appropriate design, although this would be more difficult.

In discussing the use of well-formedness to deal with generalization, Hammer and Danner state ". . . we consider this to be entirely analogous to the question of when two sentence tokens are tokens of the same sentence (Hammer & Danner (1996), p114)." Indeed it is. Again we must remind ourselves, however, that this solution is not a fully formalized account, nor is it in the case of sentences. The definitions and rules presume accurate perceptual processes that detect connected regions, for example, just as formal language descriptions presume accurate perceptual processes that detect equivalent letters in different fonts or sizes. These processes are physical processes and to be made fully precise need to be defined in physical process terms without any reliance upon poorly understood, if familiar, psychological/neural processes. Since all computations are physical processes, the rules implicitly assume certain properties of these physical processes, such as that copying a symbol from one place to another does not change it. Formalization seeks to ask very little of the physical processes, so that it is acceptable to the intuition of everyone that such processes exist and have the properties (such as permanence of identity) that are needed to implement the intended logical operations. *This strategy implicitly recognizes the necessity for an interpreter, but avoids attempting to define one precisely. Until one has a robot, complete with sense organs and a motor system, that can be presented actual physical proofs that it can recognize and study, there will remain an incompleteness to this analysis and the entire research program.*

4. Diagrammatic Reasoning in Physics

Some work has been done on representing and reasoning about physical processes. This work addresses the geometry of physical situations, but in addition considers other factors such as mass, force, and electrical properties.

Bitpict

An architecture for diagrammatic reasoning is being developed by George Furnas and colleagues [Furnas, Qu, Shrivastave & Peters (2000); Furnas (1992)]. Bitpict represents diagrams with a pixel array and provides a suite of cellular automaton-like processes for modifying them. That is, a Bitpict rule examines the context of a pixel, and based on the values in the contextual cells it alters the value of the focus pixel. The rule is applied to each pixel in the array to effect global changes.

Furnas shows how programs written with rules of this sort can simulate movement of physical objects, and do computations such as counting the number of aggregations of marked pixels and representing the result, literally, as a Roman numeral. Bitpict clearly makes use of the ordering and dimensionality properties of two-dimensional space, but exploiting additional features of space must be done by clever writing of rules and selection of initial conditions. The most interesting thing about this work is that it reduces all computations to the manipulation of pixel values, justifying the claim that it operates 'with diagrams only.' Of course the reasoning – the interpretation of results – is done by a human interpreter.

Inter-diagrammatic reasoning

A system with goals and computational style similar to Bitpict is the Inter-diagrammatic Reasoning System (IDR) of Michael Anderson and colleagues [Anderson (1996); Anderson & McCartney (1995); Anderson & McCartney (1997); Anderson & McCartney (2003)].

The similarity is that Anderson's system provides a set of processes that manipulate pixels in pixel array representations of diagrams. These processes take two or more diagrams as input, may mask them so that only specified portions are examined, and produce an output array whose pixels' values are logical combinations of the input values. There are syntactic and control structure differences between Bitpict and IDR. For example, Bitpict applies its rules to every pixel, whereas IDR can focus on portions of the diagrams. IDR examines more than one diagram whereas Bitpict makes sequential changes in a single array. In spite of these differences, the two systems can accomplish the same things, they make use of the same, limited structural features of two-dimensional space (plus other features such as color that can be encoded as pixel values), and ostensibly operate 'with diagrams only.' As with all systems (including

ARCHIMEDES), a human user must intelligently employ the computational repertoire provided to accomplish a task.

AVOW diagrams

Peter Cheng has devised a number of very clever specialized representational systems for diagrammatic reasoning. My favorite to date is AVOW (ampere, volt, ohm, watt) diagrams because they neatly illustrate a specialized partial mapping of the structure of a subject (in this case elementary circuit theory) onto a portion of the structure of two-dimensional space. See Figure 28: An AVOW Diagram Element.

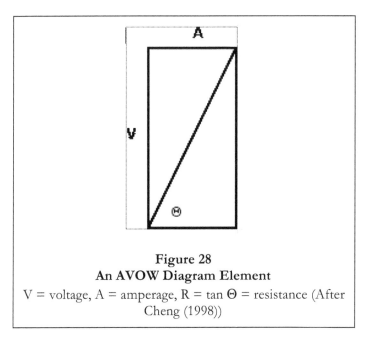

Figure 28
An AVOW Diagram Element
V = voltage, A = amperage, R = tan Θ = resistance (After Cheng (1998))

An element of an AVOW diagram is a rectangle whose width is proportional to the magnitude of an electrical current (amperage) and whose height is proportional to the magnitude of an electrical potential (voltage). Since by Ohm's Law, voltage = amperage x resistance, resistance (in ohms) is the ratio of the height to the width of the rectangle, that is, the tangent of the angle a diagonal of the rectangle makes with its amperage side. Furthermore, since voltage x amperage = wattage, the area of an AVOW rectangle represents power.

The inferencing that AVOW diagrams provide comes from the fact that each simple electrical component (a resistor, say) can be represented as a rectangle, and these can be adjoined in a manner that reflects the topology of an electrical circuit. Global properties of the circuit, such as its total voltage drop and total resistance, can then be read from the composite diagram with the same perceptual mechanisms as used for a single rectangle (i.e., measuring lengths, widths, areas, and angles). These processes exactly mirror the algebraic descriptions and solutions of the circuit using Kirchhoff's Laws (the basic laws of electrical circuits), but they represent them in a way that relates them to geometry and this has greater intuitive appeal to those without extensive experience with the algebraic analysis of circuits. See Figure 29: An AVOW Circuit.

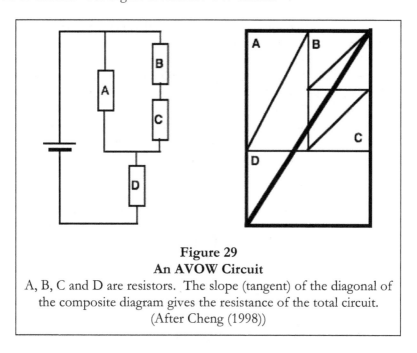

Figure 29
An AVOW Circuit
A, B, C and D are resistors. The slope (tangent) of the diagonal of
the composite diagram gives the resistance of the total circuit.
(After Cheng (1998))

5. Diagrammatic Reasoning with Graphs

The uses of spatial reasoning in the understanding of logic, geometry, and elementary physics are important subjects for study because the issues are simplified. I have called diagrammatic reasoning about Euclidean plane geometry the 'fruit-fly' of diagrammatic reasoning because it is the most simple and direct application. Of course, there are other important uses of diagrammatic reasoning, such as graphs and charts. These are ubiquitous in scientific publications as well as the popular press, and are extremely powerful ways of summarizing and conveying scientific and other knowledge because they can be used to represent arbitrary quantities and abstract relations.

Graphs in general, even simple two-axes graphs where one variable is plotted against another, use fewer spatial properties than geometric diagrams, but this makes their construction and interpretation more, not less, difficult. Indeed, while a trained scientist may find a graph highly revealing, untrained laymen often find graphs more confusing than verbal descriptions. This is because the layman has not learned the host of conventions that scientists know about the use of labels, transformed scales (such as logarithmic ones), the representation of parameters by multiple lines, and common patterns (such as that two non-parallel lines indicate an interaction of variables). The list of conventions is very long, and even trained scientists take significant time to understand a complex graph.

Another reason graphs are frequently difficult to understand is that many scientists are not very good at constructing good ones. Tufte (1983) provides a set of guidelines that if followed would improve scientific communication, but the rules themselves are not always easy to follow, and it is often difficult to predict an audience's confusion, just as it is difficult for a writer or speaker to see other than his intended meaning in an ambiguous sentence.

The situation is even more complex when graphs and other graphics attempt to render three-dimensional objects (such as the relations among three variables) on a two-dimensional plane. Again, conventions are necessary and these must be learned and widely shared in order for an observer to map the graphic onto spatial structure in the intended manner [see, e.g., Cleveland & McGill (1985); Shah (2002); Shah & Carpenter (1995); Shah, Mayer & Hegarty (1999)].

Today the situation is yet more complicated as computers and video permit dynamic presentations. Clearly it is often revealing to watch a three-dimensional structure 'rotate' and easier to detect cyclic behavior in a time-varying pattern than it is to see it in a static two-dimensional graph. However, understanding all that 3-D motion reveals may not be easy.

I will not review the literature on the psychology of graph interpretation. While the issues are complex, I feel that the way to analyze them successfully is to understand the need to relate graphs to spatial structure by explicitly mapping the relational information to be conveyed into appropriate aspects of geometric space.

. . . .

My work, described in Chapter 8, (a) makes full use of the geometry of two dimensional space, (b) manipulates representations of diagrams as a way of making inferences and forming conjectures, and (c) is motivated primarily by psychological issues, specifically the human ability to understand through the use of grounded structures, perceptual processes, and abductive thinking. The projects just described above individually address some of these issues, but none combines all of them.

8 UNDERSTANDING WITH DIAGRAMS

Behold!
(Bhaskara, 12th century CE)

1. ARCHIMEDES

I have developed a computer program called ARCHIMEDES[20] to explore a way in which understanding might be achieved through the use of structure and structural manipulation.[21] ARCHIMEDES is not a psychological model nor an intelligent program. In fact it is not a program at all. It is a programming *language* in which one may construct programs. Languages such as this, whose purpose is to construct models of human or machine intelligence, are sometimes called *cognitive architectures*. They provide a syntax, data structure formats, and an inventory of functions that allow the construction of programs of a particular computational style. Since all cognitive architectures meet the very weak requirements for computational universality, all are weakly equivalent. That is, for any program that could be written in one of them, a program that performed the same computations could be written in any other. However, they are not strongly equivalent since the behavior of weakly equivalent programs need not be identical, particularly in time and memory efficiency and in the profile of efficiency across various problems.

ARCHIMEDES is a vehicle for developing and testing a computational theory of two dimensional spatial reasoning about plane geometry. It allows one to pose and test hypotheses about how representations of geometric objects are constructed and used in reasoning. The work is primarily motivated by an interest in human psychology, specifically how humans are able to understand. This motivation differs from most other

---

[20] The name ARCHIMEDES was chosen for this system to honor the great genius Archimedes who allegedly was killed by a soldier while working on geometry by drawing diagrams in the sand [Katz (1998), page 104]. Obviously this program can make no claim to being anything like its namesake, and it is not intended in any way to claim that, nor to diminish the greatness of one of history's finest geniuses.

[21] This work was supported by grants IRI-9203946 and IRI-9526942 from the United States National Science Foundation.

work done in artificial intelligence that explores the use of diagrams. That work is primarily concerned with practical applications or with artificial intelligence theory.

The system is far from a complete implementation of all possible forms of geometric structure manipulation, and I do not intend that it ever will be. Nor do I intend that it will be a practical system for either artificial intelligence or modeling human psychology. Rather my aim is to illustrate a viewpoint about geometric understanding and to explore in reasonable detail what such ideas entail.

ARCHIMEDES and a human presumably have in common certain fundamental perceptual and cognitive abilities, albeit implemented in different computational manners. Humans and programs written in the ARCHIMEDES architecture reason by diagram construction and manipulation rather than solely by logical formulas and rules. Each autonomously notices features of the diagram and makes use of this information. Each knows the basics of arithmetic and algebra, including such things as equivalence relations, commutativity of addition and so forth. Each is able to manipulate diagrams subject to constraints, such as rigid motion. Each can, under instruction, attend to certain properties of its diagram and verify or disconfirm the validity of claims about the diagram. However, humans have many additional abilities that ARCHIMEDES lacks.

ARCHIMEDES provides a representation system for diagrams. (Recall the characterization of a representation system given in Chapter 3, page 56.) It does not have perceptions, neural events, or mental images, but rather computer analogs of these. The construction and retrieval processes are functions defined in a programming language used to implement the system, and the format for representation is the potential set of expressions that *could* be formed from these functions. An ARCHIMEDES model of the White House *architectural plans* object (not of the White House itself) would be described with a set of data expressions (percepts-images) that preserve some of the information from the architectural drawings, which in turn preserve some of the information from the physical structure in Washington.

ARCHIMEDES' representations of diagrams are treated as first-class data objects. This means that the representations play essential roles in the behavior of the system and are not used merely as adjuncts to a primarily linguistic representation. *The 'physical' properties matter, even though these properties are simulated.*

The representations implement diagrammatic processing arithmetically. Locations of points are represented in a coordinate system. Distances and directions are computed numerically. This is possible because of the isomorphism between two-dimensional Euclidean geometry and analytic geometry. Every proposition of Euclidean geometry can be stated algebraically. Since digital computers are designed for and are highly efficient at numerical and other symbolic computation, such an implementation is an appropriate use of this hardware.

It is unlikely that the brain works in the same way, or that the conscious mind explicitly does all diagrammatic manipulations by numerical calculation. This fact, if it is a fact, does not mean that ARCHIMEDES is merely treating diagrams propositionally and numerically. Earlier I discussed levels of description, arguing that there is no canonical or real level, but only levels that work well or poorly for particular purposes. The appropriate level at which to describe ARCHIMEDES is the level of diagrammatic functions (manipulations, perceptions, constructions) rather than the numerical level.

Thus while the implementation of the model is numerical, the *appropriate description* of the model is not. Rather, it is properly described as performing diagrammatic *manipulations*, such as rotations and translations, diagrammatic *perception*, such as noticing equal lengths, parallel lines, and symmetry, and diagrammatic *constructions*, such as constructing a triangle or constructing equivalent angles. In principle these operations could be performed on a non-numeric representation. However, the model should be judged by asking: Are these diagrammatic functions a *sufficient* set (rather than a *necessary* set) for modeling the human psychological abilities they are intended to explain?

2. Symbols and References

We will be talking about a model of a human agent who is thinking about diagrams that refer to abstract objects. In order to keep the many levels of abstraction and reference clear it is important to begin with some basic distinctions. It is helpful to see how diagrammatic representations are similar to and different from the more transparent and familiar linguistic representations.

A word *is* an abstraction, an element of a language whose significance derives from the language's syntax, phonology, morphology and so forth. A number *is* an abstraction, an element of a mathematical system whose significance derives from the structure of that system.

A word may be *denoted* by a sign, just as a number may be *denoted* by a numeral. For this discussion a sign is a particular physical object, say specific molecules of ink on a specific piece of paper.

A numeral-sign *refers* to a number. A word-sign may also have a referent, which may be an abstraction or may be a physical object or event. Thus an instance of "Fido" refers to Fido, a specific dog. "Fido" has four letters, Fido has four legs. An instance of the sign "dogs" refers to the abstract class of all dogs. Words may refer to arbitrarily complex abstractions.

A geometric diagram is also a sign. The diagram, and parts of it, may also have referents, which could be real objects (in the case of architectural plans, for example) or abstractions, such as the class of all right triangles. Diagrams may refer to arbitrarily complex abstract or arbitrarily complex physical objects or events. I will restrict this discussion to geometric diagrams that refer to simple abstractions such as ideal points and ideal lines and things composed of them.

A sign can be treated as an instance of an arbitrarily large class of equivalent signs that share a referent. We can choose to ignore specific features of the word-sign, such as font, size, color and so forth. This is the way word-signs are normally treated. A diagram-sign can be treated in the same way, in which case it acts simply as a non-conventional word, a logo, for example. The usual way to treat a diagram-sign, however, is to attend to its particular physical structure. We could choose to use the diagram-sign purely as decoration, in which case we could focus *only* on its physical structure and not consider any referent for it. More typically, we also treat the diagram-sign as a reference to an object, such as a particular street layout in a particular city, or as an abstraction, such as the class of all right triangles. The distinction between word-signs and diagram-signs is thus one of convention: generally we ignore the physical properties of a word-sign and consider only its referent, whereas generally we consider both the referent and the physical properties of the diagram-sign. When we treat diagram-signs for the purpose of doing geometric reasoning, we further relate the geometric properties of the diagram-sign to the physical/geometric properties of its referent. However, we may also use a diagram-sign for non-geometric reasoning, in which case we may relate its physical properties to non-geometric properties of its referent.

When one looks at a sign, a percept of the sign is generated. A percept is a mental entity, presumably implemented in brain structures and processes. Word-signs may be aural as well as written; aural signs also lead to percepts. After a word is spoken, a memory of the percept continues in the brains of the hearers (including the speaker), in auditory short-term memory, and may be mentally recalled or rehearsed to prolong the memory. It also leads to further mental activity invoking linguistic processing that elicits other cognitive (non-perceptual) memories, generates new concepts or conclusions and so forth. If the word-sign is written, the percept persists only while one's visual attention remains on it. After it is removed, say by closing one's eyes, a memory of the percept continues in the brain, in visual short-term memory. It also leads to further mental activity invoking processing that elicits other memories, generates new concepts or conclusions and so forth.

The same analysis applies to visual diagram-signs. However, if one is treating them as physical objects they may be physically altered, say with ruler and straightedge while being visually attended to. In this process the percept of the diagram-sign changes as the diagram-sign changes. After one's eyes are closed, memories of the diagram-sign may continue as images in visual short-term memory. Cognitive activity may also continue to alter these memories producing other cognitive structures, just as cognitive activity that processes words linguistically may continue after the aural or visual word-sign is removed from the perceptual field. However, the processing of diagram-sign memories may consider the remembered physical properties of the diagram-sign, whereas linguistic processing typically does not consider the physical properties of the word-sign memory.

Thus we deal with diagrams in generally the same way as we deal with words, except that for diagrams the physical properties of the sign are considered to be relevant. To emphasize this, the cognitive structures generated by diagrams are called images. They are not simply short-term memories (or afterimages). Exactly *how* this processing takes place in either mind or brain terms is exactly as mysterious as in the case of linguistic processing, even though current brain imaging technology is gathering more and more information about *where* information is stored and *where* increased metabolic activity takes place for certain tasks.

In short, we must distinguish objects from percepts from images from neural events; and we must distinguish these things both for signs and for referents of signs. When the cognitive agent is a computer program, the analogs of neural events are physical computer states, and the analogs of both perceptions and cognitions are knowledge representations stated in a programming language. This adds another complexity if we are using the computer program to model psychological processes, especially if the computer does not have human perceptual and motor capabilities, that is, is not a robot with visual and motor systems. In particular, percepts and images are conflated. When a program manipulates a diagram representation this may be construed to simulate either human perceptual-motor manipulation of a physical diagram, or human mental manipulation of the image-memory of a diagram.

For example, architectural drawing is a knowledge representation system that uses (ignoring computer-aided design) t-squares and pencils to construct drawings, and human vision, abetted by knowledge of the notational conventions of the system, to observe them. The format is a characterization of those drawings that can be constructed from paper and graphite using t-squares and pencils. Physical properties of the object at 1600 Pennsylvania Avenue in Washington, D. C. could be referred to by a specific set of pieces of paper with specific placements of graphite, called "plans and elevations of the White House" which would constitute a representation-proper that itself exists in the real world. When perceived by an architect, the plans also give rise to perceptions, which exist in the mental world, and when remembered they give rise to images that also exist in the mental world. The architect can modify the actual plans with a pencil or could imagine doing so without actually altering the plans. A program that simulates an architect without actually using writing implements would also simulate the perceptual and motor activities of the architect in the same way that it simulates the architect's thinking about images of plans. This is the case with ARCHIMEDES but in the context of geometric diagrams rather than architectural plans.

3. Overview of ARCHIMEDES[22]

ARCHIMEDES has a basic representational system embedded in a larger control system that analyzes and generates demonstrations of some classes of plane geometry propositions.

I have called the three components of a knowledge representation system the *construction processes* (the methods used to create and modify records of information), the *retrieval processes* (the methods used to access the information recorded), and the *representation-proper*, which is the data structure in which specific information is actually recorded (see Chapter 3). The *format* is the grammar of representations-proper, that is, a characterization of what data structures are permitted. The format need not be explicitly defined, although it might be, but in any case is implicit in the definition of the construction processes. A specific *object* is represented by a *model*, whose structure obeys the rules of its format.

Pixel-nets

Pixel-nets are analogs of human perceptions but they are simulated perceptions because ARCHIMEDES has no sense organs. The pixel representation used by ARCHIMEDES is numerical and coarsely digitized; specifically, all pixels have integer coordinates. This decision has several implementation consequences. One could, instead, have allowed point coordinates to be real numbers. Of course in an actual digital computer any number must be of a limited precision. As is well-known, continuous functions and processes can be approximated to any desired degree of precision digitally. One may argue, then, that the chosen integer coordinate representation could be as nearly 'continuous' as is possible in a finite computer simply by extending the size of the array on which diagrams are drawn, that is by increasing resolution arbitrarily. This is what allows digital images – on television or computer screens – to appear as clear as 'continuous tone' photographs (which of course are not really continuous in tone, either). In other words, if the observer 'stands back' far enough the digitization cannot be

---

[22] The following sections are based on material in Lindsay (1998), *Computational Intelligence. 14(2)*, pp. 222-256. (© 1998 Basil Blackwell Publishers, Inc.).

detected. Such a process however has limits because it requires unrealistic amounts of memory and processing time.

The result of the decision to treat point coordinates as integers is that certain operations performed by ARCHIMEDES are approximate. There are only eight primary directions between adjacent points (corresponding to the eight major compass directions north, northeast, east, etc.). This means that when a 'straight' line is represented as a set of contiguous points it will appear on close inspection to be jagged unless it runs in one of the eight principal directions.[23]

One method adopted to deal with the problem introduced by coarse digitization of the diagram is a parameter, called *compliance, which designates an upper limit to the program's resolution. Any differences that are smaller than some *function* of *compliance are undetectable; the particular function depends upon the comparison being made. This device allows the same representation and the same set of processes to behave with different degrees of precision.

In this way, ARCHIMEDES can model *one* of the differences (resolution) between actual diagrams – equivalent to a physical diagram in the presence of a human observer – and imaged diagrams – mental recollections or constructions. In the former case, the program is a model of a person manipulating paper, pencil, straightedge, and compass, while in the latter case it is a model of a person using imagery. (There are distinctions other than resolution between these two modes of operation.)

The *compliance parameter is also the way ARCHIMEDES handles 'rounding errors.' If we created much larger diagrams the relative errors would be smaller, indeed could be made arbitrarily small. This however would increase computation time greatly. Since the purpose of the ARCHIMEDES development is to explore the use of semantic representations of geometry, no effort has been made to achieve efficient code. The *compliance device is thus just a way to avoid problems that are not of direct concern to this research.

Structures

Structures represent propositional information about a diagram, such as the fact that a generic segment has two end points and a generic triangle has three sides. A *particular* segment structure instance may record some specific information about a particular object, such as the length of a segment or the type (equilateral, right, etc.) of a triangle. It also records information linking that object to external representations, such as printed names or graphics on a monitor. It also may record relations, such as congruency, that have been imposed between or among objects. Finally, it records information that connects the structure to corresponding elements of the pixel-net representation. This is analogous to the case of architectural drawings, to which one appends pointers to additional information, such as window and door specifications.

---

[23] ARCHIMEDES does not use *anti-aliasing*, a standard computer graphic method for making lines *appear* less jagged to a human observer.

Processes

The *construction and retrieval processes* are programs. All construction and retrieval processes are compositions of a kernel set of subprograms.

Strategy processes control the use of construction and retrieval processes to achieve goals, such as testing a conjecture, constructing a diagram, or proving a theorem.

The inputs to ARCHIMEDES are geometric facts presented in a propositional form, such as `(congruent abc def)` meaning that triangles `abc` and `def` are congruent. One could say it perceives these inputs as strings of characters with its keyboard sense organ and driver software, and then the system decodes these characters to construct models. The outputs of the system are presented as a graphic display that is isomorphic to the pixel-net, augmented by propositional statements appropriate to the task.

4. Representation-Proper

The representation-proper of an object is a set of structures that record a two dimensional geometric diagram. It is, however, better thought of at the functional level as a set of points, lines and curves with labels, plus statements about the compound geometric models (polygons, etc.) that these create.

Points

The most fundamental structure encodes the concept of a point. Structures for specific composite objects such as lines and polygons are composites of instances of point structures. There are structures corresponding to points, lines, triangles, squares, rhombuses, rectangles, quadrilaterals, parallelograms, polygons, angles, circles, and ellipses.

For each point that has been constructed on a diagram there is a pair of structures. They are called a *gridpoint* and a *pointname*. A gridpoint specifies a pair of integers that are the coordinates of the point in a two-dimensional pixelnet array (called the *beach*). The beach is a pixel-net that comprises a finite, discrete, rectangular grid with points having integer coordinates; coordinates are called *indices*.

A gridpoint may have zero, one or more associated pointname structures if the point has been or will be referenced. Not all gridpoints have pointnames, but all pointnames have a single associated gridpoint. The pair of structures associated with a point, if both exist, are interconnected by symmetric links. There is exactly one gridpoint for each pair of integers within the dimensions set for the beach. In addition, each pointname has a *displayform* which is the printable/readable form of named objects. Points have single character displayforms.

Thus each point that has been named by input results in the construction of a displayform that connects to a pointname structure that points to a gridpoint structure to which it has been assigned. The gridpoint structure points back to the pointname which points back to the displayform. Should the named point be moved by a manipulation of the diagram, a different gridpoint would be associated with the pointname. A pointname can have other information associated with it (such as, perhaps, that it must remain fixed in location, that is, its assigned gridpoint may not be changed) and it can be referred to by other structures. Displayforms and gridpoints cannot be so annotated.

Table 12: ARCHIMEDES Point Structures presents the organization of the structures for points. Note that gridobjects record location and metric information and objectnames record constraints that have for one reason or another been placed on the associated object. A *predicate* is a function that evaluates to either true or false. It is possible that the gridpoint associated with displayform a is also associated with another pointname whose displayform is c, and that the gridpoint associated with b is associated with another pointname whose displayform is d. (See Figure 30: Relations of pointname, gridpoints, coordinates, other point information.)

Table 12
ARCHIMEDES Point Structures
pointnames properties (value types)
displayform (a string)
gridpoint (a gridpoint structure)
constraints (a predicate)
locationstatus ("arbitrary," "fixed," or "constrained")
condition ("free" or "held")
gridpoints have these properties and (value types)
names (a list of pointname structures)
labels (a list of pointname structures)
x-index (an integer)
y-index (an integer)
color ("black," "white," etc.)
east-neighbor (a gridpoint structure)
northeast-neighbor (a gridpoint structure)
north-neighbor (a gridpoint structure)
northwest-neighbor (a gridpoint structure)
west-neighbor (a gridpoint structure)
southwest-neighbor (a gridpoint structure)
south-neighbor (a gridpoint structure)
southeast-neighbor (a gridpoint structure)
east-pull (a floating point number)
northeast-pull (a floating point number)
north-pull (a floating point number)
northwest-pull (a floating point number)
west-pull (a floating point number)
southwest-pull (a floating point number)
south-pull (a floating point number)
southeast-pull (a floating point number)

CHAPTER 8: UNDERSTANDING WITH DIAGRAMS

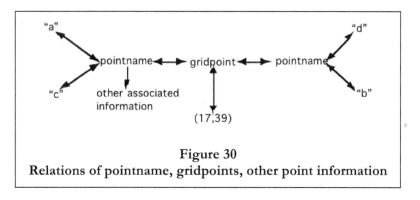

Figure 30
Relations of pointname, gridpoints, other point information

Each class of geometric *object* (line segment, triangle, square, etc.) that ARCHIMEDES can deal with has an analogous set of three structures associated with it: displayform, objectname, and gridobject. For each instance of an object type that has been constructed on a particular beach there is an instance of a gridobject, at least one instance of an objectname, and for each objectname there is at least one displayform. For example, a line segment from point a to point b has a segmentname with displayforms ab and ba and each of these segmentnames is associated with the same gridsegment. ARCHIMEDES may *notice* (see below) that a line segment exists between c and d, and will construct a gridsegment with a segmentname which has two displayforms, cd and dc. Thus there is a many-to-one mapping of displayforms onto objectname for all object types. In fact all 'natural' displayforms are created for an objectname to make reference easy. Thus a triangle whose vertices are points a, b, and c has six displayforms abc, acb, bac, bca, cab, and cba. If the usual convention of counter-clockwise naming were followed, only three would be needed. All six are made available simply for convenience. A square whose vertices are d, e, f, and g has only four displayforms defg, efgd, fgde, and gdef, preserving the convention of naming the object in the counterclockwise order of its vertices to shorten the list of possible names.

Constructing points and objects

Objects may come into being in two ways. They may be explicitly defined by the person who is exploring the system behavior (by *instruction*) or they may arise through action of the system (*noticing*). If three segmentnames have been constructed (either by instruction or by noticing) and these three form a triangle, then a gridtriangle and a trianglename are automatically constructed and associated with its six displayforms that are the permutations of the concatenated pointname displayforms. Since points may have multiple names, two coincident triangles may have two trianglenames with a total of 12 or more displayforms. Thus ARCHIMEDES treats the coincident triangles as distinct objects with different sets of names. This, for example, permits the movement of one of them while the other remains fixed. See Figure 31: Coincident triangles. The purpose of the automatic creation of displayforms is simply to reduce the burden of memory on the user interacting with it.

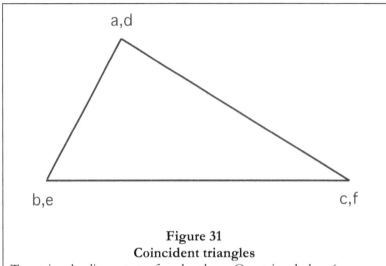

Figure 31
Coincident triangles
Two triangles lie on top of each other. One triangle has 6 names, corresponding to the 6 permutations of abc, and the other has 6 names corresponding to the 6 permutations of def. There is no triangle "abf" or other such mixtures unless and until one is noticed.

The structures for segments and triangles are shown in Table 13: Archimedes Rectilinear Objects. The structures for the other rectilinear figures have essentially the same format as that of triangles. The structures of the non-rectilinear figures (circles and ellipses) are given in Table 14: Archimedes Curvilinear Objects.

The explicit construction of three segments that cross one another could yield a triangle, as in Figure 32: Implicitly Constructed Triangle. If the points of intersection have not been previously defined and hence lack names, neither the segments that are the sides of the triangle nor the triangle itself will be known to ARCHIMEDES, that is, no gridtriangle or trianglename will be constructed. If the system is in a noticing mode, which may be by instruction or because it is automatically monitoring its diagram, the intersection points will be named, the side segments will be constructed and named, the triangle will be named and all the appropriate structures and displayforms will be created.

A particular instance of an ARCHIMEDES object corresponds to what for a person would be an annotated diagram on a piece of paper, plus associated knowledge about that class of objects, plus specific information about this one instance.

Table 13
ARCHIMEDES Rectilinear
Objects
segmentnames
have these slots (value types):
displayform (a string)
gridsegment (a gridsegment structure)
lengthstatus ("arbitrary" or "fixed")
lengthconstraints (a predicate)
bearingstatus ("arbitrary" or "fixed")
bearingconstraints (a predicate)
premises (a list of conditions)
gridsegments
have these slots (value types):
names (a list of segmentname structures)
labels (a list of segmentname structures)
end-1 (a pointname structure)
end-2 (a pointname structure)
segmentpoints (list of gridpoints)
segmentcolor ("black" or "white")
length (a floating point number)
bearing (a floating point number)
trianglenames
have these slots (value types):
gridtriangle (gridtriangle structure)
scalene (t or nil)
isoceles (t or nil)
equilateral (t or nil)
right (t or nil)
vertex-1-type (string)
vertex-2-type (string)
vertex-3-type (string)
side-1-type (string)
side-2-type (string)
side-3-type (string))
gridtriangles
have these slots (value types):
names (list of trianglename structures)
vertex-1 (gridpoint structure)
vertex-2 (gridpoint structure)
vertex-3 (gridpoint structure)
side-1 (gridsegment structure)
side-2 (gridsegment structure)
side-3 (gridsegment structure)

Table 14
ARCHIMEDES Curvilinear
Objects
Circlenames
have these slots (value types):
displayform (a string of letters)
gridcircle (a gridcircle structure)
sizestatus ("arbitrary" or "fixed")
sizeconstraints (a predicate)
positionstatus (a symbol)
gridcircles
structures have these slots (value types):
names (a list of circlenames)
radius (a floating-point number)
center (a gridpoint)
circumference-points (a list of gridpoints)
area (a floating-point number)
ellipsenames
have these slots (value types):
displayform (a string of letters)
gridellipse (a gridellipse structure)
sizestatus ("arbitrary" or "fixed")
sizeconstraints (a predicate)
positionstatus "arbitrary" (a symbol)
gridellipses
structures have these slots (value types):
minor-axis-length (a floating-point number)
focus-1 (a gridpoint)
focus-2 (a gridpoint)
circumference-points (a list of gridpoints)
area (a floating-point number)

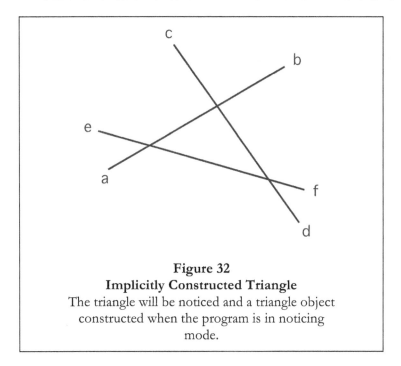

Figure 32
Implicitly Constructed Triangle
The triangle will be noticed and a triangle object
constructed when the program is in noticing
mode.

5. Construction Processes

The construction processes are intended to correspond to the abilities that I presume humans routinely use in reasoning with geometric diagrams. They embody both a knowledge of spatial relations and how constraints restrict alterations of diagrams. Propositional knowledge about a diagram may be stated and used, but in the service of manipulation rather than deduction.

There are four classes of processes that create and modify representations-proper.

Description constructions are instructions about how to construct and alter a diagram to illustrate a proposition. One type of description construction specifies that a new segment or other component of the diagram is to be created with a specified relation to already created components. For example, (`construct-triangle a b c`) creates a structure for three points and assigns them coordinates if they do not already exist, and constructs three segments and one triangle. *Propositional-notations* permit the explicit introduction of algebraic and geometric knowledge that has not been previously available to the system, for example, a formula for the area of a figure.

A second type of construction specifies *situation constraints*. These are properties that the program is to attribute to already existing components, for example that a specific segment must remain of fixed length or that a specific object is rigid. Thus (`congruent abc def`) establishes a constraint property predicate that evaluates true when **ab** = **de**, etc. Situation constraints contrast with the constraints that follow from spatial properties (topological and geometric relations) that are inherent in the representation scheme itself and are always enforced.

A third type of construction is a *simulation construction*, in which one or more objects are moved with the remaining components being altered as required by the spatial and situation constraints of the problem. For example, (move a b) moves point a to the location of b, and 'drags along' anything rigidly attached.

A fourth type of construction is the *rearrangement construction* in which part of a diagram is moved elsewhere not by the gradual movement of simulation, but by a discrete jump. Such constructions depend upon the existence of specific knowledge by which the system knows such movements are permitted and will 'work.' Such knowledge is given to the system in a variety of ways, but is not always available. For example, *if* the system knows that congruent triangles may be superimposed *and* that two triangles are congruent if their corresponding sides are of equivalent lengths, then it may make the rearrangement construction that moves one on top of the other. In the course of this, the system creates a simulation construction program, expressed as ARCHIMEDES functions, that could perform this movement (for example, translate point a to point d while bringing along triangle abc, then rotate triangle abc about point a until it coincides with triangle def).

Description constructions

ARCHIMEDES has no visual input system; it must be given a diagram by explicit definition of components. For each object type there is a process that creates an instance, another that copies an instance, and another that erases an instance.

One can define a point, giving it a displayform and a location. This causes the construction of a pointname structure, a gridpoint structure, and a pointname-displayform variable denoted by a single character, with their properties set to default values unless otherwise specified. Points thus constructed may be referred to by functions that construct segments, that is, that create a segmentname structure, a gridsegment structure, and two segmentname-displayforms.

One can construct a triangle by first constructing three points and the three segments connecting them, and then constructing a triangle (that is, the structures) by explicitly calling a triangle construction function. It is also possible to simply call the triangle construction function once its vertices have been constructed; the segments will be constructed automatically.

Another way to construct a triangle is to construct its vertices and sides, and then evaluate the **notice-new-objects** function, described below. This will discover that the three segments do in fact form a triangle, and will construct the required structures to represent it. The same procedure can be used with other rectilinear figures. Curvilinear figures (circles and ellipses) can only be constructed by instruction; they cannot be noticed.

The repertoire of construction functions includes means to construct a variety of constrained situations. For example, (**construct-and-name-perpendicular-from-pointname** *segment:de point:c*) constructs a segment perpendicular to an existing line from a point not on the line.

In addition to these basic functions there are a number of more complex description constructions that are composed of the basic ones. For example, (**construct-square-on-segment** *:segment ab :direction clockwise*) constructs a square with *ab* as one side. *direction* determines on which side of *ab* the square will lie: *clockwise* means point c lies to the right of directed segment a to b.

CHAPTER 8: UNDERSTANDING WITH DIAGRAMS

Construction of situation constraints

There are a number of construction functions that serve to establish constraints on a particular diagram. For example (`fix-pointname a`) will record that the position of point *a* is not to be altered, by marking the property location-status as "fixed." If *a* is the endpoint of a segment and its other endpoint *b* is also fixed, then the segment will not be movable. If *b* is not fixed, moving it may cause a stretching or shrinking of the segment since *a* is not allowed to move. If the length of the segment has also been fixed along with point *a*, any attempt to move *b* other than to rotate it around *a* will fail because the segment cannot stretch or shorten. If length is fixed but neither endpoint is fixed, moving one endpoint will cause a rigid translation of the segment in the direction of motion of its endpoint. One may also constrain a segment's orientation so that it will only move in ways that maintain this orientation. Most other features of diagram components also have values that may be marked fixed, including angle sizes and orientations, circle radii, and major and minor axes of ellipses.

Situation constraints may also require that certain relations among objects be maintained. Thus one can specify that two line segments must always remain of equal length; in fact, one can specify any predicate to define the relation, such as that one segment must always be double the length of the other. Similarly, one can state that two segments must remain perpendicular or parallel, that two triangles must remain congruent, and so forth. One can also require that a particular point remain on a particular segment. Any attempts to alter these constraints will be resisted, which in turn could lead to other alterations or to a failure of the invoked manipulation.

Simulation constructions

A simulation is an alteration that has these four attributes: (1) a *particular* diagram, rather than an abstract description of a class of diagrams, is represented; (2) the parts of the diagram interact according to explicit causal laws; (3) the behavior is restricted to obey certain constraints; and (4) the process is incremental.

The most straightforward implementation of this process with representations of geometric diagrams would be to simulate physical situations by employing the classical methods of mathematical physics, in which the laws of Newtonian mechanics supplement the Cartesian description of space with laws that describe the acceleration of mass under the influence of forces.

The complexity of these computations makes this approach, at least in its most general form, impractical for human mental computation. However, we can restrict the analysis to *critical points*, such as endpoints of line segments and intersections of curves, and interpolate the connecting lines and curves or reconstruct them after each movement of a critical point. This immensely simplifies the simulation of the behavior of points interacting under the effects of connectivity. In this way, basic spatial relations may be more readily captured by a simulation on contemporary hardware and could, conceivably, be done in brain circuitry, or with paper and pencil, in a related fashion.

However, the imposition of additional situation constraints, such as requiring certain pairs of distances to remain equal or requiring that a point remain on a given curve, adds new computational burdens. Such constraints are essential in the statement of theorems and the representation of problems and puzzles. As noted, these situation constraints are in addition to the constraints of space and physics that the representation embodies by virtue of its structure. In the general case, adding constraints stated algebraically will lead to sets of non-linear equations for which there are no general solution methods that are polynomial time in complexity, that is, the computation time increases exponentially, rather than geometrically, with the scale – roughly the number of critical points – of the problem. There are alternatives to finding closed algebraic solutions, however. For example, Kramer (1992) uses degree of freedom analysis to create a system that is able to plan a sequence of movements that will bring a set of objects into compliance with a collection of constraints of the sort employed here, even though they begin in an arbitrary configuration of non-compliance. His system is computationally efficient.

Pixel representations can address this problem by taking advantage of the inherent parallel processing the representation affords. For example, with Furnas's BitPict the rules of movement could in principle be applied simultaneously and such features as detecting collisions will happen 'automatically' without solving equations. This is a fundamental computational advantage of diagrammatic representations over algebraic representations.

Additionally in an ARCHIMEDES simulation the computation is easier than with an algebraic representation because it is computationally much less expensive to *maintain* constraints under incremental changes than it is to discover a configuration that obeys them, and ARCHIMEDES makes essential use of this fact. Thus, once a diagram has been constructed from a propositional description, it is possible to forego repeating that task while generating future legal states with a high degree of accuracy and much less computation. See also Bier & Stone (1986); Gleicher & Witkin (1991a); Gleicher & Witkin (1991b). Modifying diagrams incrementally provides an 'envisionment' of the geometric system in the sense that qualitative simulations of kinematics (Forbus (1984)) and dynamics (de Kleer & Brown (1984)) do for simulated physical systems. The envisionment may then be used in problem solving and conjecturing by noting what states it can and cannot achieve.

The simulation-construction function of ARCHIMEDES works in an incremental fashion by making prescribed movements of specified critical points and then checking to see if the situation constraints are violated. If no violation has occurred, the program tests to see if a prescribed stopping condition has been achieved and, if so, it interpolates the remaining points and halts with success. If the stopping condition has not been achieved and no situation constraints are violated, the program repeats this *cycle* by making the next alteration that is called for.

If one or more constraints are violated as a result of movement during a cycle, the program enters an inner iteration loop at each *step* of which the violated constraints are examined. Each violation yields a stress on certain points. For example, if a segment is too long, its endpoints are stressed in the directions that would move them closer. After all violated constraints add stresses, net stresses are computed and movements are proposed in those directions that could reduce the net stress. Generally there are a number of such movements and combinations of movements possible, and the one leading to the least overall stress in the diagram is chosen. This may or may not result in the satisfaction of all constraints; if not, the others are tried in turn until one is found that produces a constraint-satisfied diagram (at which point the inner iteration ends and the next cycle is begun), or all have failed. If all fail, the best is chosen and another step taken to resolve the impasse. If success is not achieved in this manner, and the stopping condition has not been achieved, the simulation ends with failure.

For example, if an endpoint of a line segment has a fixed location and the line segment has a fixed length, any pulls on the non-fixed endpoint in the direction of the line segment, or its opposite, will fail, but other pulls will lead to rotations of the line about its fixed point. The simulation constructions can only translate and rotate objects, although the objects may be either rigid or flexible in whole or in part (that is, some or all of the dimensions may be held fixed or allowed to freely vary by specifying situation constraints).

Clearly the numerical computations underlying simulation constructions are implausible as the basis of a psychological model. However, considered at a higher level of description, the level describing the function of the simulation in the context of its purpose, they illustrate computations that are psychologically plausible.

Rearrangement constructions

A rearrangement is the rigid displacement of one object, or a copy of one object, from one location in the diagram to another as a unit rather than point by point. If a copy is moved the original is unchanged and the copy is assigned a new name with new component names. The object could be a segment, a triangle, a square, and so forth. The new location is specified by giving the target locations of one or more points of the to-be-moved object. The object's components (points, segments, etc.) will be moved in such a way that the shape of the object is unchanged.

Simulation constructions cannot flip over objects in 3-space. Thus it is possible that two objects are congruent but are mirror images and thus cannot be superimposed by a simulation construction. In that case a rearrangement construction requested to make such a superposition will do so, but will indicate that it could not be done by simulation.

6. Retrieval Processes

Retrieval processes are the components of a knowledge representation that examine a representation-proper and return information or answer questions about it. In ARCHIMEDES these processes examine the pixel-net and structures that represent a collection of objects, *i.e.,* a diagram. For example, there are functions that can determine if two segments are of the same length, are perpendicular or parallel, and so forth. Other retrieval functions determine whether an object, say a square, is partitioned into other objects, say a pair of triangles created by a diagonal of the square.

Since such information is often needed for the construction of objects, the retrieval functions are also frequently components of the construction processes. Thus the use of a representation is more dynamic and fluid than a straightforward data base, such as an address book, in which information is added by a recording process and later retrieved by an access process. The central idea of ARCHIMEDES is that a diagram may be altered and the results of the alteration noticed by the system. ARCHIMEDES can create a diagram by evaluating a program of description constructions. Generally this will result in a structure that contains more objects than were explicitly mentioned in the description constructions. The same is true after an alteration is made by a simulation construction: new objects may arise, and some old ones may have disappeared. The graphic display of the program's progress could be examined by a human, who would, through his processes of perception, notice the new objects, and the disappearance of some old objects. ARCHIMEDES'S 'perceptual' processes are called *noticing* functions, and they are created from the basic construction and retrieval processes.

Noticing and observing

Human perception is an active process that works automatically whenever one visually attends to a diagram. In contrast, ARCHIMEDES must explicitly invoke its noticing processes, and generally does so after any alterations have been made, although for efficiency the user may delay noticing until several alterations have been completed and the diagram is in a quiescent state.

Suppose, for example, that ARCHIMEDES were instructed to construct a parallelogram and drop an altitude from one vertex to an opposite side. See Figure 33: Understanding the Area of a Parallelogram. It would notice that a triangle was thus implicitly formed. The system would also notice that the original parallelogram is partitioned into a triangle and a quadrilateral by the altitude construction. ARCHIMEDES could then be instructed to translate the newly formed triangle across the parallelogram stopping when a rectangle is formed. It would notice that this results in the formation of a rectangle and that the rectangle is partitioned into the same quadrilateral plus a copy of the same triangle, relocated. This could be the basis for reasoning that the area of the parallelogram is the same as the area of the rectangle.

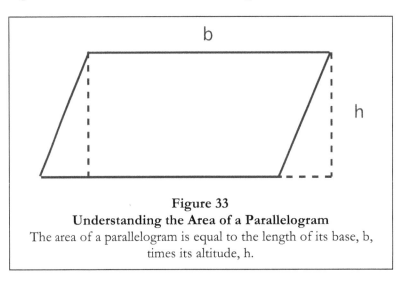

Figure 33
Understanding the Area of a Parallelogram
The area of a parallelogram is equal to the length of its base, b,
times its altitude, h.

Constant monitoring of a diagram, even just of quiescent states, can be computationally expensive. Even humans do not notice every feature of their visual field, but search it serially (with discrete eye movements called saccades) and usually not completely. Just as a teacher might call a student's attention to an overlooked feature of a diagram, it is possible for the ARCHIMEDES user to call its attention to one feature, say an object, and ask the system to verify something about it, such as whether it is a right triangle, or a parallelogram, or is congruent to another object. This confirmation of a question about the diagram is called *observing* (to distinguish it from noticing), and it uses the same set of retrieval processes.

Observing partitions

One class of complex noticing-operations includes those that notice that one object is exactly partitioned into a set of other objects (or that it is not). For example, Figure 34: Overlapping Figures shows a rectangle that is divided in half by a diagonal and thus is partitioned into two triangles. Human perception is very fast and accurate at detecting such cases provided the diagram is not very complicated. Computing such observations from an algebraic representation is fast for very simple cases, but each case requires a different computation, and more complex cases such as irregular polygons and curves of non-constant curvature are not computationally tractable algebraically.

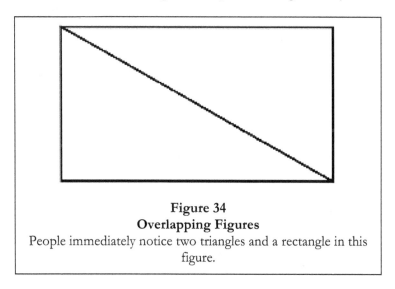

Figure 34
Overlapping Figures
People immediately notice two triangles and a rectangle in this
figure.

ARCHIMEDES relies upon the implicit topology of its pixel-net to do these computations in a general and efficient manner, much as BitPict does. The technique employs *color-spreading,* a method suggested by Ullman (1985). Points in the pixel net may be temporarily assigned arbitrary 'colors' (really just distinct labels) and these can be used to record computational results. This process is analogous to a human coloring-in an enclosed area of a diagram with a crayon, or tracing the outline of an object with a colored pencil. For example, suppose one wishes to know if, in Figure 34, the rectangle is exactly partitioned into the two triangles. One may re-color the black border of the rectangle one color, say blue, then begin tracing the borders of the triangles. If a triangle point is initially black it is assigned a different color, say green, indicating that it has not been visited before. If it is blue, it is assigned yet a different color, say yellow, indicating that it is on the rectangle border as well as a triangle border. If it is green, it has already been marked as an interior triangle side and is now being traced a second time, so is marked, say red. After all sides of all objects have been traced, if any blue points remain then the putative partitioning is not true because some part of the rectangle is uncovered. If any points are red or green then the partitioning objects do not all have shared borders.

Thus it is possible to determine whether the putative partitioning is a fact. This process will work with non-linear and irregular shapes as well.

Noticing symmetries

Human vision is extremely good at noticing certain kinds of symmetries, and ARCHIMEDES attempts to capture these abilities. For example, people can quickly recognize mirror symmetries, that is bilateral symmetry about an axis. This is particularly easy if the axis of symmetry is vertical. The actual computation to detect and check such symmetry is fairly elaborate. The axis must be located, and for each point its symmetric partner must be found.

The human body is approximately symmetric about a sagittal plane. However, the symmetry is only approximate. When shown a photograph constructed from two copies, one reversed, of the same side of a person's face, one will notice that it does not look quite right. When looking at simple geometric diagrams, however, even small departures from symmetry are readily noted, while at the same time one recognizes near symmetry.

Knowing that a figure is bilaterally symmetric means that one knows a large number of equivalences. For example, symmetric partner segments are known to be of equal length even though their orientations differ. Thus the ready detection of symmetry is a powerful tool for many inferences.

ARCHIMEDES is able to notice vertical or horizontal axes of mirror symmetry and thereby notice the numerous equivalences these entail. It notices by computing an average horizontal (and vertical) coordinate, and then checking each named point and segment to see if it has a symmetric partner. Radial symmetries are also noticed with a similar computational scheme.

As mentioned above, humans appear to have a preference for vertical axes, but they are also quite good at obliques. Noticing mirror symmetries about oblique axes could also be implemented but has not been. Symmetry noticing is one of the most powerful inferential abilities of humans and of ARCHIMEDES.

7. Higher Organization of System Knowledge

Lemmas

ARCHIMEDES is able to remember a sequence of constructions, including simulation and rearrangement constructions. It remembers these in a generalized form, that is, not as applying to a specific object, say **abc**, but as applying to any triangle that has the same constraint structure as **abc**. Associated with this sequence of constructions is a conclusion, perhaps something that it noticed. The conclusion is also stated generally. These sequences and conclusions are called lemmas, and they can be invoked as macro operators when the 'same' situation arises, or is pointed out. This makes use of the *syntactic symmetry* frequently found in diagram demonstrations and manipulations.

Syntactic symmetry is a notion introduced by Gelernter (1959). The idea is that any two logical expressions or sequences of such expressions that can be transformed into one another by a consistent and systematic substitution of variables have the same logical form, and hence entail the same consequences, *mutatis mutandis*. Thus a proof of one statement, once discovered, can be transformed immediately by the same substitution of variables into a proof of another statement that is syntactically symmetric. This ability substantially aided Gelernter's geometry machine to avoid duplication of effort. The same principle is adopted in part by ARCHIMEDES' lemma mechanism.

Episodes

The process of discovering interesting properties of diagrams, as opposed to merely checking that a conclusion is supported, is often brought about by playing with a diagram, either on paper or in the imagination. This ability is implemented in ARCHIMEDES by *episode* structures. The user (or, someday perhaps, the program) can suggest a sequence of incremental changes and mention a set of diagram properties to be monitored. ARCHIMEDES will sequentially make the changes, including whatever follows from these changes by constrained simulation, and record the values of the monitored properties. This record, the episode, associates the values of the specifically manipulated features with the values of the monitored properties. Episodes are then examined for patterns of certain types, for example monotonic changes in a set of values, or an increase to a maximum followed by a decrease. Critical values, such as beginning and ending limits, maxima, and the appearance of any of a number of configurations of special interest (such as right angles or parallel lines) are then detected and an attempt is made to correlate them with other features.

Strategy processes

The machinery thus far described is not able to do anything of interest by itself. It must be combined into programs to achieve goals, such as testing an hypothesis or demonstrating a theorem. The specification of these programs may be done by the user or by higher-level programs. Every classical program[24] yet devised is limited in the way that ARCHIMEDES is limited: it must be told what to do and why. Programs (somewhat like pets trained to dance or fetch) are not self-motivated, they do not set their own goals; unlike human agents, they do not understand the very process of problem-solving that they are exhibiting, but learn it by reinforcement of associations. Thus I have not created an autonomous intelligence that does what people do, but rather a system that can be told how to do some things that people do in ways that are more human-like than those that traditional systems use.

Several strategies have been developed and will now be examined in detail to illustrate some of what the ARCHIMEDES architecture has been used to do.

8. Behavior of ARCHIMEDES Models

I will describe three tasks of increasing scope and illustrate each with a few specific examples that ARCHIMEDES has actually accomplished, with a little help from its friends. The tasks are (1) Verifying demonstrations, (2) Discovering demonstrations, and (3) Discovering interesting conjectures. Finally I will show how each of these is a

---

[24] Evolutionary programs such as Genetic Programming (Koza (1992)) are an exception. Although they too are 'told' what to do by providing a goal (fitness function), the telling is so indirect and non-explicit that they constitute a different type of AI altogether.

component of understanding, and discuss what is missing and would still be missing even if each of these abilities were fully perfected.

STUDENT: Verifying demonstrations

ARCHIMEDES STUDENT is a program written within the ARCHIMEDES architecture. It follows demonstrations supplied by a person. It constructs diagrams as instructed, including the propositional information associated with diagram components. At each step of the construction the program verifies that the construction is legitimate according to the constraints of geometry and the situation constraints imposed by the person. When an inference is pointed out to the program, it verifies that the inference is correct, if it is. It also makes inferences by examining what it has constructed. At some point, the program is informed of the proposition that is being demonstrated, and ultimately it attempts to verify that the proposition is in fact true of the diagram it has constructed and modified. Constructions generally include simulation constructions that are imposed by the person supplying the demonstration.

The Pythagorean theorem

To illustrate this behavior in more concrete detail, consider a classic demonstration of the Pythagorean theorem. See Figure 35: Pythagorean Theorem Demonstration by Chou pei suan ching. This is one of the most simple and direct 'proofs' available, and is attributed to Chou pei suan ching, circa 200 BCE (Pythagorean Proof I from Nelsen (1993)). The demonstration, which employs two static diagrams, is assumed to be so transparent that no words are necessary to convey it. Of course, as I have been noting repeatedly, that is only the case if the observer knows the right things. 'Words' are necessary, but often can be supplied by the observer. For example, if the observer has never heard of the Pythagorean Theorem and is unfamiliar with the conventions of diagram drawing, then the demonstration will likely not be followed, and perhaps be construed as samples of bathroom tile patterns instead.

ARCHIMEDES STUDENT must therefore be presented with more information when asked to verify this demonstration. First, instructions are given for the construction of one of the figures (say the left side of Figure 35). ARCHIMEDES STUDENT will spontaneously notice certain things about this figure, such as that it contains four right triangles and two squares. It notices that the four triangles are congruent, by observation, not by proof. Explicit instructions are then given for moving parts about until the other configuration is attained. The simulated movements are done under the constraint that the moved objects are rigid. ARCHIMEDES STUDENT 'knows' that rigid motion of an object maintains its area. ARCHIMEDES STUDENT notices that the final arrangement includes four right triangles equivalent to the original four, and concludes that their total area is the same in each figure by reasoning from area preservation under rigid motion and algebraic equivalences involving sums of areas. The demonstrator does not need to prod ARCHIMEDES STUDENT to draw these conclusions. It also notices that the final configuration contains, in addition to the four triangles, two small squares, and that the large square has not been altered. It notices that the large (border) square in the first figure has been decomposed into its components as is the border square in the final figure.

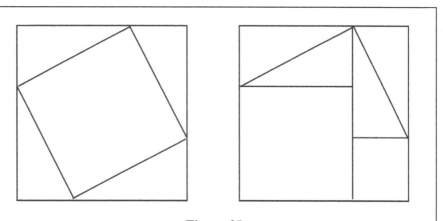

Figure 35
Pythagorean Theorem Demonstration by Chou pei suan ching
The triangles in the left square can 'obviously' be rearranged as in the right
square which is of equal area.

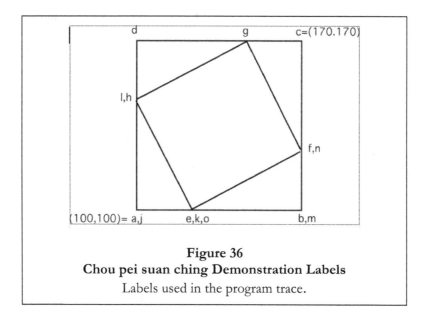

Figure 36
Chou pei suan ching Demonstration Labels
Labels used in the program trace.

The demonstrator explicitly points out to ARCHIMEDES STUDENT that in the
original figure the interior square is the square on the hypotenuse of (each) triangle. In
the final diagram, the demonstrator explicitly points out to ARCHIMEDES STUDENT
that the two small squares in the final configuration correspond to the squares on the two
non-hypotenuse sides of (each) triangle. The demonstrator then explicitly asks if the
hypotenuse square from the first configuration is equal in area to the sum of the areas of
the two small squares in the second configuration. ARCHIMEDES STUDENT confirms
this by algebraic manipulations of the area equivalence relations it has noticed.

There are a number of obvious differences between the behavior of ARCHIMEDES
STUDENT and that of a hypothetical human student who is observing the

demonstration. The demonstration as usually presented to a human student contains two configurations and does not give explicit manipulations for transforming one into the other. Presumably, however, a sufficiently clever human observer does essentially what ARCHIMEDES STUDENT is told to do. The human student presumably knows the Pythagorean Theorem and discovers without instruction that Figure 35 is related to it. ARCHIMEDES STUDENT knows no such thing and must be explicitly told. ARCHIMEDES STUDENT does not know the practical and historic significance of the Theorem, and cannot be told because it has no knowledge structures that deal with such information.

In short, ARCHIMEDES STUDENT has a perceptual and cognitive style that in some ways is like human style, but ARCHIMEDES STUDENT lacks the context of knowledge, experience, practicality, and historical perspective in which the human's cognitive acts are embedded.

The following is an abbreviated outline of the steps of the demonstration and is accompanied by comments added to aid the reader, not the program. Semicolons precede descriptive comments that are not part of the program's operation. Figure 36: Chou pei suan ching Demonstration Labels indicates the points that are constructed, and whose names are assigned by the program. Note that 'a refers to a displayname, (locus a) to a gridpoint, and a to a pointname (similarly for other objects). Also '(eq x y) denotes a predicate which, when evaluated, in turn yields true or false, depending on whether x and y are identical. The notation :variable-name variable has been employed in some places for clarity.

Pythagorean Theorem Demonstration (Chou pei suan ching)

```
;Step 1: Constructing Initial Square
(construct-point 100 100)    ;This constructs point a
(construct-point 190 100)    ;This constructs point b
(construct-segment 'ab)      ;This constructs segment ab
(construct-squarename-on-segmentname ab)
(construct-point 130 100)    ;point e
(construct-point 190 130)    ;point f
(construct-point 160 190)    ;point g
(construct-point 100 160)    ;point h
(construct-segment 'fg)      ;To form unmoved triangle cgf
(construct-segment 'gc)
(construct-segment 'cf)
(construct-segment 'gh)      ;To form unmoved triangle dhg
(construct-segment 'hd)
(construct-segment 'dg)
(construct-copy-of-point a)  ;point j = a
(construct-copy-of-point e)  ;point k = e
(construct-copy-of-point h)  ;point l = h
;Next create triangles jkl and mno that will later be moved
;Note that any polygon can be referred to by listing its
;vertices in any perimeter order
(construct-segment 'jk)    ;segment jk coincides with segment ae
(construct-segment 'kl)    ;kl coincides with eh
(construct-segment 'lj)    ;lj coincides with ah
                           ;the sides of jkl now exist
```

```
(construct-copy-of-point b)   ;point m = b
(construct-copy-of-point f)   ;point n = f
(construct-copy-of-point e)   ;point o = e = k
(construct-segment 'mn)    ;mn coincides with bf
(construct-segment 'no)    ;no coincides with fe
(construct-segment 'om)    ;om coincides with eb
                           ;the sides of mno now exist
      ;There are now 16 segments and one square (abcd) created
(notice-new-facts)   ;This notices the triangles whose sides
                     ;were constructed above
      ;Many other object names are noticed because several
      ;points have multiple displayforms
      ;This includes 42  implicitly created segments
      ;and 28 trianglenames (from only distinct figures)
      ;and 15 more square names (e.g., mcdj)
```

;Step 2: Point out decomposition of large square into small
square and 4 triangles
```
(observe-decomposition :object abcd :components (efgh jkl mno
dhg cgf)) ;This confirms that
          ;abcd is composed of the other five objects
(notice-new-facts)   ;Nothing new is noticed
```

;Step 3: Translate jkl along segment hg until l falls on g
```
      ;The next three lines define the intended movement
      ;but do not yet execute it
(translate-rigid-triangle-along-curve 'jkl hg :stop-when '(eq
(locus l) (locus g)) :direction 'counter-clockwise)
(fix-namedpoints)    ;Holds all points fixed
(unfix-points i j k)    ;except triangle vertices
      ;The following performs the movement as just instructed
(simulation-construction :namedpoints '(j k l) :namedsegments
'(jk kl jl))
(notice-new-facts)    ;Nothing new is noticed
```

;Step 4: Translate mno along fg until n falls on l, which is
now at g
```
(translate-rigid-triangle-along-curve 'mno fg :stop-when '(eq
(locus n) (locus l)))
(fix-namedpoints)
(unfix-points m n o)
(simulation-construction :namedpoints '(m n o) :namedsegments
'(mn no mo))
(notice-new-facts)    ;Nothing new is noticed
```

;Step 5: Form small squares by dropping perpendicular from j to
ab at p
```
(construct-and-name-perpendicular-from-pointname-to-segment j
ab :direction 'clockwise)
(construct-segmentnamedf :segmentdf 'pm);This segment must be
                                        ;explicitly constructed
(notice-new-facts)    ;The squares are noticed and constructed
```

;Step 6: Point out the area decomposition of abcd into 2 squares and 4 triangles
```
(observe-decomposition :object abcd :components (bjio aoln ijk
lmn dhg cgf)) ;Program confirms
```

;Step 7: Observe Target
```
(construct-remember-goal-proposition ('equal-area (efgh) (bkjp
apmo)))
(observe-target)     ;This step will generates area equivalence
        ;relations and stop when it finds the target among them.
```

Archimedes-Student reports:

YES, I SEE THAT. I HAVE VERIFIED THE DEMO.

ARCHIMEDES STUDENT of course does not *understand* the demonstration. It has merely followed it and verified that each step is justified based on its knowledge of geometry, diagram conventions, and simulation. While a person can readily see that the exact proportions of the four right triangles are irrelevant to the demonstration, this generalization is unknown to ARCHIMEDES STUDENT. Indeed it is unknowable with the machinery used in this example.

Extensions of ARCHIMEDES STUDENT to be described later will add additional perceptual and cognitive abilities to the system that capture further human qualities. In the end, however, a large gap will remain, as is always the case in psychological models, whether computational or not.

Another Pythagorean demonstration

The second Pythagorean demonstration from Nelsen (1993) is also a classic of simplicity that Nelsen attributes to Bhaskara, 12th century CE. It is labeled simply Behold! See Figure 37: Behold! ARCHIMEDES STUDENT proceeds in a manner similar to the previous example, moving the triangles around. In this case the original figure is not converted to the final figure *in situ*, rather copies of the components of the left square are made, reoriented, and moved to the right to build the final configuration. ARCHIMEDES STUDENT must also be instructed to draw the final boundary not shown in Nelsen's figure, dividing the large, irregular hexagon into two squares. It can then confirm that the two squares correspond to the squares on the triangles' legs. The original square is the square on the hypotenuse, and the original small square, which remains after the translations, is subtracted from both total areas to yield the conclusion.

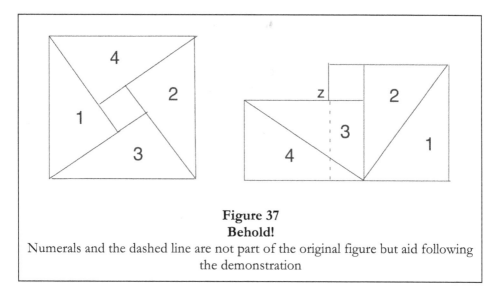

Figure 37
Behold!
Numerals and the dashed line are not part of the original figure but aid following
the demonstration

The following is an outline of the steps in this demonstration. The actual code is not presented for this example.

Pythagorean Theorem Demonstration (Bhaskara)

```
Step  1 . . . Construct Initial Bhaskara Square
Step  2 . . . Translate copy of triangle [1] to the right
Step  3 . . . Rotate the copy of triangle [1]
Step  4 . . . Translate and rotate copy of triangle [2] to form
              rectangle
Step  5 . . . Translate and rotate copy of triangle [3]
Step  6 . . . Translate and rotate copy of triangle [4]
Step  7 . . . Translate copy of small square
Step  8 . . . Rotate small square
Step  9 . . . Drop perpendicular from z to base
Step 10 . . . Observe-decomposition of figure into two squares
Step 11 . . . Finally the goal is stated: (area of original
              left square = area of right hexagon). The
              program is told to verify this and it does so
              successfully.
```

During this verification the program constructed 17 points and many segments and other objects. All of these are present in the Bhaskara diagram, many of whose components have multiple names because it is necessary to make copies to perform movements. Human perception deals with these complexities easily, but something like the bookkeeping done by the program nonetheless must be going on as part of the perceptual and motor processes.

More complex Pythagorean demonstrations

The following is a more complex demonstration, found in Loomis (1940). It involves translations of both squares and triangles, and rotations of triangles, plus more complex decomposition verifications.

While this procedure is more elaborate and requires additional functionality of ARCHIMEDES STUDENT, the verification still amounts only to a confirmation that each step is consistent with the architecture's theory of space. It understands the demonstration only in the sense that a logic-based proof checker understands a proof that it verifies. This is by no means a trivial task for either ARCHIMEDES STUDENT or a proof-checker, but it is of limited achievement in comparison to human understanding.

Figure 38: Diagrammatic Demonstration of Loomis (1940) illustrates each of the steps of the demonstration, given below. The numbers in the Figure refer to the construction steps.

Pythagorean Theorem Demonstration (Loomis)

```
Step   1 . . . Construct right triangle
Step   2 . . . Construct square on the hypotenuse
Step   3 . . . Construct square on the long-leg
Step   4 . . . Construct square on the short-leg
Step   5 . . . Set target of demonstration: abde = acfg + cbih
Step   6 . . . Construct extension of long-leg square side
Step   7 . . . Construct extension of short-leg square side
Step   8 . . . Construct perpendicular to first construction
Step   9 . . . Observe Decomposition of hypotenuse square into 3
               triangles and a quadrilateral
Step  10 . . . Construct and rotate copy of triangle akb by
               simulation
Step  11 . . . Observe Area-equivalence abde = mnb + oep + ejl +
               bkjd

Step  12 . . . Observe newly formed hexagon bklepn
Step  13 . . . Observe Decomposition of the hexagon into 3
               triangles and a quadrilateral
Step  14 . . . Construct segment jq
Step  15 . . . Observe Decomposition of hexagon into 2 squares
Step  16 . . . Construct and translate copy of square bkqn by
               simulation
Step  17 . . . Construct and translate square north, then east
Step  18 . . . Observe Decompositions rsuv=acfg and wz$% = cbih
Step  19 . . . Observe Area-equivalences bkqn=acfg and lepq=cbih
Step  20 . . . Verify target proposition
```

Step 9 is an instruction to observe that the hypotenuse square has now been decomposed into four objects, that is, that the four objects are entirely contained within the boundary of the square, and every point within the square is contained in exactly one of the four objects. While such a computation could be done by arithmetic on coordinate points, this would be very complex and in the general case of arbitrary shapes might be intractable. Instead ARCHIMEDES STUDENT uses the method described in Section 8.6: Retrieval Processes.

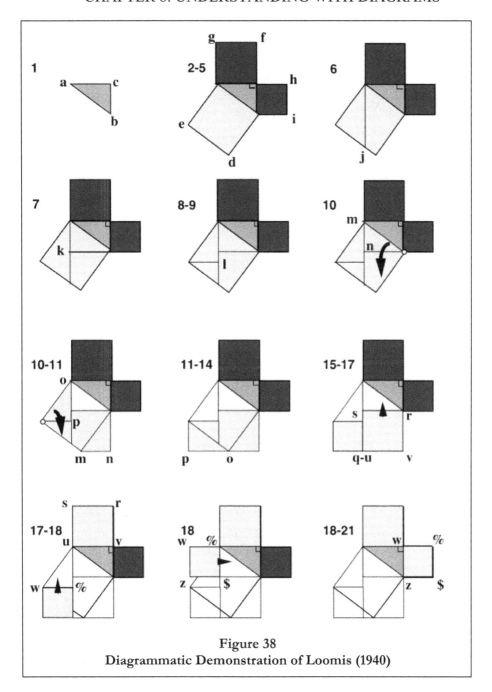

Figure 38
Diagrammatic Demonstration of Loomis (1940)

An algebraic Pythagorean demonstration

This demonstration is based on the construction of similar triangles that are then used to generate equations based on the fact that the lengths of sides of a triangle stand in the same ratio to corresponding sides of a of similar triangle. See Figure 39: An Algebraic Pythagorean Demonstration. These facts can be imparted to ARCHIMEDES STUDENT by construction and measurement, or by informing ARCHIMEDES STUDENT either explicitly or implicitly of the above fact about similar triangles. The detection of pairs of similar triangles can also be done in two ways, either by construction and measurement of the lengths of sides, or by employing theorems that specify conditions under which two triangles are similar. In this example, the appropriate theorem is that two triangles are similar if their corresponding angles are equal in measure. Those facts can in turn be determined, once again, either by construction and measurement or from theorems. In this example, a relevant theorem is that two angles are equal if their corresponding sides are perpendicular. Another relevant theorem is that any angle inscribed in a circle such that it is subtended by a diameter is a right angle; combined with the construction of a right angle, this establishes the equality.

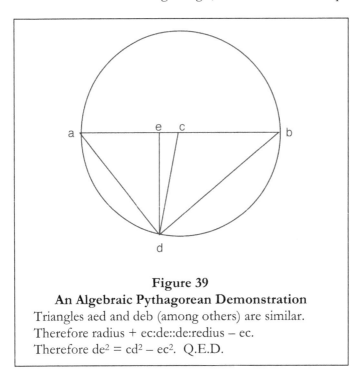

Figure 39
An Algebraic Pythagorean Demonstration
Triangles aed and deb (among others) are similar.
Therefore radius + ec:de::de:radius − ec.
Therefore de² = cd² − ec². Q.E.D.

In the experiment described here, facts about angle equality were made by measurement; discovery of pairs of similar triangles and equal ratios of lengths were discovered by prior knowledge of theorems. The proportionality noted in the figure yields the equation (where radius = cd)

$$(cd + ec)/ de = de/(cd − ec)$$

Finally, algebraic manipulations were performed in a purely forward chaining fashion, that is, the program applied transformations of terms and equalities, and substitutions of variables in all possible ways until it was able to verify that the target proposition had been generated.

Pythagorean Theorem Demonstration (Similar Triangles)

```
Step 1 . . . Construct a circle and a diameter
Step 2 . . . Pick random point d on circumference and construct
             triangle by dropping perpendicular to ab
Step 3 . . . Set target of demonstration: cd2 = de2 + ce2
Step 4 . . . Notice similar triangles and equalities based on
             ratios of sides
Step 5 . . . Observe the truth of the target proposition by doing
             the algebra
```

DISCOVERER: Discovering demonstrations[25]

Verifying demonstrations in the above fashion is a limited form of understanding that avoids the problem of determining the manipulations that underlie the demonstration; that problem is solved by the inventor of the demonstration. The program has been extended so that it can discover some demonstrations by finding sequences of manipulations that achieve a particular end. Note that the system still must be given a goal proposition; it has no way to decide what might be an interesting proposition to demonstrate. It must also be given the diagram appropriate to the goal. The program is called ARCHIMEDES DISCOVERER

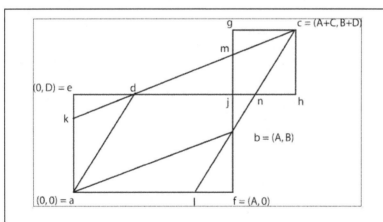

Figure 40
A 2 x 2 Determinant is the Area of a Parallelogram
From R. B. Nelsen, *Proofs without words. Exercises in visual thinking,*
1993, page 133. Copyright the Mathematical Association of
America 1993. All rights reserved. Reprinted by permission.

---

[25] For an extended account see Lindsay (2000), in S. O'Nuallian (Ed.) *Spatial Cognition* (pp. 199-212). © 2000 John Benjamins Publishing Co.

Consider Figure 40: A 2 x 2 Determinant is the Area of a Parallelogram, taken from Nelsen (1993). An instance of this diagram was 'drawn' for the program, which assigned names to the points as indicated and then noticed – and constructed in its memory – structures corresponding to each of the figures that were implicitly created by the construction of the major segments.

The program noticed the following objects.

points (13):   (n m l k j h g f e d c b a)

segments (42): (fg bg eh dh fm bm en dn bj dj jn hn jm gm km dm cm ln bn cn bf de cl fl al bl ck ek ak dk gj cg ch hj ae ej fj af ad cd bc ab)

triangles (14): (afb alb bcg bcm blf bnj adk ade cdn cdh cnh cgm dek djm)

rectangles (2): (cgjh afje)

parallelograms (4):   (bcda bmka alnd cmkd)

quadrilaterals (54):   (jekm flnj dekm djmk cmdn cmjn clfm cnek cndk cgfl cgmk cgjn ckeh cmdh ckdh clnh cmjh cdnl cdjm cdjg cgmd cked alck alne afmk afjd afmd akmd alcd akcd bndm bmcn bgcn bnlf bjnl bmcl bgcl bjnc bnlc bflc bckm bnhc bjhc bcdn bcdj bcdm baln balc bcka bnea bjea bnda bjda bmda)

This may appear to be a large number of objects, particularly of quadrilaterals, in that they do not all leap out at the human observer. However, each object can readily be found from its name and, with great care and good record keeping, one can produce these lists from an examination of the diagram. However, some of the objects listed above are degenerate, such as parallelogram *cmdk* whose vertices are collinear, that is the 'parallelogram' looks like a line segment. Such 'objects' are not routinely detected by human perception (or perhaps more correctly are ignored by human cognition). The program does not cull these degenerate cases, though to do so would be straightforward.

Once the diagram has been drawn and the program has noticed this inventory of objects, it is given the target proposition: The area of rectangle *afje* (=AD) equals the sum of the areas of rectangle *cgjh* (=BC) and parallelogram *bcda*. That is, the area of the large rectangle is the area of the large parallelogram plus the area of the small rectangle: AD = BC + area of *bcda*. If one assigns point *a* to the origin and point *b* to (A, B), point *c* to (A+C, B+D) and *d* to (0, D), then the dimensions of the large rectangle are AxD and of the small rectangle are BxC. The 2 X 2 determinant

$$\begin{vmatrix} A & B \\ C & D \end{vmatrix} = AD - BC$$

is thus the difference in the areas of the two rectangles. The proposition as stated by Nelsen is that the value of this determinant equals the area of the parallelogram. Transforming this statement to eliminate the minus sign yields the target proposition stated above.

ARCHIMEDES DISCOVERER also works in exactly the same form for other demonstrations that depend upon establishing an area equivalence, including the examples presented in the previous section. ARCHIMEDES DISCOVERER first attempts to see if it can verify the target from what it knows already. It does this by consulting a list of known area-equivalences (which initially is empty) and attempting to combine them by substitutions of equivalences and by using the properties of symmetry and transitivity of the equivalence relation. The knowledge of the properties of the equivalence relation and of substitution of equals is built into the program and is not related to its knowledge of space.

ARCHIMEDES DISCOVERER next examines each side of the target proposition equation. Each object mentioned on either side is considered in turn. For each of these objects, every possible decomposition into a set of other objects is detected, such that the set exactly covers the initial object without overlap. For example, triangle *ade* can be decomposed into triangle *adk* plus triangle *dek*.

These computations are not done algebraically, but make use of the pixel representation and its underlying eight neighborhood relations that permit one to find the immediate neighbors of a given pixel. The method is a 'color-spreading' iteration similar to the method described earlier for finding common boundaries, although here the *interiors* of objects are colored. The interior of an object is marked by first labeling the border with one 'color', say red. Starting with an interior point of the object, that point is colored a different color, say orange, and each neighbor is examined. If a neighbor is border-colored or interior-colored already, it is ignored. Other neighbors are colored the interior-color and added to the list of points whose neighbors remain to be examined. The iteration continues until no more pixels remain on that list. Notice that this procedure works for closed objects of any shape, including non-convex polygons, circles, and any closed curve. Note also that it implicitly makes use of the geometric (topological) structure of the diagram.

The discovery of an interior point is an interesting problem itself. This is a problem that human perception appears readily able to solve, provided the object is not too complex. Exactly what makes an object too complex for human perception is a matter of empirical study, but it is easy to find non-trivial examples such as Figure 20: More Difficult Perception of Inside-Outside (Section 6.7: Representation of Geometric Diagrams). Unlike the simple cases of Figure 19: Perception of Inside-Outside, where a person can immediately determine if a point is within a given object, examining Figure 20 requires a slower, sequential analysis, perhaps aided by pointing and tracing with a pencil. A color-spreading method would also work in many cases, but again for complex boundaries this would entail the physical use of a pencil (or crayon) by a person.

Here ARCHIMEDES DISCOVERER relies on the fact that its objects are polygons. It discovers interior points by examination of several candidates such as the intersection of diagonals (which always works for non-degenerate convex polygons). The general problem of finding an interior point cannot be solved by ARCHIMEDES DISCOVERER, and is indeed a subtle perceptual computation in the general case if the representation is a pixel array.

The next step in finding decompositions is to determine which other objects are contained within the putative container object. This is true of a polygon if its vertices are now either the interior-color or the border-color. This is not a sufficient condition for complete containment (consider a non-convex container), but partially overlapping false candidates are eliminated in later steps. Next, the collection of all subsets of the set of contained objects is enumerated. For example if there are three objects a, b, and c, there are seven non-null subsets: {a}, {b}, {c}, {a,b}, {a,c}, {b,c}, and {a,b,c}. In general with n objects there are $2^n - 1$ non-null subsets. Each of these subsets may or may not exactly decompose the initial object. There may be a very large number of such subsets to try. In the Figure 40 example, there are nine objects that are at least partly within parallelogram *bcda*, yielding 511 subsets to examine. To cull this large number, ARCHIMEDES DISCOVERER first considers the nine objects pair-wise and determines which pairs overlap; any two objects that overlap cannot both be part of an exact decomposition. Testing for overlap is done with a color-spreading procedure also. First the interior of one member of the pair is colored a distinct color, say yellow, and then the second interior is colored differently, say orange, but coloring stops if yellow is encountered. Culling the 511 subsets mentioned above in this way leaves only 38 to be checked for exact fit.

This last step is done by tracing the boundary of the putative container and then tracing the boundaries of the subset of partially contained objects, halting if the number of retracings is inconsistent with exact decomposition. The details are given in Lindsay (1998).

The result of these steps is to produce a set of area equivalences of the form: the area of the container equals the sum of the areas of the contained. With these additions to the list of known area equivalences, a test is again made to see if the target proposition follows from these by substitution, symmetry, or transitivity.

If this fails, as it does in this example, ARCHIMEDES DISCOVERER determines all possible congruencies that it sees in the diagram. For example, each pair of triangles is considered in turn. The program determines if one can be rotated and translated onto the other. If so, it generates the program that could demonstrate this by using the simulation construction algorithm. This program could actually be executed to effect the demonstration. However, here it is assumed that the program at this stage of its education 'knows' that two triangles are congruent if they have sides that are equal pair-wise in the same order. (If they are equal but not in the same order they are still in fact congruent but one of them would have to be flipped in three-space to achieve coincidence, and ARCHIMEDES DISCOVERER does not 'know' this because it does not know about flipping, so it cannot generate a simulation-construction program to do this and fails to detect this form of congruency by superposition.)

Every pair of congruent figures yields an area equivalence statement, and these are added to the list of known equivalences. In our example, this yields enough information to verify the target proposition.

PLAYER: Discovering Interesting conjectures[26]

We have seen how the system has been explored as a means of verifying diagrammatic demonstrations of classical geometric propositions and for constructing diagrammatic demonstrations of conclusions supplied for the system. The process of *discovering* propositions to be demonstrated is a more difficult task. Central to the

---

[26] This material is summarized from R. K. Lindsay, Playing with Diagrams, in M. Anderson, P. Cheng, and V. Haarslev (Eds.) *Theory and application of diagrams*, pages 300-313. Copyright 2000 Springer-Verlag. Used with kind permission of Springer Science+Business Media.

discovery process is systematic manipulation of diagrams and observation of consistent relations among features of the diagram as manipulations are made and observed. I call this *playing with diagrams*. The play results in the creation of an *episode* of diagram behaviors that is examined for regularities from which a general proposition might be proposed. This section illustrates this process and discusses the advantages and limitations of this system and of other computational models of diagrammatic reasoning.

Exploring the Pythagorean theorem

There are literally hundreds of diagrammatic demonstrations of the Pythagorean Theorem that involve construction of the squares on the sides of a right triangle followed by various manipulations that demonstrate the theorem (*e.g.*, see Loomis (1940)); we have seen a few of these above. Each such demonstration is performed on a particular instance of a right triangle. To convince oneself of its generality, demonstrations might be performed on a variety of exemplars, provided they were chosen in such a way that no 'accidental' property was essential to the demonstration. Thus a 45 degree right triangle might be a special case for which the theorem is true simply because 45 degrees is a special angle measure. There is no procedure for choosing exemplars that guarantees that all such special cases have been eliminated so that the proposition is true in general for all

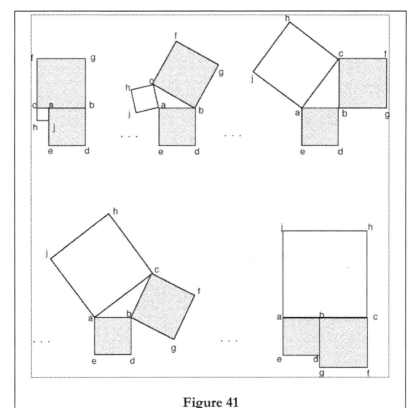

Figure 41
Exploring the Generalized Pythagorean Relation
Shown are a selected stage of squares on the sides of a triangle as angle abc goes from 0 to 180 degrees.

right triangles (although see Miller (2000), who addresses this issue). Conventional propositional proofs avoid some of these problems by using size-, position-, and orientation-independent characterizations: basically some of the problems are defined away. Suppose one wished to gain a deeper understanding or a greater sense of assurance that the Pythagorean Theorem is true. One way is to note that it is not true of (some examples of) non-right triangles. Furthermore, one may notice that the relation between hypotenuse square and the sum of the other squares changes *monotonically* with the critical angle, and the relation holds exactly only as the critical angle passes through 90 degrees. This observation can be made diagrammatically by constructing a triangle and allowing one of its angles to increase from acute to obtuse while observing the sizes of the squares. Consider the following experiment. Start with two line segments of arbitrary length and use them to construct a degenerate triangle, that is, one with one straight angle and two null angles. Then increase the measure of one of the null angles while holding the original sides fixed in length. Increase the angle until it is 180 and the other two angles are null. See Figure 41: Exploring the Generalized Pythagorean Relation.

ARCHIMEDES PLAYER is a program that performed this experiment and took 'snapshots' at various stages including the critical values of 0, 90, and 180 for the altered angle. For each snapshot the diagram was examined and several parameters were recorded. Among these were size of the critical angle *cba*, critical angle class, and the areas of the three squares on the sides. Also the program looked for symmetries in the diagrams, but found none.

The sequences of parameter values recorded is an *episode*, as introduced earlier. For this experiment a portion of it looked like this:

EPISODE FROM PT WATERSHED DEMO

```
Conditions ={angle-cba varied}

(<cba class) = {null acute acute acute acute acute right obtuse obtuse obtuse
                obtuse obtuse straight}
(<cba size) = {0  13  32  53  72  87  90  103 122 143 162 177 180}
(abde area)={900   900   900   900   900   900   900   900   900   900   900
              900   900}
(bcfg area)={1600  1602  1597  1600  1588  1604  1600  1602  1597
              1600  1588  1604  1600}
(achj area)={100   162   457   1060  1768  2384  2500  3042  3757
              4420  4768  4804  4900}
symmetries={nil   nil   nil   nil   nil   nil   nil   nil   nil   nil
              nil   nil}
```

CHAPTER 8: UNDERSTANDING WITH DIAGRAMS

A series of noticing processes then examined this episode to look for key features. It found the following.

```
EPISODIC REGULARITIES NOTICED:

CONSTANTS:
(abde area):value=900 position=all
(bcfg area): value=1600 position=all
symmetries: value=nil position=all
INCREASING SIZES:
(achj area): max=4900 position=13
```

MAXIMA FOR ANGLE SIZES:
```
(<cba size): max=180 position=12
             {000  013  032  053  072  087  090  103  122  143
              162  177  180}
```

MINIMA FOR ANGLE SIZES:
```
(<cba size): min=000 position=0
             {000  013  032  053  072  087  090  103  122  143
              162  177  180}
```

Thus the program has noticed that two of the squares have remained approximately constant in area while the third has increased monotonically. All measures in the model are considered approximate because of the discrete array used. Equality is determined if differences fall within a tolerance that is determined by the *compliance parameter.

A suite of additional noticing functions is also routinely applied to the regularities. In this case it notices that the critical angle is a right angle only once, and at that point it verifies the Pythagorean relation, whereas the relation is not true for any other values of the critical angle.

For a person, these observations comprise an understanding of the critical, or watershed, condition. That is, not only is the Pythagorean relation true of right triangles, it is not true of any others because of the monotonic increase of the area of the hypotenuse square. The observations might also suggest for one who is mathematically more sophisticated than the program that, since the relation proceeds smoothly from a less-than inequality through equality to a greater-than inequality, there might be a more general relation for which the Pythagorean is a special case (there is).

The program does not in fact understand any of this deeper insight nor could it perform the generalization. What it can do is what it has done, explore the relation among triangle sides and angles by diagram manipulation.

Exploring circles and ellipses

In this second example, ARCHIMEDES PLAYER was instructed to explore the behavior of angles inscribed within ellipses as the dimensions of the ellipse were systematically altered. The model constructed a sequence of ellipses with a fixed horizontal axis of length 300 units and vertical axes of 100, 200, 300, 400 and 500 (the third ellipse was thus a circle). See Figure 42: Playing with Ellipses. For each ellipse a sequence of pairs of points on its perimeter was selected beginning with each end of the horizontal axis and proceeding counter-clockwise along the top and bottom in equal steps. For each pair of points in turn each point was connected to the ends of the horizontal axis. Thus for the first pair the connecting lines were of zero length. At each subsequent stage this results in the formation of several angles, including two inscribed angles subtended by the horizontal axis, plus at least two triangles and a parallelogram. The model discovered these objects as they appeared during the construction. At each stage, the model recorded angle sizes and symmetries in the diagrams. The entire period of play generated a series of five episodes, one for each ellipse.

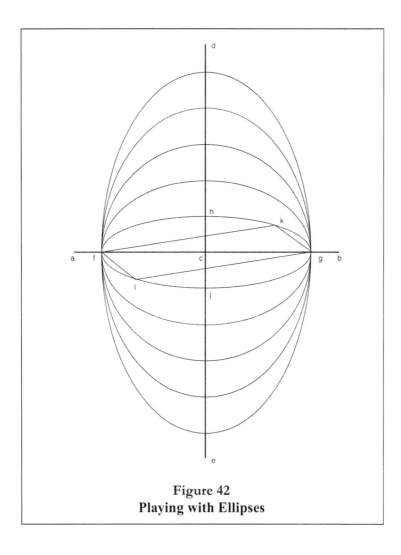

Figure 42
Playing with Ellipses

CHAPTER 8: UNDERSTANDING WITH DIAGRAMS

EPISODE FROM ELIPSE INSCRIBED ANGLE DEMO

```
EPISODE 1   length 7
Conditions =   {(horizontal-axis 300)   (vertical-axis 100)
                   (number of points 7)}
(<glf size)=  {90   132   140   142   140   131    90}
(<fkg size)=  {90   132   140   142   140   131    90}
(<fgl size)=  { 0     8    13    19    27    41    90}
(<gfk size)=  { 0     8    13    19    27    41    90}
(<lfg size)=  {90    40    27    19    13     7     0}
(<kgf size)=  {90    40    27    19    13     7     0}
symmetries =   {nil ((flg gkf)) ((flg gkf)) ((fgk gfj)(gkl fjh)
                   (ghl fjh)   (gkj fjh)   (flg ghf)   (fjg ghf)
                   (flk  ghj) (flh  ghj) (fjk  ghj) (fjh  ghj))
                   ((flg gkf))   ((flg gkf)) nil}


EPISODE 2   length 7
Conditions =   {horizontal-axis 300)   (vertical-axis 200)
                   (number of points 7)}
(<glf size)=  {90   104   111   113   111   104    90}
(<fkg size)=  {90   104   111   113   111   104    90}
(<fgl size)=  { 0    13    23    34    47    64    90}
(<gfk size)=  { 0    13    23    34    47    64    90}
(<lfg size)=  {90    63    46    34    23    12     0}
(<kgf size)=  {90    63    46    34    23    12     0}
symmetries =   {nil ((flg gkf)) ((flg gkf)) ((fgk gfj) (gkl fjh)
                   (ghl fjh)   (gkj fjh)   (flg ghf)  (fjg ghf)
                   (flk ghj)   (flh ghj)   (fjk ghj)  (fjh ghj))
                   ((flg gkf))   ((flg gkf)) nil}
EPISODE 3   length 7
Conditions =   {(horizontal-axis 300)   (vertical-axis 300)
                   (number of points 7)}
(<glf size)=  {90    90    90    90    90    90    90}
(<fkg size)=  {90    90    90    90    90    90    90}
(<fgl size)=  { 0    16    31    45    60    75    90}
(<gfk size)=  { 0    16    31    45    60    75    90}
(<lfg size)=  {90    74    59    45    30    15     0}
(<kgf size)=  {90    74    59    45    30    15     0}
symmetries =   {nil ((flg gkf)) ((flg gkf)) ((fgk gfj) (gkl fjh)
                   (ghl fjh)   (gkj fjh)   (flg ghf) (fjg ghf)
                   (flk ghj)   (flh ghj)   (fjk ghj) (fjh ghj))
                   ((flg gkf)) ((flg gkf)) nil}
EPISODE 4   length 7
Conditions =   {(horizontal-axis 300)   (vertical-axis 400)
                   (number of points 7)}
(<glf size)=  {90    82    76    74    77    83    90}
(<fkg size)=  {90    82    76    74    77    83    90}
(<fgl size)=  { 0    18    35    53    69    80    90}
(<gfk size)=  { 0    18    35    53    69    80    90}
(<lfg size)=  {90    80    68    53    35    17     0}
```

185

```
(<kgf size)=   {90    80    68    53    35    17     0}
symmetries=    {nil ((flg gkf)) ((flg gkf)) ((fgk gfj) (gkl fjh)
                (ghl fjh)  (gkj fjh)  (flg ghf)  (fjg ghf)
                (flk ghj)  (flh ghj)  (fjk ghj)  (fjh ghj))
                ((flg gkf))  ((flg gkf)) nil}
EPISODE 5  length 7
conditions=    {(horizontal-axis 300)  (vertical-axis 500)
                (number of points 7)}
(<glf size)=   {90    77    67    62    67    78    90}
(<fkg size)=   {90    77    67    62    67    78    90}
(<fgl size)=   { 0    20    39    59    74    82    90}
(<gfk size)=   { 0    20    39    59    74    82    90}
(<lfg size)=   {90    82    74    59    39    20     0}
(<kgf size)=   {90    82    74    59    39    20     0}
symmetries=    {nil  ((flg gkf))  ((flg gkf))  ((fgk gfj)   (gkl
                fjh)   (ghl fjh)   (gkj fjh)   (flg ghf)
                (fjg ghf)   (flk ghj)   (flh ghj)   (fjk ghj)
                (fjh ghj))  ((flg gkf))  ((flg gkf)) nil}
```
The model then applied its noticing functions to each episode, resulting in information about constants, increasing, and decreasing values. For example, for Episode 1 this yields
```
INCREASING ANGLE SIZES:
(<gfk size):max=090 position=6   000 008 013 019 027 041 090)
(<fgl size):max=090 position=6   000 008 013 019 027 041 090)
NON-DECREASING ANGLE SIZES:
(<gfk size):max=090 position=6   000 008 013 019 027 041 090)
(<fgl size):max=090 position=6   000 008 013 019 027 041 090)
DECREASING ANGLE SIZES:
(<lfg size):min=000 position=0   090 040 027 019 013 007 000)
(<kgf size):min=000 position=0   090 040 027 019 013 007 000)
NON-INCREASING ANGLE SIZES:
(<lfg size):min=000 position=0   090 040 027 019 013 007 000)
(<kgf size):min=000 position=0   090 040 027 019 013 007 000)
MAXIMA FOR ANGLE SIZES:
(<glf size):max=142 position=3   090 132 140 142 140 131 090)
(<fkg size):max=142 position=3   090 132 140 142 140 131 090)
(<fgl size):max=090 position=6   000 008 013 019 027 041 090)
(<gfk size):max=090 position=6   000 008 013 019 027 041 090)
(<lfg size):max=090 position=0   090 040 027 019 013 007 000)
(<kgf size):max=090 position=0   090 040 027 019 013 007 000)
MINIMA FOR ANGLE SIZES:
(<fgl size):min=000 position=0   000 008 013 019 027 041 090)
(<gfk size):min=000 position=0   000 008 013 019 027 041 090)
(<lfg size):min=000 position=6   090 040 027 019 013 007 000)
(<kgf size):min=000 position=6   090 040 027 019 013 007 000)
```

The remaining episodes yield similar results. For each episode it is noted among other things that angle $<gfk$ increases from 0 to a maximum of ninety degrees, and that angle $<fkg$ reaches an extreme value when the moving points lie on the vertical axis. Furthermore, the program noticed that for the third case (the circle), angle $<fkg$ was constant and furthermore was a right angle.

Finally, the model then examined the set of episodes itself in search of regularities across them, using similar methods. It noticed that the extreme values reached by $<fkg$ changed monotonically and achieved a critical value of right angle for episode 3, the circle. This is a potential watershed because horizontal and vertical axes are equal for this episode and no other. That is, for the first two episodes, $<fkg$ increased to a maximum (which was smaller in the second episode but always obtuse) and then decreased to its original value, while for episodes four and five the angle decreased to a minimum (which was smaller in the fifth episode and always acute) and then increased to its original value. Thus, the sequence of extreme values decreased monotonically as one proceeds through the episodes, passing through 90 degrees for the circle.

The information in this series of episodes thus suggests that the circle is a watershed case for which the inscribed angles are right angles, which of course is a true proposition about circles. The program has not proven this nor even constructed a demonstration of it in the sense that term was used earlier. Rather it has found a conjecture.

Episodes may be examined for indication of other key features as well. Two examples are asymptotes and cyclic behavior. The latter is not of much value in geometric contexts, but could be very important in many other applications.

A yet more complex discovery task than those addressed by ARCHIMEDES PLAYER is to discover conjectures that might then lead to the construction of demonstrations. This is an open-ended and extremely difficult extension that blends into the problem of modeling mathematical creativity itself. As such, there is little chance that progress will be made on this task in the general case until breakthroughs have been made on fundamental questions about the nature of intelligence.

ARCHIMEDES PLAYER's exploration of episodes is similar in approach and goals to several other explorations of scientific discovery, notably BACON [Langley (1978); Langley, Bradshaw & Simon (1981); Langley, Bradshaw & Simon (1983)], AM and Eurisko (Lenat (1976)), and HAMB [Buchanan & Livingston (2004); Livingston, Rosenberg & Buchanan (2001); Livingston, Rosenberg & Buchanan (2003), Buchanan & Waltz (2009)]. In each of these systems sets of data or examples are examined for regularities in order to draw general conclusions. BACON examined relatively small sets of numerical data that could have been generated by experiments, and was able to induce classical physical laws, such as Kepler's Third Law of planetary motion and the ideal gas law relating pressure, temperature and volume. AM successfully discovered interesting conjectures in elementary set theory. HAMB discovered regularities in experimental attempts to crystallize proteins for crystallographic examination to determine the protein's structure. A large number of subsequent projects have addressed similar issues in areas where sometimes massive amounts of numerical and other data are available in data bases. That field is called data-mining.

While ARCHIMEDES PLAYER generates and examines some numerical data, the discovery process envisioned depends on the human perceptual processes more generally. Specifically ARCHIMEDES PLAYER should be driven by the detection of features such as symmetry and containment that are efficient and natural for human reasoners. The systems just mentioned, which emphasize engineering artifacts rather than psychological theory, take a more general approach to the problem of discovery.

It is interesting to note that the success of AM depended critically upon the fact that the representation it used – lists – provided a good match to the structure of elementary set theory, and AM's success failed to generalize to other domains (Lenat & Brown

(1984)). Similarly, Eurisko, which attempted to use more general, domain non-specific representations, was unable to achieve equivalent successes. These experiences support the argument made in this essay that the essence of understanding is finding and exploring the structure of the subject matter. One way of doing so is to examine specific cases, as I suggested in Lindsay (1973).

This is not to say that there are no powerful domain-independent methods for discovering regularities in data; there doubtless are. All of the systems mentioned, including ARCHIMEDES PLAYER, employ domain-general methods. However, ARCHIMEDES PLAYER and AM also employ highly structured domain specific models to generate the data to which the discovery processes are applied.

9. Summary of ARCHIMEDES

The main difference among cognitive architectures is in the mode of understanding they provide. ARCHIMEDES provides an architecture that is designed for dealing with Euclidean geometry in a computational style that conceives of operations that manipulate the geometric structure of geometric diagrams in certain ways. The architecture makes use of the (simulated) physical structure of diagrams, rather than treating them as word-signs or logos whose physical properties are only of significance for sign-category discrimination or aesthetic qualities. That is, in ARCHIMEDES, *geometric diagrams are primary computational objects*. This is not the case for most other architectures that address geometric reasoning.

ARCHIMEDES has no visual apparatus; it does not look at a physical diagram with a video camera and record a diagram in its memory. Nonetheless, construed as psychological models, ARCHIMEDES–implemented models *use* physical diagrams. The internal representation of a diagram (pixel nets and predicative structures) models the interpreted diagram that is available to a human observing the physical diagram.

ARCHIMEDES makes available five major classes of computational abilities, corresponding to the four types of construction processes plus the ability to notice several kinds of features.

- First, it can augment its representation of a diagram on the basis of new information provided to it by a programmer. That is, it can add new points, lines, and other objects to an existing representation and the result is a new representation that is still well-formed so that it can be further manipulated.
- Second, it can impose situation constraints and enforce them.
- Third, it can manipulate its representation in a simulation mode. Simulation in ARCHIMEDES is not the equivalent of physical manipulation of a real object. Rather, it is an approximation to such manipulation. The approximation takes the form of selecting certain key points, moving them a finite but small distance, and then modifying the remainder of the representation in ways that preserve all applied constraints – both those of geometry and those that have been specified by the programmer (the situation constraints).
- Fourth, it can make wholesale manipulations of its representation when it has the underlying enabling knowledge necessary.

- Fifth, it can notice properties of its representation, such as symmetries, area decompositions, and other new or altered properties that arose from changes it has made.

Psychological models and ARCHIMEDES

The models that I have programmed in ARCHIMEDES and described in the previous sections could be construed as psychological models of how a person might think about diagrams by mentally manipulating them. I have done no experiments with human subjects to verify these models in the usual manner of experimental psychology. I believe that to do so is unnecessary since the models are manifestly too coarse and brittle to model successfully even a small set of human subjects' behavior. They certainly do not describe the full range of abilities humans bring to this class of problems. Furthermore they do not attempt to model other ways in which some humans approach these problems, much less the fact that the majority of humans cannot do these problems at all. What then is the point of these ARCHIMEDES models?

I view these models as an illustration of a style of thinking about geometry that is important although not the only one. It is a style that treats representations of diagrams as first-class computational objects that are manipulated directly and used as means of making inferences. It is a style that demonstrates how geometric representations can preserve and use the structure of two-dimensional space to reason, so that reasoning is grounded in the perceptual-motor abilities humans possess. It is a style that uses constraints rather than deduction to produce inferences. It is a style that integrates predicative representations and predicative knowledge with geometric representations, acknowledging that this integration is an essential aspect of reasoning. It makes clear that there is no such thing as purely diagrammatic reasoning, because reasoning requires more than the perceptual motor abilities we share with the primates.

Most importantly, the exercise of actually constructing an architecture and using it to model geometric reasoning eliminates the vagueness that characterizes most classical, non-programmed psychological models. To do this modeling requires the construction of precise access processes and formats, and the specification of precise sequences of operations that do in fact accomplish a task. I have been careful not to overstate the abilities or potential of this system, as has often been done in other AI reports. Hopefully this exercise has provided specific examples of a computational style that can be critiqued and built upon, and that will move us beyond the debates that pit one ill-formed conception against another.

The Imagery Debate and ARCHIMEDES

The Imagery Debate has taken two forms. One branch of the debate, primarily advanced by AI researchers, is that diagrammatic reasoning does not have a special status because all such reasoning can be represented and carried out in a formal language such as the predicate calculus. Furthermore there are some reasoning tasks, most notably discovering generalizations, that cannot be done simply by observing diagrams. Still ARCHIMEDES embodies the position that there is indeed an important distinction between diagrammatic and non-diagrammatic reasoning. The defining characteristic of diagrammatic reasoning is that it makes explicit use of some of the structure of space by using the physical properties of diagrams. It need not use all of the structure of space, but if it uses none then it is not diagrammatic even if diagrams are involved. This position does not commit one to a particular form of representation; in particular it does not choose between predicate calculus and some sort of pixel-net or other raster representation. Either can underlie diagrammatic reasoning and either can instantiate non-diagrammatic reasoning. ARCHIMEDES does, however, make clear that reasoning, including but not limited to drawing general conclusions, requires an ability to represent general, quantified statements, which entails the use of variables. ARCHIMEDES also demonstrates that the discovery of general principles can be accomplished by appropriate diagrammatic manipulations in the context of a goal driven architecture, so that such discovery need not be done solely within a formal predicative representation that maintains geometric structure axiomatically.

The second branch of the debate, which has been of greater interest to psychology, involves the status of images rather than percepts. A visual percept results when one is actually looking at the physical world. A visual image is the phenomenological presence of something 'like' a percept in the absence of an actual physical stimulus. The debate is over whether *images* are manipulated *visually*. Note that there are two components to the debate: what is imaged and how is it used.

One side of the debate is often caricatured as the 'pictures in the head' view: images are like pictures in the head which are examined by the 'mind's eye.' The alternative view is that images are not actually represented in the brain, rather the coding is of descriptions of images, which are processed in some verbal or logic-like fashion.

The 'picture-in-the-head' view holds great intuitive appeal especially to those who are adept at thinking in images. The caricature can and has been ridiculed on the grounds that it simply puts off the real questions by adding an unnecessary additional layer of analysis. However, the general idea does not require an infinite regress of homunculi looking in each other's heads. It simply asserts that images actually are represented in the brain, just as are percepts, and that imaging processes treat images in ways similar to the perceptual processes that apply to percepts. To be images, however, they must be depictive. That is, they must make certain information (specifically, but not exclusively, geometric information) readily available. This view does not deny the existence of other non-depictive representations; it only denies that all representations are non-depictive.

When one looks at a diagram of a triangle, for example, a cascade of neural processes takes place. The image is projected onto the retina by the lens, where is it transduced into bursts of nerve action potentials coursing through the optic nerve on a long journey 'inward.' At the visual cortex (Area 17) the pattern of activity can still be seen to be retinotopic (it maintains the same topological organization, though geometrically distorted). The topographic integrity of the cortical firing is maintained in some but not all of the downstream areas. However, signals eventually go to many higher visual centers (a few dozen of which have been identified) and these detect or record differing aspects of the original stimulus, such as its location in space relative to the perceiver, its shape and color, and so forth.

There is substantial evidence from recent studies, including brain imaging, that indicates that some areas of the brain that are active during perception are also active during imaging. Kosslyn, Thompson & Ganis (2006) review this evidence and argue that perceptual and imagery memory traces are present in a form that makes depictive information readily available. For example, they argue that the fact that cortical activity maintains certain properties of the stimulus (such as topology) means that such properties can be easily 'used' by the brain. Of course this argument is based on the assumption that there are retrieval processes (my terminology) that effect this ease of access. Since we know essentially nothing about the nature of these processes it is difficult to evaluate this argument: the information is 'there' only if it can be accessed and used in some fashion, and while retinotopic correspondence seems to keep the information 'there' it is a leap to suggest that it is 'there' for the brain. It is a plausible suggestion, however: since visual processes acting on perceptual records must be available in any case, why would they not work on similar image generated information?

The non-depictive side of this debate has been advanced primarily by psychologist-computer scientist Zenon Pylyshyn and philosophers Jerry Fodor and Daniel Dennett. They consider images to be epi-phenomena – phenomenological but not functional. Pylyshyn (1999) bases his objection on his concept of cognitive penetrability (Pylyshyn (1984)). In brief, he distinguishes two classes of visual processes. The *early vision* processes are direct and immediate and *cannot be altered by beliefs and knowledge.* For example, we simply 'see' that an object appears red (in certain conditions) and we cannot choose to see it as blue (although we could *say* we see it as blue to fool someone else, we cannot fool ourselves). Pylyshyn says that these early visual processes are not cognitively penetrable. The other class of visual processes *are* cognitively penetrable. For example, if asked the effect of superimposing two color filters, we can readily 'image' that result, but we can just as readily image the wrong result as the correct result. In other words, it is our beliefs and knowledge, not our vision *per se*, that make the inferences. Pylyshyn believes that cognitively penetrable processes underlie almost all that passes for imagistic reasoning.

Even if Pylyshyn is correct, however, this does not mean that the cognitive processes are best described as general logical manipulations. Kosslyn may also be correct if the penetrability does in fact make use of 'explicit and accessible' depictive information. In other words, imagistic thinking could be cognitively penetrable *and* depictive. The information must be (readily) accessible by virtue of whatever access processes can be applied to the brain-record. Requiring that the brain-record be 'explicit' is irrelevant; it is explicit if and only if it is readily accessible.

An important issue is the 'automaticity' of the processes involved. The early visual processes presumably just happen. Cognition cannot control their course or the amount of time they take. In contrast, processes under cognitive control may be altered in function and timing. Evidence that image processes are automatic would support Kosslyn. However, even if many important processes are under cognitive control, they may still be depictive, and hence this would not undermine the Kosslyn theory.

The representations used by ARCHIMEDES are not literally percepts since they do not arise from sensory processes. Since they are internal representations that are manipulable by programs, they might be construed as images. However, what they most closely model is what might be going on within a person's brain while he is viewing a physical diagram. Better yet, they model what a person might be doing while actually manipulating a physical diagram by erasing and redrawing lines, although the planning of the constructions is done cognitively, and limited but crude mental experiments are done before more careful physical manipulations are made.

Thus although ARCHIMEDES does not make a commitment about the *de novo* creation and manipulation of visual images, the models it supports are clearly of a cognitively penetrable *and* depictive style. ARCHIMEDES must simulate visual processes to the extent that it can examine its representations and detect their properties, and it can manipulate them by incremental simulations, but all under cognitive control. ARCHIMEDES does not assume that there are any automatic, non-cognitively penetrable visual processes involved in reasoning, other than the equivalents of these simple perceptual feature detection processes. All other processing, including simulations (which are not perceptual processes by any stretch), are cognitive. Nonetheless they make use of 'depictive' information of the sort that human perception makes accessible.

9 SUMMARY

Beauty is Truth
– John Keats (1795–1821)

1. Introduction

In 2011 a computer named Watson beat the two most successful human Jeopardy[27] players in a not very close contest. This fact is remarkable for two reasons.

First a computer was able to best humans at what many had considered a classical example of an intellectual task requiring a high level of intelligence.

More remarkable still, at least in hindsight, is the fact that the computer did not shut out the humans entirely.[28] Anyone who has played Jeopardy will recognize that word association with extensive memory is how most human players play, as does Watson (see my earlier discussion in Chapter 3). One difference is that humans do not have primarily text based memories,[29] and do not produce dozens or hundreds of candidate solutions for checking, but quickly zero in on one or a few possibilities, a difference this contest shares with Deep Blue vs. Kasparov. Watson's major advantage is that it is very fast.[30]

---

[27] Jeopardy is a popular television game show in which "answers" are posed in English and the contestants must reply with a "question" for which the answer is appropriate. The "answers" can range over essentially any topic that can be posed with text, and speed of reply is essential to successful play. For the competition, the rules of the game were altered to disallow pictorial and audio clues normally permitted, since Watson could not deal with these.

[28] In the competition, Watson won 58% of the total 'points' earned; the two humans shared the remainder. In more extensive tests against other human opponents in 55 contests, Watson's winning rate was about 70%.

[29] Watson's memory is 4 trillion bytes of text, far larger than human *text* memory, which typically consists of a few song lyrics, poems, and a couple of speeches. Thus while humans use word association, the retrievals are from a much more structured database, more like CYC than Watson.

[30] Indeed early versions of Watson took two hours to answer a question. By adding more hardware this was reduced to the three second response time needed to beat good human

Given that human players work in a similar way but without the luxury (at least at the moment) of being able to employ more memory and processors[31] (as Watson's developers did during its development) it is surprising that the humans were able to answer any of the questions *before* Watson did. In short, Jeopardy was an excellent choice for this challenge because it can be successfully played without understanding natural language or any of the topics of the questions.

Both Watson and Deep Blue were developed by the research department of IBM. Unfortunately the IBM promotional message repeatedly has been that Watson understands natural language, a claim with superficial validity since the input is arbitrary text and replies are words or phrases. This use of "understanding" is quite different from my use of that word in this essay: Watson makes no use of the full structure of 'answer/questions,' it does not understand the meanings of words in a human way (notwithstanding that it had access to the text of a dictionary), it does not have a comprehensive ability to analyze or produce utterances even at the level of a human child, and its knowledge is not grounded in experience or episodic memory. It does not know anything about the topics of the game other than how words are statistically correlated to its database of text. The IBM claim is equivalent to asserting that computers 'understand number theory' because they input and process numerals to produce numerical answers. Not surprisingly, the popular press[32] eagerly picked up on the IBM exaggeration so that it is now part of popular belief.

Watson is a significant engineering achievement which will certainly have many important applications as a general question answering system that truly finds relevant responses to an unbounded set of questions. It will eventually be extended to use other forms of memory and thus have greater application yet. It is not the case, however, that it understands in human fashion, anymore than do Google or ELIZA. Thus, while it is an excellent piece of *engineering*, it does not move us closer to a *scientific* understanding of *human* understanding and intelligence.

---

players. Speed was Watson's major advantage. Had the rules been modified to allow all contestants to answer (within, say, 5 seconds) and be rewarded and penalized for their answers (much as in the 'Final Jeopardy' round) the scores would have been much more even, with all contestants getting the vast majority (about 90% judging by prior performance) of replies correct.

[31] Watson and its support systems fill a large room several orders of magnitude greater than a human brain, and additional processors and memory could be added as modules without limit.

[32] For example, CBS's Sunday Morning program on February 20, 2011 preposterously proclaimed that Watson is "able to understand language with all its nuances." Laymen are easily fooled. Eliza was an early and very primitive 'natural language' system from the 1960's, created by Joseph Weisenbaum to illustrate how readily we attribute intelligence even to a simple system. It also accepted arbitrary text input and produced responses in English – without much more than a key-word trigger of canned phrases – yet many thought its responses were relevant and even insightful.

2. Human Understanding

Understanding and the abilities that underlie it are the basis of uniquely human cognitive abilities – language, story-telling and literature, mathematics, science, art, music and dance, religion. Attempting to understand is our human quest. In spite of its limitations, understanding is the essential way in which we cope with the world. It remains the key concept of human psychology, and understanding understanding is an essential intellectual goal of psychology.

Artificial Intelligence originally addressed the scientific task of creating a theory of a complete human intelligence, and even aspired ultimately to creating a super-human intelligence. As the difficulty of these tasks became ever more apparent, AI increasingly emphasized its other, engineering, aspect: creating artifacts that do intelligent things in limited specialties for practical reasons. The engineering effort now dominates the field, and has achieved substantial success with many applied problems. There remains the belief among many that the engineering route will eventually achieve the scientific goal. This opinion is incorrect. The problem is not so much the achievement of *intelligence* in artifacts, but capturing the uniquely *human* cognitive system which is intelligent and which *understands* what it is intelligent about, whether that involves complex technical knowledge or everyday living.   The successful modeling of human cognition must await new conceptualizations that go well beyond those now available, and most importantly such developments will surely require a great deal of further empirical work on both brain and behavior before the issues are fully clarified.

The conception of understanding I have outlined in this essay is a departure from many traditional cognitive modeling approaches, from Associationism, to stochastic modeling, to symbolic artificial intelligence. Human cognitive life, on my view, is tied in an essential way to the ability to construct and use models, to the ability to understand and relate structures abstractly, to linguistic abilities such as abstraction by quantification, to perceptual motor processes, and to one's representation and memory of experience. Understanding and problem solving as performed by humans rely extensively on the ability to imagine situations and events that flow from a model, and to run mental experiments that allow inference, prediction, and planning.

The ability to understand the world and one's actions in it is a characteristic of humans that is not shared fully by other forms of life. Understanding is a complex ability that depends on several uniquely human cognitive abilities that are superimposed upon other essential abilities that are shared by chimpanzees and in most cases by all mammals.

3. Understanding Understanding

My proposed analysis of understanding is the following:

- Understanding requires the ability to represent knowledge abstractly. This includes the representation of objects and events that are not perceptually present, the representation of non-physical abstractions, the use of variables that range over members of a set, the use of various kinds of quantification over variables, and the ability to generate representations systematically, iteratively, and recursively. These abilities are not available in lower life forms.

- Understanding requires the ability to recognize structure in the perceptual world and also in the abstract world of knowledge representations. Structure is the interconnected set of constraints on what is possible within the bounds of required relations among entities. This ability is not fully available in lower life forms.

- Understanding requires the ability to relate perceptions, actions, and symbolic thoughts to structure, so that selected relations are maintained in the structure while others are ignored. This permits a human to perceive a situation abstractly, ignoring certain perceptual features, and treating it as-if it were something that it is manifestly not. This ability is not available in lower life forms.

- Understanding requires the ability to form hypotheses and theories, using analogy, metaphor, and other structural knowledge, that is, to think theoretically (abductively) through the manipulation of structured representations in ways that preserve the constraints of the structure, permitting the agent to observe the constrained behavior of the representation and thus to make inferences. This ability is not fully available in lower life forms.

- Understanding requires core cognitive abilities based upon but supplementing the previous abilities mentioned. Core abilities provide basic structured representations of world knowledge. These include intuitive geometry, intuitive physics, intuitive biology, and intuitive Theory of Mind. These abilities are not fully shared with lower life forms.

- Human experience requires an extensive episodic memory that records events, including remembered perceptions, cognitions, and actions. Episodic memory is not a passive record but can be examined and 'penetrated' by the cognitive system to produce structured descriptions of previously experienced events and to generate representations of non-experienced events. Other primates have a limited version of episodic memory but lack the full ability to abstract.

- Understanding by humans critically depends on the subhuman cognitive abilities humans share with other mammals, in particular perceptual skills, motor skills, emotion, intentionality, consciousness, and social skills that connect one to the world.

- Understanding is ultimately grounded in experience and in core human cognitive abilities. Since understanding requires both experience and core abilities, other primates do not have the ability to understand in human fashion.

Limitations of current approaches to understanding

Artificial Intelligence artifacts to date have explored only piecemeal a few of the abilities underlying understanding, generally by building them in directly and studying them in isolation. While this work has produced practical computational artifacts it has provided no insight into the full issue of human mental capacity and does not appear to be on a path to do so. Current cognitive theories and AI techniques are not adequate to the task of explaining understanding.

Current models such as expert systems and neural nets have only a little more computational sophistication than the chimpanzee's perceptual-association skills. Indeed they are essentially the same in spirit, although symbolic models do permit abstract representations, including abstractions of abstractions, variables, and recursive computation not fully available to chimpanzees. To achieve artificial intelligence of human breadth will require extension to encompass model construction, analogy formation, metaphor, and understanding; many researchers in AI and psychology have recognized these needs. Although inventing sound theories of these abilities is a daunting task, attempting to circumvent them is futile. Specifically, experience cannot be captured in a lexicon or encyclopedia, but only through complex multi-sense perceptual processes and complex motor skills applied not only to the external world but in episodic memory as well. Furthermore, understanding cannot be represented *directly* in the form of conditional rules or logical statements. Rather, understanding understanding will require the development of several layers of description to account for the above abilities.

On this analysis of understanding, there is a qualitative difference between human understanding and the cognitive activities of chimpanzees, and perforce all other species, even though those organisms are goal directed and conscious, are capable of learning, and even though some are capable of solving non-trivial problems, including the use of tools and intraspecies communication.

Also, there is a qualitative difference between what I have called cook-book understanding and real understanding. The former is achieved by many human technicians and even by expert system artifacts. Deep Blue understands chess in the cook-book manner because it has a store of factual knowledge that it successfully applies to its assigned task, just as a television repairman can locate and repair faults by following a troubleshooting guide. Deep Blue does not fully understand chess competition in the sense a chess master does.

Abduction

The ability to operate in hypothetical worlds allows one to devise models that can be mentally manipulated to generate and test conjectures and solve problems. The hypothetical worlds may involve only the physical, or they may include emotional and social aspects. *This abductive ability is the capstone achievement of human cognition.* It requires linguistic abilities – referring, variables, quantification, and abstraction. It also requires the ability to adopt the intentional stance. It is why we can, and do, think in a distinctively human manner. It is why science is possible. It is why human culture is possible.

Understanding something requires being able to construct a model of it, a model that makes use of the structure of the subject, and to explore the implications of this structure. By abstracting the structure of one domain, such as space, one can project another domain onto it. Thus understanding is a process of seeing structure. Some domains, such as space, are primitive in the sense that evolution has provided us with a representation that is adequate to the tasks of survival and reproduction. Therefore spatial reasoning provides an important paradigmatic case of understanding by structural analogy, although it is not the only form of structure so used. Lower animals necessarily have this structural knowledge in order to survive and explore the world. However, they lack the other mechanisms whereby this structure can be exploited in complex reasoning.

Hierarchy

Understanding highly complex concepts and systems is achieved in steps, by connecting the highest abstraction to another lower one, which in turn is connected to another, and so on until a base level is reached. The connections need not all be held in mind simultaneously; indeed that is why the levels are important. The interconnection of two levels is how understanding is achieved. The connection of the lower level to the base level (grounding in core knowledge and experience) is necessary to the final achievement.

The base levels are built-in in the sense that they are fundamental processes, such as perceptual motor processes plus human core abilities, with which we connect to our environment and which are essential for success, that is, the adaptive success that underlies their evolution.

Emergence

I am not arguing for a reductionist approach to understanding. Indeed if understanding understanding could not be achieved until conceptual accounts and models were reduced to an ultimate base level there would be no understanding of understanding until the programs of physical science were complete. They may never be. Even if complete, reducing theories of understanding to the level of physical processes would be too complex to be illuminating. Worse yet, such descriptions would miss the important generalizations of concepts that emerge at higher levels of organization.

New properties and phenomena emerge at higher levels of description. This does not mean that they are causally disconnected from the lower levels. It does mean, however, that they are not predictable nor subsumable by the lower levels. Many emergent properties are the result of the way lower level items are organized, and such structure does not exist at the lower levels: a water molecule is not wet, a single bird does not flock. Yet wetness and flocking are important notions.

The scientific community is in the process of trying to understand the important idea of emergence. Emergence does not yet have a proper definition, but emergence certainly will play an important role in the understanding of the scientific enterprise.

4. Diagrammatic Reasoning

Diagrammatic reasoning is one form of uniquely human understanding that provides an example of these ideas. Diagrams are seen by humans not merely as perceptual objects but as representations of abstract and general situations. A diagram can be seen as-if it were what it is not. Diagrammatic reasoning calls upon intuitive geometry to recognize the geometric structure of the abstracted diagram, it calls upon our perceptual-motor-memory systems to simulate modifications of a diagram, and it calls upon linguistic-related skills to represent generalizations gleaned from these processes. Diagrammatic reasoning is not merely looking at an image in the mind's eye. Predicative knowledge must be brought to bear, and this abstract knowledge is not available to subhumans.

Diagrammatic reasoning makes use of some of the structure of space. A diagram that makes use of very little of this structure supports only an impoverished form of diagrammatic reasoning. For example, if a diagram only maps a simple ordering relation onto a single spatial dimension, then it uses the structure of space no more fully than does a natural (or a formal) language, which also relies on a spatial (or temporal in the case of spoken language) ordering of symbols along a single dimension. However, if a diagram uses other aspects of spatial structure such as topological relations or dimensionality or a distance metric, then it is using spatial structure in a way not *directly* available to the syntax of language. To be sure, language can discuss such relations, but it does so in a fundamentally different way, by axiom and inference rather than constraint satisfaction. This is what distinguishes diagrammatic (and spatial) reasoning from formal logical reasoning.

Whether this difference makes a difference depends entirely on how the processes are implemented. This is an issue that has been almost universally confused in the imagery debate. A format for recording information is only one part of a knowledge representation system. Processes that create and access knowledge in that format must also be specified. Neither diagrams nor text have inherent meaning, independent of an interpreting agent. Unless the creation and access processes are fully specified, the description of the representation system is incomplete and representations in different systems cannot be compared in any useful way. Since these essential descriptions are seldom given, many arguments about descriptive versus depictive representations are meaningless. Ultimately the processes must be described as physical processes, as must all computations.

Diagrammatic reasoning also necessarily involves linguistic processes, specifically the ability to refer, and to use variables and quantification. Diagrams that lack annotations and do not rely on verbalized conventions do not directly support these abilities. Thus there is no such thing as purely diagrammatic *reasoning*, even though diagrammatic reasoning is not the same as linguistic reasoning. Diagrams are cognitively penetrable, and must be in order to serve any inferential purpose or to support understanding. One can actively manipulate them mentally, and we do so to understand, to conjecture, and to discover.

It is significant that diagrammatic reasoning is limited to humans. To be sure, other animals, particularly primates, have rudimentary versions of some components of this ability, but the differences are so great as to constitute a difference in kind, not just degree. For example, while chimpanzees can through extensive training learn to use hundreds of distinct symbols to refer to perceptual objects, and sometimes do so for objects not previously seen by them, this still leaves them far short of a human language capability. All humans, barring accident or serious developmental problems, learn language without any laborious training procedure, merely by exposure to a speaking community. Furthermore, the human language ability is vastly richer than that of the most well-trained chimpanzee, both in syntax and in representational power.

Much of the discussion about these issues in the psychological literature has been pursued at the level of armchair philosophy, where it is easy to ignore the real problems because their solutions are taken for granted. Therefore I chose to actually implement as a computer system my notions of geometric reasoning with diagrams. While far from achieving an autonomous cognitive system, the discipline of the exercise has illuminated many of the issues, and forced me to recognize problems even when they were not solved. ARCHIMEDES is a concrete illustration of how complex abstractions can be related to existing intuitions of geometry that are common to modern educated people. The form the relation takes is to identify abstract structure with a partially isomorphic structure of specific concrete instances, in this case geometric diagrams.

The ARCHIMEDES architecture has been used only to illustrate cognition-by-simulation of geometrically structured representations of diagrams. Other than that limited illustration it does not approach an explanation of understanding because it is not embedded in a system that has had experience of the world.

5. Scientific Understanding of Understanding

I have provided a coarse road map of a theory of understanding. The Devil, as we are often reminded, is in the details, none of which I have provided. Even my highly specific ARCHIMEDES architecture, which is quite precise in some aspects, does not address the really fundamental problems. Unfortunately, no other work does either.

A solid understanding of cognition requires grounding in things we understand. The obvious candidates for psychological theories are neural structures and processes, and evolution-genetics.

Many contemporary psychological models are stated as actual computer programs, and many more are couched in the language of computation without being actually implemented in computer code. Computational models are a potential third type of grounding for a theory of understanding. They serve for the moment as important way stations by giving precise functional descriptions of psychological processes. However, ultimately they themselves will need to be related to (not 'reduced to') biology.

Take but one simple example of a cognitive ability that has been studied by primatologists and developmental psychologists: the ability for mirror self-recognition. This is an ability all humans have. It has also been observed in other species, and there are yet other species that may or may not possess it. We have a more or less clear test for it: place a mark on an animal in a spot where the animal cannot see it except in a mirror; does the animal reach, on its body, for the mark when it sees its image?

But what could underlie success at this test? It is often said that the animal must 'have a representation' of itself that includes its body structure, must 'see' that the image corresponds to this representation, must be able to note 'something unexpected' in the image, and must be able to locate on its body the place 'corresponding to' the imaged object. However, these descriptions do not give an adequate account of exactly how the organism is doing these things, either in computational, neural, or genetic terms. We are a long way from understanding the neural circuitry that implements mirror self-recognition. We do not know where in the brain 'representations' lie, or how they do the work we assume they do. Evolutionary psychology tells us that self-recognition must have 'adaptive significance' but it does not tell us how the genome was modified from an organism without the ability to one with it.

We could, with some effort and creativity, create a robot that exhibits mirror self-recognition, but we would still lack understanding of how this engineering device could be implemented biologically or how it arises from the genetic code of an organism. Further, we would not know how this specific ability is an instance of some more general ability or how it is integrated with other capacities, nor exactly how it gives a species a reproductive advantage.

Similar observations hold for all cognitive bases of the mammalian perceptual motor skills. By 'cognitive bases' I mean not just the abilities to run, intercept, catch, and so forth, but the abilities that relate these activities to cognitive functions such as tool use and construction, social cooperation, way-finding, and a host of other perceptual-motor skills. Without solid neural, computational, or genetic explanations of these fundamental abilities, we will not be able to find similarly well-grounded explanations of the human core cognitive abilities that underlie human level understanding.

Currently new techniques for imaging brains are providing much new information, and older techniques of anatomical tracing, measurement of evoked potentials, and biochemical analysis of synapses and neurons are also making new strides. In genetics other enormous strides have been taken with the mapping of the genomes of many organisms and studies of development and gene regulation. We have a long way to go, but methods will continue to improve.

However, neither brain research, nor genetics, nor computational modeling alone or together will be able to solve the real problems of understanding understanding until all are combined and related to functional descriptions of cognitive abilities. At the moment the three fields are speaking different languages. I feel that the integration necessary will require *new conceptualization* that will rewrite our way of looking at these problems in ways as powerful as the ways in which relativity and quantum mechanics re-wrote classical physics and evolution and genetics re-wrote classical biology.

I make these observations not because I think understanding the human mind is impossible, nor to disparage the important work that has been done, but in hopes that others will see the limitations of the explanations that have been thus far offered, and, even if they are not able to set the ship of science on the proper course, they will at least understand where it is we need to go.

APPENDICES

1. Appendix A: Hilbert's Axiomatization of Euclidean Geometry

A version of the Hilbert axioms is given here. They obviously must be augmented by carefully constructed definitions that I have not included but are straightforward. Note also that this list is not a strictly formal axiom set, but is stated in English (here) and requires that the reader understand the meanings of many words (*e.g.*, *emanates*, among many others).

(It is understood that "two points" means "two distinct points" etc. throughout.)

Axioms of incidence

I.1 For every two points A, B there exists a line L that contains each of the points A, B.

I.2 For every two points A, B there exists no more than one line that contains each of the points A, B.

I.3 There exist at least two points on a line. There exist at least three points that do not lie on a line.

I.4 For any three points A, B, C that do not lie on the same line there exists a plane *alpha* that contains each of the points A, B, C. For every plane there exists a point which it contains.

I.5 For any three points A, B, C that do not lie on one and the same line there exists no more than one plane that contains each of the three points A, B, C.

I.6 If two points A, B of a line L lie in a plane *alpha* then every point of L lies in the plane *alpha*.

I.7 If two planes *alpha*, *beta* have a point A in common they have at least one more point B in common.

I.8 There exist at least four points which do not lie in a plane.

Axioms of order

II.1 If a point B lies between point A and point C then the points A, B, C are three distinct points of a line, and B then also lies between C and A.

II.2 For two points A and C, there always exists at least one point B on the line AC such that C lies between A and B.

II.3 Of any three points on a line there exists no more than one that lies between the other two.

II.4 Let A, B, C be three points that do not lie on a line and let L be a line in the plane ABC which does not meet any of the points A, B, C. If the line L passes through a point of the segment AB, it also passes through a point of the segment AC, or through a point of the segment BC. (A *segment* has been defined to be a pair of points, and *points of a segment* is defined as the set of points between the pair of points.)

UNDERSTANDING UNDERSTANDING

Axioms of congruence

III.1 If *A, B* are two points of a line *L*, and *A'* is a point on the same or on another line *L'* then it is always possible to find a point *B'* on the line *L'* on a given side of *A'* such that the segment *AB* is congruent or equal to the segment *A'B'*.

III.2 If a segment *A'B'* and a segment *A"B"* are congruent to the same segment *AB*, the segment *A'B'* is also congruent to the segment *A"B"*.

III.3 On the line *L* let *AB* and *BC* be two segments which except for *B* have no point in common. Furthermore, on the same or another line *L'* let *A'B'* and *B'C'* be two segments which except for *B'* also have no point in common. In that case, if *AB* is congruent to *A'B'* and *BC* is congruent to *B'C'* then *AC* is congruent to *A'C'*.

III.4 Let angle (*h,k*) be an angle in a plane *alpha* and *L'* a line in a plane *alpha'* and let a definite side of *L'* in *alpha'* be given. Let *h'* be a ray on the line *L'* that emanates from the point *O'*. Then there exists in the plane *alpha'* one and only one ray *k'* such that the angle (*h,k*) is congruent or equal to the angle (*h',k'*) and at the same time all interior points of the angle (*h',k'*) lie on the given side of *L'*. Every angle is congruent to itself. (An angle is defined as two rays emanating from a single point.)

III.5 If for two triangles *ABC* and *A'B'C'* the congruences *AB A'B'*, *AC A'C'* and angle *BAC* angle *B'A'C'* hold, then *ABC* is congruent to *A'B'C'*

Axiom of parallels

IV.1 Let *L* be any line and *A* a point not on it. Then there is at most one line in the plane, determined by *L* and *A*, that passes through *A* and does not intersect *L*.

Axioms of continuity

V.1 (Axiom of Archimedes). If *AB* and *CD* are any segments then there exists a number *n* such that *n* segments *CD* constructed contiguously from *A*, along the ray from *A* through *B*, will pass beyond the point *B*.

V.2 (Axiom of line completeness). An extension of a set of points on a line with its order and congruence relations that would preserve the relations existing among the original elements as well as the fundamental properties of line order and congruence that follows from Axioms I-III, and from V.1 is impossible.

Summary of Hilbert's axiomatization

Hilbert defines three sets of objects – points, lines, and planes – the structure of which the axioms will specify. He divides his axioms into five groups. The 8 Axioms of Incidence specify the basic relations among the three sets of objects: that two points determine a unique line, that three non-collinear points determine a plane. They also introduce dimensionality by asserting that there are non-collinear points and non-coplanar points. Dimensionality is limited to 3 by requiring that any two non-parallel planes intersect in exactly one line. (Axiom I.7 expresses the fact that space has no more than three dimensions. Axiom I.8 expresses the fact that space has no less than three dimensions.)

The 4 axioms of order formalize the concept of betweeness. The vagueness of this notion and that of containment in Euclid was the source of many problems.

There are 5 axioms of congruence that define a relation among figures that is free from the notions of superposition and movement that underlie both intuitive and Euclidean geometry.

There is but one axiom of parallels, and it is essentially Euclid's although stated differently. Hilbert proved that it is independent of his other axioms, ending centuries of debate on this issue.

The final group of axioms consists of two axioms of continuity. These are the most puzzling of the formalization. Hilbert showed that without Archimedes's axiom, the remaining set is inconsistent. This is because the first groups of axioms together are satisfied by (have as a model) the points on a line, but without Archimedes's axiom it is always possible to adjoin to the model other points and still have a consistent model; thus the axiom of line completeness is inconsistent with the remainder unless Archimedes's axiom is included. However the completeness axiom is not a consequence of Archimedes's axiom.

The modern method of formalizing continuity is the use of the concept of a limit (see Chapter 4). Neither of Hilbert's axioms of continuity makes direct reference to that concept. Remarkably, however, taken together they are equivalent to the limit formulation of continuity. Furthermore, it is possible thus to show that Hilbert's geometry is identical to Cartesian geometry.

Thus we have a full axiomatization of intuitive/Euclidean geometry for which Cartesian geometry is a model. This result means that an artificial intelligence formalism based on Cartesian (numerical, algebraic) geometry can capture the human intuitive structure of space.

2. Appendix B: Non-Euclidean Geometries

The algebrization of geometry was the force that led ultimately to the development of non-Euclidean geometries, among many other things. This required precise definitions of the intuitive notion of curvature.

It is natural to think that curvature of a line or surface requires that the object in question be embedded in a space with at least one more dimension than the object: one may define the curvature at a point of a (one-dimensional) line in two dimensional space and the curvature at a point of a two dimensional surface in three dimensional space. We may also speak of the curvature of a line in three-space, in which case the curvature may differ with direction. We may also speak of the curvature of a two-dimensional surface in three-space or higher. By extension, we may conceive of the curvature of a three dimensional volume in four-space, as well as the curvature of surfaces and lines in that same space. This view leads to an *extrinsic* definition of curvature.

Riemann and Gauss were the first to introduce analytic definitions of geometry that formalized the notions of straightness and curvature. This field of mathematics is called differential geometry. Gauss defined curvature *intrinsically* in a way that does not require an embedding in a higher dimensional space. With the methods of differential geometry, curvatures are defined as differentials. The (constant) curvature of a sphere is $1/r^2$ (=1 for the unit sphere), the curvature of a plane is 0. Surprisingly, the curvature of any surface that a plane can be mapped onto while preserving distance, such as a cylinder, is also 0. With an intrinsic definition of curvature one may discuss the curvature of three dimensional space without reference to a fourth dimension and discuss the curvature of the four dimensional spacetime of Einstein's general relativity without reference to five dimensions.

Lobachevsky extended Gauss's notion of curvature to develop an axiomatic geometry in which 3 dimensional space has a negative curvature. In this geometry, the parallel postulate is not true; in fact there are an *infinite* number of lines parallel to a given line through a given point. He showed that his *hyperbolic geometry* was relatively consistent, that is, if Euclidean geometry leads to no contradictions, then neither does hyperbolic geometry. Later Hilbert proved that under his axiomatization Euclidean geometry is consistent, so hyperbolic geometry is as well.

Later yet, Riemann showed that another version of the parallel postulate yielded a consistent geometry, Riemannian or *elliptical geometry*. In this geometry, space has a positive curvature, such as that of a sphere in three dimensional space. In fact, a spherical surface is a model of two dimensional Riemannian geometry, in which straight lines are segments of great circles. A great circle is a geodesic, that is, the shortest distance between two points on the surface. Note that two distinct great circles, such as lines of longitude on the idealized earth, have transversals (the latitudes) that intersect at right angles, but great circles violate Euclid's Postulate 5 because they intersect (*e.g.*, at the North and South Poles). In elliptical geometry there are *no* parallel lines.

3. Appendix C: Hammer-Danner Venn Analysis

Table 15: Construction Rules for Venn Diagrams reproduces Hammer and Danners's statement of the rules of transformation for Venn Diagrams. The transformation rules are already in the form of construction processes. I omit definitions of several terms that are included in the original paper since they are not needed to convey the spirit of the system. To illustrate the Shin/Hammer-Danner system, consider Figure 43: Construction Rules for Venn Diagrams Illustrated, demonstrating the syllogism

$$(\exists x)(x\varepsilon A \text{ or } x\varepsilon B), \text{ All } B \text{ are } C, \text{ therefore } (\exists x)(x\varepsilon A \text{ or } x\varepsilon C).$$

Table 15
Construction Rules for Venn Diagrams

With kind permission from Springer Science+Business Media and the authors: Journal of Philosophical Logic, Towards a model theory of diagrams, 25, 1996, pages 471-472, E. Hammer and N. Danner, "Rules of Inference." © 1996 Kluwer Academic Publishers – Dordrecht.

Erasure of part of an x-sequence. D' is obtainable from D by this rule if and only if D' results from D by erasure of some link of an x-sequence that falls in a shaded region of D, provided the two halves of the sequence are reconnected by a line.

Spreading x's. D' is obtainable from D by this rule if and only if D' results from the additon of a new link to any sequence of D.

Erasure of a diagrammatic object. A diagram D' is obtainable from D by this rule if and only if D' results from the erasure of any entire x-sequence, or from the erasure of the shading of any region, or by the erasure of any closed curve in accordance with the following condition: the shading of any minimal region of D that would fail to cover an entire minimal region upon erasure of the curve must also be erased, and if the erasure of the curve would result in some x-sequence having two links in some minimal region of D', then one of those links must be erased (and the two halves rejoined).

Introduction of new basic regions. D can be asserted at any line if D consists of a rectangle within which is a single closed curve but no shading or sequences, or else D consists of a single rectangle.

Conflicting information. D' is obtainable from D by this rule if D' is any diagram and D has a region that is both shaded and has no x-sequence.

Unification of two diagrams. Diagram D is obtainable from D_1 and D_2 by unification if and only if the following hold:
1. The set of labels of D is the union of the set of labels of D_1 and the set of labels of D_2.
2. If a region r of either D_1 or D_2 is shaded, then there is a counterpart of it in D which is also shaded. Likewise, if any region r of D is shaded, then there is a counterpart of it in either D_1 or D_2 which is also shaded.
3. If r is a region having an x-sequence in either D_1 or D_2, then there is a counterpart of it in D which also has an x-sequence. Similarly, if any region r of D has an x-sequence, then there is a counterpart of it in either D_1 or D_2 which also has an x-sequence.

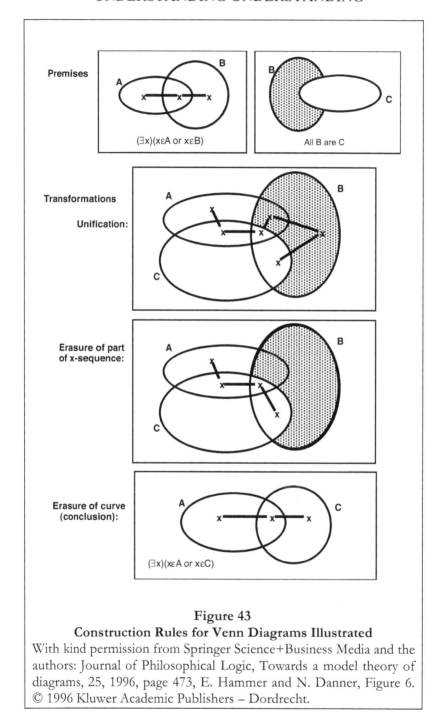

Figure 43
Construction Rules for Venn Diagrams Illustrated
With kind permission from Springer Science+Business Media and the
authors: Journal of Philosophical Logic, Towards a model theory of
diagrams, 25, 1996, page 473, E. Hammer and N. Danner, Figure 6.
© 1996 Kluwer Academic Publishers – Dordrecht.

How do these methods handle the problem of generalization? Hammer & Danner
(1996) treat this by defining equivalence classes of diagrams. Each member of an
equivalence class is called a token of the type (the class). The definitions are prescriptions
for ignoring differences that depend on metric properties of the diagram, such as size,

shape, and direction. This amounts to focusing on a subset of the structure of geometry that will carry meaning. This is similar to the convention of ignoring absolute size and orientation when discussing properties of geometric diagrams, thus permitting diagrammatic demonstrations to apply to implicit classes of diagrams. Further restrictions to provide appropriate generalizations are more difficult to define, for example a restriction to right triangles.

4. Appendix D: Peirce Beta Graphs

A *Line of Identity* is any network of lines connecting individuals, and its interpretation is that all connected individuals are the same. Cuts that enclose part or all of a line of identity express quantification, expressed as negation. If the outermost part of a line of identity is *evenly* enclosed in cuts, this expresses the existence of that which is enclosed. If the outermost part of a line of identity is *oddly* enclosed in cuts, this expresses universal quantification. Figure 44: A Peirce Beta Graph (a) expresses that there exists a mortal human, and (b) expresses that everything human is mortal.

To use these diagrams, one begins with a predication (or proposition) and creates a diagram expressing it. One then augments this diagram so that it also represents additional predications. Finally, the resulting diagram is 'read' to determine what has been implied by the inputs. Reading means translating a diagram into a symbolic expression. The diagram does inferential work because the diagrams 'make' inferences by virtue of obeying the structure of physical space. In the case of logic diagrams, very little of spatial structure is involved. As noted in Section 7.3, Peirce alpha graphs use only the ordering property of space. Beta graphs are truly diagrammatic because they use the two dimensional structure of space as well, although not its metric properties. However, the reading methods do not make full use of humans' powerful perceptual processes, and thus these graphs do not have the immediate intuitive connection of Venn diagrams.

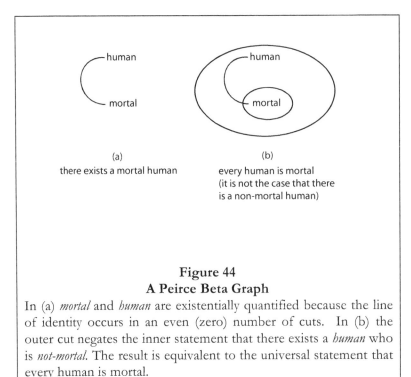

human

mortal

human

mortal

(a)
there exists a mortal human

(b)
every human is mortal
(it is not the case that there
is a non-mortal human)

Figure 44
A Peirce Beta Graph

In (a) *mortal* and *human* are existentially quantified because the line of identity occurs in an even (zero) number of cuts. In (b) the outer cut negates the inner statement that there exists a *human* who is *not-mortal*. The result is equivalent to the universal statement that every human is mortal.

Indeed the reading methods (which involve among other things providing labels and determining the parity of cut embedding) are awkward. Furthermore, different reading methods produce different, though logically equivalent, symbolic expressions.

Nonetheless, the graphs are interesting and diagrammatic because the inference mechanism through graph construction and augmentation makes real use of spatial constraints.

Peirce suggested a reading method that was not fully stated algorithmically. Roberts (1973) and Zeman (1964) have proposed other reading methods, but these do not make full use of the diagrammatic features of the system. Shin (2000) defined a new reading method for Peirce beta graphs, and this is presented in Table 16: Retrieval Rules for Peirce Beta Graphs primarily to illustrate its complexity. (I have not fully explained the notation and motivation underlying this method, but refer the interested reader to the article just cited). Note that the Zeman reading of the graph in Figure 45: Another Peirce Beta Graph is $-\exists x(Px \ \& \ \exists y \exists z(x=y \ \& \ y=z \ \& \ -(Qy \ \& \ Rz)))$. The Shin reading method yields $\forall x[-Px \ \text{or} \ (Qx \ \& \ Rx)]$. The two are logically equivalent, but the latter is much simpler. This is a clear example of the fact that access and retrieval processes are a critical part of any representation system, affecting not only the naturalness (to humans) of the system, but the ease of interfacing it with other representational systems.

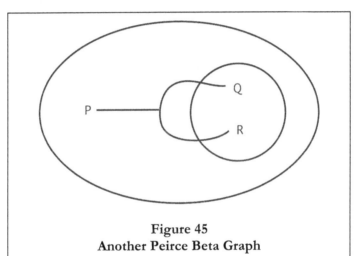

Figure 45
Another Peirce Beta Graph
$-\exists x(Px \ \& \ \exists y \exists z(x=y \ \& \ y=z \ \& \ -(Qy \ \& \ Rz)))$
P is universally quantified because it is enclosed in an odd number of cuts. Q and R are existentially quantified because they are enclosed in an even number of cuts.

Table 16

Retrieval Rules for Peirce Beta Graphs

From S.-J. Shin (2000), Reviving the Iconicity of Beta Graphs. In M. Anderson, P. Cheng, and V. Haarslev (Eds.), *Theory and application of diagrams* (pp. 58-73). Berlin: Springer-Verlag. ©2000 Springer-Verlag. With kind permission from Springer Science+Business Media and the author.

1. Erase a double cut (when one lies within the other and nothing lies between).

2. Assign variables to a "Line of Identity" (LI) network:

    (a) If no portion of an LI network crosses an odd number of cuts entirely, then assign a new variable to the outermost part (*i.e.* its least enclosed part) of the LI networks.

    (b) If a portion of an LI network crosses an odd number of cuts entirely (*i.e.* an odd number of cuts clips an LI into more than one part), then

        i. assign a different type of a variable to the *outermost* part of each clipped part of the network, and

        ii. at each joint of branches inside the *innermost* cut of these odd number of cuts, write $v_i = v_j$, where v_i and v_j are assigned to each branch into which the line is clipped by the cuts.

3. Write atomic formulas for LI's (Let us call it a quasi-Beta graph and let [ ] represent a cut):

    (a) For an end of an LI with a predicate, say P, replace P with $Pv_1 \ldots v_n$, respecting the order of endpoints in a clockwise direction, where v_1 (or $[v_1]$) , . . . , and v_n (or $[v_n]$) are assigned to the lines hooked to P.

    (b) For each loose end of an LI, *i.e.* an end without a predicate, write T.

    (c) For an LI which does not get any atomic formula or T, *i.e.* a cycle whose part is not clipped, write T at the outermost part and at the innermost part of the LI.

4. Obtain a complex formula: Let G be a simple quasi-Beta graph (an atomic formula, a single cut of an atomic formula, T, an empty space, or an empty cut). The following f is a basic function:

$$f(G) = \alpha \qquad \text{if G is atomic formula } \alpha.$$
$$f(G) = \neg\alpha \qquad \text{if G is a single cut of atomic formula } \alpha.$$
$$f(G) = \mathsf{T} \qquad \text{if G is } \mathsf{T}.$$
$$f(G) = \neg\mathsf{T} \qquad \text{if G is a single cut of } \mathsf{T}.$$
$$f(G) = \mathsf{T} \qquad \text{if G is an empty space.}$$
$$f(G) = \neg\mathsf{T} \qquad \text{if G is an empty cut.}$$

Table 16 continued
Retrieval Rules for Peirce Beta Graphs

Now we extend this function f to $\bar{f}$ to translate a quasi-Beta graph into a complex formula:

(a) $\bar{f}(G) = f(G)$ if G is a simple quasi-Beta graph.

(b) $\bar{f}([[G]]) = \bar{f}(G)$.

(c) $\bar{f}(G_1 \ldots G_n) = \bar{f}(G_1) \wedge \ldots \wedge \bar{f}(G_n)$.

(d) $\bar{f}([G_1 \ldots G_n]) = \bar{f}([G_1]) \vee \ldots \vee \bar{f}([G_n])$.

5. Obtain sentences. For each variable v_i in the formula obtained by the previous step,

(a) if v_i is written in an evenly enclosed area in step 2, then add $\exists v_i$ immediately in front of the smallest sub-formula containing all occurrences of v_i, and

(b) if v_i is written in an oddly enclosed area in step 2, then add $\forall v_i$ immediately in front of the smallest sub-formula containing all occurrences of v_i.

UNDERSTANDING UNDERSTANDING

REFERENCES

Anderson, M. (1996). Reasoning with diagram sequences. In J. Seligman & D. Westerfahl (Eds.), *Logic, language and computation*. Stanford, CA: CSLI Publications.

Anderson, M. & McCartney, R. (1995). Inter-diagrammatic reasoning. *Proceedings of the Fourteenth International Joint Conference on Artificial Intelligence* (Montreal) (pp. 878-884). San Francisco: Morgan Kaufmann.

Anderson, M. & McCartney, R. (1997). Learning from diagrams. *International Journal of Machine Vision and Graphics, 6*(1), 57-76.

Anderson, M. & McCartney, R. (2003). Diagram processing: Computing with diagrams. *Artificial Intelligence, 145*, 181-226.

Baillargeon, R. (1994). A model of physical reasoning in infants. In C. Rovee-Collier & L. Lipsitt (Eds.), *Advances in infancy research*. Norwood, NJ: Ablex.

Baillargeon, R. & DeVos, J. (1991). Object permanence in young infants: Further evidence. *Child Development, 62*, 1227-1246.

Barker-Plummer, D. & Bailin, S. C. (1992). Proofs and pictures: Proving the diamond lemma with the GROVER theorem proving system. In *Reasoning with Diagrammatic Representations. Technical Report SS-92-02* (pp. 99-104). Menlo Park, CA: American Association for Artificial Intelligence.

Barr, A. & Feigenbaum, E. A. (1982). *Applications-oreiented AI Research: Science*. Reading, MA: Addison-Wesley.

Barwise, J. & Etchemendy, J. (1992). Hyperproof: Logical reasoning with diagrams. In *Reasoning with Diagrammatic Representations. Technical Report SS-92-02* (pp. 77-81). Menlo Park, CA: American Association for Artificial Intelligence.

Barwise, J. & Etchemendy, J. (1996). Visual information and valid reasoning. In W. Zimmerman & S. Cunningham (Eds.), *Visualization in teaching and learning mathematics* (pp. 9-24). Washington, DC: Mathematical Association of America.

Bickhard, M. & Terveen, L. (1995). *Foundational issues in artificial intelligence and cognitive science: Impasse and solution*. Amsterdam: North-Holland.

Bier, E. A. & Stone, M. C. (1986). Snap-Dragging. *SIGGRAPH '86* (pp. 233-240).

Boysen, S. T. (1993). Counting in chimpanzees: Nonhuman principles and emergent properties of number. In S. T. Boysen & E. J. Capaldi (Eds.), *The development of numerical competence* (pp. 39-60). Hillsdale, NJ: Erlbaum.

Brannon, E. M. & Terrace, H. S. (1998). Ordering of numerosities 1 to 9 by monkeys. *Science, 282*, 746-749.

Brett, W. F., Feldman, E. B. & Sentlowitz, M. (1974). *An introduction to the history of mathematics, number theory, and operations research.* New York: MSS Information Corporation.

Britten, R. J. (2002). Divergence between samples of chimpanzee and human DNA sequences is 4% counting indels. *Proceedings of the National Academy of Science (USA), 99*(21), 13633-13635.

Brooks, R. A. (1986). A robust layered control system for a mobile robot. *IEEE Journal of Robotics and Automation, RA-2*(April), 14-23.

Brooks, R. A. (1991). How to build complete creatures rather than isolated cognitive simulators. In K. VanLehn (Ed.) *Architectures for intelligence* (pp. 225-239). Hillsdale NJ: Lawrence Erlbaum.

Buchanan, B. B. & Livingston, G. R. (2004). Toward automated discovery in the biological sciences. *AI Magazine, 25*(1), 69-84.

Buchanan, B. B. & Waltz, D. (2009). Automating Science. *Science, 3324*(5923), 43-44.

Buchanan, B. G. & Feigenbaum, E. A. (1978). DENDRAL and Meta-DENDRAL: Their applications dimension. *Artificial Intelligence, 11*, 5-24.

Buchanan, M. (2000). *Ubiquity.* New York: Three Rivers Press.

Byrne, R. W. (2000). Evolution of Primate Cognition. *Cognitive Science, 24*(3), 543-570.

Call, J. (2000). Representing space and objects in monkeys and apes. *Cognitive Science, 24*(3), 397-422.

Carey, S. (in press). On the origin of concepts. *Mind and Reality: A Multidisciplinary Symposium on Consciousness* (Columbia University).

Carey, S. & Spelke, E. S. (1996). Science and core knowledge. *Philosophy of Science, 63*, 515-533.

Carey, S. & Spelke, E. S. (unpublished manuscript). *Bootstrapping the integer list: Representations of number.*

Cheney, D. L. & Seyfarth, B. M. (1990). *How monkeys see the world: Inside the head of another species.* Chicago: Chicago University Press.

Cheng, P. C.-H. (1998). AVOW Diagrams: A novel representational system for understanding electricity. In P. Olivier (Ed.) *Thinking With Diagrams 98. Is there a science of diagrams?* (Aberystwyth, Wales) (pp. 86-93). The University of Wales.

Chomsky, N. (1965). *Aspects of the theory of syntax.* Cambridge, MA: MIT Press.

Chou, S.-C. (1988). *Mechanical geometry theorem proving.* Dordrecht, Boston, Lancaster, Tokyo: D. Reidel Publishing Company.

Cipra, B. A. (1995). Catching Fly Balls: A New Model Steps up to the Plate. *Science*, 268 (April 1995), 502.

Claverie, J.-M. (2001). What if there are only 30,000 Human Genes? *Science, 291*(5507), 1255-1257.

Cleveland, W. S. & McGill, R. (1985). Graphical perception and graphical methods for analyzing scientific data. *Science, 229*(30 August), 828-833.

de Kleer, J. & Brown, J. S. (1984). A qualitative physics based on confluences. In D. G. Bobrow (Ed.) *Qualitative reasoning about physical systems* (pp. 7-83). Amsterdam: Elsevier.

Dehaene, S. (1997). *The number sense: How the mind creates mathematics*. New York: Plenum Press.

Dehaene, S. (2000). Cerebral bases of number processing and calculation. In M. Gazzaniga (Ed.) *The new cognitive neurosciences* (2nd edition) (pp. 987-998). Cambridge, MA: MIT Press.

Dennett, D. C. (1978). *Brainstorms: Philosophical essays on mind psychology*. Montgomery, VT: Bradford Books.

Dennett, D. C. (1987). *The intentional stance*. Cambridge, MA: Bradford Books/MIT Press.

Dennett, D. C. (1991). *Consciousness explained*. Boston, Toronto, London: Little, Brown and Company.

Deutsch, D. (1997). *The fabric of reality*. New York: Penguin Putnam.

Diamond, J. M. (1992). *The third chimpanzee: The evolution and future of the human animal*. New York: Harper Collins.

Diamond, J. M. (1997). *Guns, germs, and steel: The fates of human soceties*. New York: W. W. Norton.

Dunham, W. (1990). *Journey through genius: The great theorems of mathematics*. New York: Wiley.

Estes, W. K. (1988). Toward a framework for combining connectionist and symbol-processing models. *Journal of Memory and Language, 27*, 196-212.

Evans, T. G. (1968). A program for the solution of geometric-analogy intelligence-test questions. In M. Minsky (Ed.) *Semantic information processing* (pp. 271-353). Cambridge, MA: MIT Press.

Fauconnier, G. & Turner, M. (2002). *The way we think: Conceptual blending and the mind's hidden complexities*. New York: Basic Books.

Ferrucci, D., Brown, E., Chu-Carroll, J., Fan, J., Gondeck, D., Kalyanpur, A. A., Lally, A., Murdock, J. W., Nyberg, r., Prager, J., Schlaefer, N. & Welty, C. (2010). The AI behind Watson – The technical article. *AI Mgazine, 31*(3).

Fodor, J. A. (1983). *The modularity of mind*. Cambridge, MA: M.I.T. Press.

Fodor, J. A. & Pylyshyn, Z. (1988). Connectionism and cognitive architecture: A critical analysis. *Cognition, 28*, 3-71.

Forbus, K. (1984). Qualitative process theory. In D. G. Bobrow (Ed.) *Qualitative reasoning about physical systems* (pp. 85-168). Amsterdam: Elsevier.

Frith, U. (1989). Autism and "theory of mind". In C. Gillberg (Ed.) *Diagnosis and treatment of autism* (pp. 33-52). New York: Plenum Press.

Furnas, G., Qu, Y., Shrivastave, S. & Peters, G. (2000). The use of intermediate graphical constructions in problem solving with dynamic, pixel-level diagrams. In M. Anderson, P. Cheng & V. Haarslev (Eds.), *Theory and application of diagrams* (pp. 314-329). Dordrecht: Springer-Verlag.

Furnas, G. W. (1992). Reasoning with diagrams only. In *Reasoning with diagrammatic representations. Technical Report SS-92-02* (pp. 115-120). Menlo Park, CA: American Association for Artificial Intelligence.

Gallup, G. G. J. (1970). Chimpanzees: Self-recognition. *Science, 167*, 86-87.

Garber, P. (1989). Role of spatial memory in primate foraging patterns: *Saguinus mystax* and *Saguinus fuscicollis*. *American Journal of Primatology, 19*, 203-216.

Gelernter, H. (1959). Realization of a geometry theorem proving machine. *International Conference on Information Processing* (pp. 273-282). Paris: UNESCO House.

Gelernter, H., Hansen, J. R. & Loveland, D. W. (1960). Empirical explorations of the geometry theorem proving machine. *Proceedings of the Western Joint Computer Conference* (pp. 143-147). New York: National Joint Computer Committee.

Gergely, G., Nadasdy, Z., Gergely, C. & Biro, S. (1995). Taking the intentional stance at 12 months of age. *Cognition, 56*, 165-193.

Glasgow, J. & Papadias, D. (1992). Computational imagery. *Cognitive Science, 16*(3), 355-394.

Gleicher, M. & Witkin, A. (1991a). *Creating and manipulating constrained models.* (Report CMU-CS-91-125) Carnegie-Mellon University.

Gleicher, M. & Witkin, A. (1991b). *Differential Manipulation.* (Report CMU-CS-91-123) Carnegie-Mellon University.

Gold, E. M. (1967). Language indentification in the limit. *Information and Control, 10*(5), 447-474.

Gopnik, A. & Melzoff, A. (1997). *Words, thoughts, and theories.* Cambridge, MA: MIT Press.

Greene, B. (2000). *The elegant universe.* New York: Vintage Books.

Hammer, E. (1996). Peircean graphs for propositional logic. In G. Allwein & J. Barwise (Eds.), *Logical reasoning with diagrams* (pp. 129-147). Oxford: Oxford University Press.

Hammer, E. & Danner, N. (1996). Towards a model theory of Venn diagrams. In G. Allwein & J. Barwise (Eds.), *Logical reasoning with diagrams* (pp. 109-127). Oxford: Oxford University Press.

Hauser, M. & Carey, S. (1998). Building a cognitive creature from a set of primitives. In C. Allen & D. Cummins (Eds.), *The evolution of mind* (pp. 51-106). London: Oxford University Press.

Hauser, M. D. (2000). *Wild minds: What animals really think.* New York: Henry Holt.

Hauser, M. D., Chomsky, N. & Fitch, W. T. (2002). The faculty of language: What is it, who has it, and how did it evolve? *Science, 298*(5598), 1569-1579.

Hauser, M. D., Kralik, J., Botto-Mahan, C., Garrett, M. & Oser, J. (1995). Self-recognition in primate phylogeny and the salience of species-typical features. *Proceedings of the National Academy of Science (USA), 92*, 10811-10814.

Heyes, C. M. (1998). Theory of mind in nonhuman primates. *Behavioral and Brain Sciences, 21*(1), 101-134.

Hilbert, D. (1930). *Grundlagen der Geometrie.* (7th ed.). Leipzig: Teubner.

Holland, J. H. (1999). *Emergence: From chaos to order.* Reading, MA: Perseus Books Group.

Jamnik, M. (2001). *Mathematical reasoning with diagrams: From intuition to automation.* Stanford, CA: CSLI Publications.

Johnson, S. C., Slaugher, V. & Carey, S. (1998). Whose gaze will infants follow? The elicitation of gaze-following in 12-month olds. *Developmental Science, 1*, 233-238.

Kaplan, R. (1999). *The nothing that is: A natural history of zero.* Oxford: Oxford University Press.

Karpinski, L. C. (1915). *Robert of Chester's Latin translation of the algebra of Al-Khowarizmi, with an introduction, critical notes and English version.* New York: The Macmillan Company.

Katz, V. J. (1998). *A history of mathematics: An introduction.* (2nd ed.). Reading, MA: Addison-Wesley.

Kaufman, S. G. (1991). A formal theory of spatial reasoning. *Proceedings of the Second Conference on Knowledge Representation* (Cambridge MA) (pp. 347-356). Morgan Kaufmann.

Kline, M. (1972). *Mathematical thought from ancient to modern times.* Oxford: Oxford University Press.

Koedinger, K. R. & Anderson, J. R. (1990). Abstract planning and perceptual chunks: Elements of expertise in geometry. *Cognitive Science, 14*, 511-550.

Kohler, W. (1927). *The mentality of apes.* (2 ed.). New York: Vintage Books.

Kosslyn, S. M., Thompson, W. R. & Ganis, G. (2006). *The case for mental imagery.* New York: Oxford University Press.

Koza, J. R. (1992). *Genetic programming: On the programming of computers by means of natural selection.* Cambridge, MA: MIT Press.

Lakoff, G. & Johnson, M. (1980). *Metaphors we live by.* (2nd ed.). Chicago: University of Chicago Press.

Lakoff, G. & Nunez, R. (2001). *Where mathematics comes from: How the embodied mind brings mathematics into being.* New York: Basic Books.

Langley, P. (1978). BACON-1: A general discovery system. *Proceedings of the Second National Conference of the Canadian Society for Computational Studies in Intelligence* (Toronto, Ontario) (pp. 173-180).

Langley, P., Bradshaw, G. L. & Simon, H. A. (1981). BACON-5: Discovery of conservation laws. *Proceedings of the Seventh International Joint Conference on Artificial Intelligence* (Vancouver) (pp. 121-126). Menlo Park CA: American Association for Artificial Intelligence.

Langley, P., Bradshaw, G. L. & Simon, H. A. (1983). Rediscovering chemistry with the BACON system. In R. S. Michalski, J. G. Carbonell & T. M. Mitchell (Eds.), *Machine learning: An artificial intelligence approach* (pp. 307-329). Palo Alto, CA: Tioga Press.

Larkin, J. H. & Simon, H. A. (1987). Why a diagram is (sometimes) worth ten thousand words. *Cognitive Science, 11*, 65-100.

Lenat, D. (1976). *AM: An artificial intelligence approach to discovery in mathematics as heuristic search.* Doctoral dissertation, Stanford University, Computer Science Department.

Lenat, D. B. & Brown, J. S. (1984). Why AM and EURISKO appear to work. *Artificial Intelligence, 23,* 269-294.

Leslie, A. M. (1994). ToMM, ToBy, and Agency: Core architecture and domain specificity. In L. Hirschfeld & S. Gelman (Eds.), *Mapping the mind: Domain specificity in cognition and culture* (pp. 201-233). New York: Cambridge University Press.

Lindsay, R. K. (1961). *Toward the development of a machine which comprehends.* Doctoral dissertation, Carnegie-Mellon University.

Lindsay, R. K. (1973). In defense of *ad hoc* systems. In R. Schank & K. Colby (Eds.), *Computer models of thought and language* (pp. 372-395). San Francisco: W. H. Freeman.

Lindsay, R. K. (1974). Behaving man. *Science, 184*(4135), 455-457.

Lindsay, R. K. (1976). Turing's test. *SIGART Newsletter (ACM),* (58), 3-4.

Lindsay, R. K. (1998). Using diagrams to understand geometry. *Computational Intelligence, 14*(2), 222-256.

Lindsay, R. K. (2000). Using spatial semantics to discover and verify diagrammatic demonstrations of geometric propositions. In S. O'Nuallian (Ed.) *Spatial Cognition* (pp. 199-212). Amsterdam: John Benjamins.

Lindsay, R. K. (2000). Playing with diagrams. In M. Anderson, P. Cheng & V. Haarslev (Eds.), *Theory and application of diagrams* (pp. 300-313). Dordrecht: Springer-Verlag.

Lindsay, R. K., Buchanan, B. G., Feigenbaum, E. A. & Lederberg, J. (1980). *Applications of artificial intelligence for organic chemistry: The DENDRAL Project.* New York, NY: McGraw-Hill.

Lindsay, R. K., Buchanan, B. G., Feigenbaum, E. A. & Lederberg, J. (1993). DENDRAL: A case study of the first expert system for scientific hypothesis formation. *Artificial Intelligence, 61*, 209-261.

Livingston, G. R., Rosenberg, J. M. & Buchanan, B. G. (2001). Closing the loop: An agenda- and justification-based framework for selecting the next discovery task to perform. In N. Cercone, T. Y. Lin & X. Wu (Eds.), *First IEEE International Conference on Data Mining* (San Jose, CA) (pp. 385). Washington, DC: IEEE Computer Society.

Livingston, G. R., Rosenberg, J. M. & Buchanan, B. G. (2003). An agenda-and justification-based framework for discovery systems. *Knowledge and information systems, 5*(2), 133-161.

Loomis, E. S. (1940). *The Pythagorean proposition: Its proofs analyzed and classified and bibliography of sources for data of the four kinds of proofs.* (2nd ed.). Ann Arbor, MI: Edwards Brothers.

Matsuyama, T. & Nitta, T. (1995). Geometric theorem proving by integrated logical and algebraic reasoning. *Artificial Intelligence, 75*(1), 93-105.

Matsuzawa, T. (Ed.) (2001). *Primate origins of human cognition and behavior.* Tokyo: Springer-Verlag.

Mayell, H. (2002). *Painting Elephants get Online Gallery.* http://news.nationalgeographic.com/news/2002/06/0626_020626_elephant.html: National Geographic News.

McBeath, M. K., Shaffer, D. M. & Kaiser, M. K. (1995). How baseball outfielders determine where to run to catch fly balls. *Science, 268*(28 April), 569–573.

McCarthy, J. (1988). Mathematical logic in artificial intelligence. *Daedalus,* (Winter, 1988), 297-310.

McCloskey, M., Caramazza, A. & Green, B. (1980). Curvilinear motion in the absence of external forces: Naive beliefs about the motion of objects. *Science, 210*(4474), 1139-1141.

McCloskey, M. & Kohl, D. (1983). Naive physics: The curvilinear impetus principle and its role in interactions with moving objects. *Journal of Experimental Psychology: Learning, Memory, & Cognition, 9*(1), 146-156.

McCloskey, M., Washburn, A. & Felch, L. (1983). Intuitive physics: The straight-down belief and its origin. *Journal of Experimental Psychology: Learning, Memory and Cognition, 9*(4), 636-649.

McDougal, T. F. (1993). Using case-based reasoning and situated activity to write geometry proofs. *Annual Meeting of the Cognitive Science Society* (pp. 711-716). Hillsdale, NJ: Lawrence Erlbaum.

Miller, A. I. (1984). *Imagery in scientific thought.* Boston: Birkhauser.

Miller, A. I. (1998). Imagery and representation in 20th century physics (abstract of unpublished manuscript of invited talk). *Thinking with Diagrams* (Aberystwyth, Wales). University of Wales.

Miller, G. (1956). The magical number seven plus or minus two: Some limits on our capacity to process information. *Psychological Review, 63*(81-97).

Miller, G. A. (1962). *Psychology. The science of mental life.* New York: Harper & Row.

Miller, N. (2000). *Case analysis in Euclidean geometry.* Department of Mathematics, Cornell University.

Nahin, P. J. (1998). *An imaginary tale: The story of i.* Princeton, NJ: Princeton University Press.

Narayanan, N. H. (1992). *Imagery, diagrams and reasoning.* Doctoral dissertation, Ohio State University, Department of Computer and Information Science.

Nelsen, R. B. (1993). *Proofs without words: Exercises in visual thinking.* Washington, D.C.: The Mathematical Association of America.

Netz, R. (2000). The origins of mathematical physics: New light on old questions. *Physics Today, 53,* June 2000, 32-37.

Newell, A. (1990). *Unified theories of cognition.* Cambridge, MA: Harvard University Press.

Newell, A., Shaw, J. C. & Simon, H. A. (1957). Empirical explorations with the logic theory machine. *Proceedings of the Western Joint Computer Conference* (pp. 218-239).

Nilsson, N. J. (1980). *Principles of artificial intelligence.* Palo Alto, CA: Tioga Publishing Company.

Novak, G. (1977). Representations of knowledge in a program for solving physics problems. *Proceedings of the Fifth International Joint Conference on Artificial Intelligence* (Cambridge, MA) (pp. 286-291). Pittsburgh, PA: Carnegie-Mellon University.

Perner, J., Leekam, S. R. & Wimmer, H. (1987). Three-year olds' difficulty with false belief. *British Journal of Developmental Psychology, 5,* 125-137.

Povinelli, D. J. (2000). *Folk physics for apes. The chimpanzee's theory of how the world works.* Oxford: Oxford University Press.

Povinelli, D. J. & Bering, J. M. (2002). The mentality of apes revisited. *Current Directions in Psychological Science, 11,* 115-119.

Povinelli, D. J., Bering, J. M. & Giambrone, S. (2000). Toward a science of other minds: Escaping the argument by analogy. *Cognitive Science, 24*(3), 509-541.

Powers, W. T. (1973). *Behavior: The control of perception.* Chicago: Aldine Publishing Company.

Premack, D. & Premack, A. (2003). *Original intelligence: Unlocking the mystery of who we are.* New York: McGraw-Hill.

Premack, D. & Woodruff, G. (1978). Does the chimpanzee have a theory of mind? *Behavioral and Brain Sciences, 1*(4), 515-526.

Pylyshyn, Z. (1999). Is vision continuous with cognition? The case for cognitive impenetrability of visual perception. *Behavioral and Brain Sciences, 22*(3), 341-423.

Pylyshyn, Z. W. (1984). *Computation and cognition: Toward a foundation for cognitive science.* Cambridge, Massachusetts: MIT Press.

Rauff, J. V. (2003). Counting on your body in Papua New Guinea. *Mathematical Connections, 2,* 20-41.

Ritt, R. F. (1938). Differential equations from an algebraic standpoint. In *AMS Colloquium Publications.* New York: American Mathematical Society.

Rival, I. (1987). Picture puzzling: Mathematicians are rediscovering the power of pictorial reasoning. *The Sciences, 27,* 41-46.

Roberts, D. (1973). *The existential graphs of Charles S. Peirce.* The Hague: Mouton.

Rumelhart, D. E. & McClelland, J. L. (1986). *Parallel distributed processing. Explorations in the microstructure of cognition.* Cambridge, MA: MIT Press.

Samuel, A. L. (1963). Some studies in machine learning using the game of checkers. In E. A. Feigenbaum & J. Feldman (Eds.), *Computers and thought* (pp. 71-108). New York: McGraw Hill.

Searle, J. R. (1980). Minds, brains, and programs. *The Behavioral and Brain Sciences, 3,* 417-424.

Searle, J. R. (2002). *Consciousness and language.* Cambridge, MA: Cambridge University Press.

Seife, C. (2000). *Zero, the biography of a dangerous idea.* Harmondsworth: Viking Penguin.

Shah, P. (2002). Graph comprehension: The role of format, content, and individual differences. In M. Anderson, B. Meyer & P. Olivier (Eds.), *Diagrammatic representation and reasoning* (pp. 173-186). London: Springer-Verlag.

Shah, P. & Carpenter, P. A. (1995). Conceptual limitations in comprehending line graphs. *Journal of Experimental Psychology, General, 124,* 43-61.

Shah, P., Mayer, R. E. & Hegarty, M. (1999). Graphs as aids to knowledge construction: Signaling techniques for guiding the process of graph comprehension. *Journal of Educational Psychology, 91,* 690-702.

Shastri, L. & Ajjanagadde, V. (1993). From simple associations to systematic reasoning: A connectionist representation of rules, variable and dynamic bindings using temporal asynchrony. *Behavioral and Brain Sciences, 16,* 417-494.

Shin, S.-J. (1994). *The logical status of diagrams.* Cambridge: Cambridge University Press.

Shin, S.-J. (1999). Reconstituting beta graphs with an efficacious system. *Journal of Logic, Language and Information, 8,* 273-295.

Shin, S.-J. (2000). Reviving the iconicity of beta graphs. In M. Anderson, P. Cheng & V. Haarslev (Eds.), *Theory and application of diagrams* (pp. 58-73). Berlin: Springer-Verlag.

Skinner, B. F. (1953). *Science and Human Behavior.* New York: The Macmillan Company.

Skinner, B. F. (1957). *Verbal behavior.* New York: Appleton-Century-Crofts.

Smolensky, P. (1987a). The constituent structure of connectionist mental states: A reply to Fodor and Pylyshyn. *The Southern Journal of Philosophy, 26 (supplement),* 137-161.

Smolensky, P. (1987b). *On variable binding and the representation of symbolic structures in connectionist systems.* (Report CU-CS-355-87) University of Colorado at Boulder.

Smolensky, P. (1990). Tensor product variable binding and the representation of symbolic structures in connectionist systems. *Artificial Intelligence, 46,* 159-216.

Smullyan, R. M. (1961). *Theory of formal systems.* Princeton, NJ: Princeton University Press.

Spelke, E. S. (1994). Initial knowledge: Six suggestions. *Cognition, 50,* 431-445.

Spelke, E. S., Breinlinger, K., Macomber, J. & Jacobson, K. (1992). Origins of knowledge. *Psychological Review, 99,* 605-632.

Spelke, E. S., Phillips, A. & Woodward, A. L. (1995). Infants' knowledge of object motion and human action. In D. Sperber, D. Premack & A. Premack (Eds.), *Causal cognition: A multidisciplinary debate* (pp. 44-78). Oxford: Clarendon Press.

Sperber, D., Premack, D. & Premack, A. (1995). *Causal cognition: A multidisciplinary debate.* Oxford: Clarendon Press.

Stark, H. (1978). *An introduction to number theory.* Cambridge, MA: MIT Press.

Stenning, K. & Oberlander, J. (1991). Reasoning with words, pictures and calculi: Computation versus justification. In J. Barwise, J. M. Gawron, G. Plotkin & S. Tutiya (Eds.), *Situation theory and its applications* (pp. 607-621). Chicago: University of Chicago Press.

Stenning, K. & Oberlander, J. (1992). Implementing logics in diagrams. In *Reasoning with Diagrammatic Representations. Technical Report SS-92-02* (pp. 88-92). Menlo Park, CA: American Association for Artificial Intelligence.

Suppes, P. (1960). *Axiomatic set theory.* Princeton, NJ: D. Van Nostrand.

Terrace, H. S., Petitto, L. A., Sanders, R. J. & Bever, T. G. (1979). Can an ape create a sentence? *Science, 206*(4421), 891-902.

Terrace, H. S., Son, L. K. & Brannon, E. M. (2003). Serial expertise in Rhesus and Macaques. *Psychological Science, 14*(1), 66-73.

Thompson, R. K. R. & Oden, D. L. (2000). Categorical perception and conceptual judgments by nonhuman primates: The paleological monkey and the analogical ape. *Cognitive Science, 24*(3), 363-396.

Tomasello, M. (1999a). *The cultural origins of human cognition.* Cambridge, MA: Harvard University Press.

Tomasello, M. (1999b). The human adaptation for culture. *Annual Review of Anthropology, 28,* 509-529.

Tomasello, M. (2000). Primate cognition: Introduction to the issue. *Cognitive Science, 24*(3), 351-361.

Tomasello, M. & Call, J. (1997). *Primate cognition.* Oxford UK: Oxford University Press.

Touretzky, D. S. (1990). Dynamic symbol structures in a connectionist network. *Artificial Intelligence, 46*, 5-46.

Touretzky, D. S. & Hinton, G. E. (1985). Symbols among the neurons: Details of a connectionist inference architecture. In A. Joshi (Ed.) *Proceedings of the Ninth International Joint Conference on Artificial Intelligence* (Los Angeles) (pp. 238-243). San Francisco: Morgan Kaufmann.

Tufte, C. (1983). *The visual display of quantitative information.* Cheshire, CN: Graphics Press.

Turing, A. M. (1950). Computing machinery and intelligence. *Mind, 59*(236), 433-460.

Ullman, S. (1985). Visual routines. In S. Pinker (Ed.) *Visual Cognition* (pp. 97-159). Cambridge, MA: MIT Press.

Venn, J. (1971). *Symbolic logic.* (2nd ed.). New York: Burt Franklin.

Venter, J. C. & others. (2001). The sequence of the human genome. *Science, 291*(5507), 1304-1351.

Wang, D. (1995). *Studies on the formal semantics of pictures.* Doctoral dissertation, University of Amsterdam, Institute for Logic, Language, and Computation.

Wellman, H. M. (1990). *The child's theory of mind.* Cambridge, MA: Bradford Books/MIT Press.

Wellman, H. M. (2002). Understanding the psychological world: Developing a theory of mind. In U. Goswami (Ed.) *Handbook of cognitive development* (pp. 167-187). Oxford: Blackwell.

Wimmer, H. & Perner, J. (1983). Beliefs about beliefs: Representation and constraining function of wrong beliefs in young children's understanding of deception. *Cognition, 13*, 103-128.

Wrangham, R. & Peterson, D. (1996). *Demonic males: Apes and the origins of human violence.* Boston: Houghton Mifflin.

Wu, W. (1978). On the decision problem and the mechanization of theorem proving in elementary geometry. *Scientia Sinica, 21*, 157-179.

Wynn, K. (1992). Addition and subtraction by human infants. *Nature, 358*(749-750).

Zeman, J. (1964). *The graphical logic of C. S. Peirce.* Doctoral dissertation, University of Chicago.

Zimmerman, W. & Cunningham, S. (Eds.). (1991). *Visualization in teaching and learning mathematics.* Washington, D. C.: The Mathematical Association of America.

ABOUT THE AUTHOR

Robert Kendall Lindsay is Professor Emeritus of Psychology at the University of Michigan and Research Professor Emeritus of Computer Science at the University of Michigan Medical School. He received a Bachelor of Science degree in physics from Carnegie Mellon University (formerly Carnegie Institute of Technology), a Master of Arts degree in psychology from Columbia University, and a Ph.D. from Carnegie Mellon, where his mentors were Artificial Intelligence pioneers Herbert A. Simon and Allen Newell.